# SCHEMERS

## *Blackmail Never Felt So Good*

A NOVEL

VICTOR McGLOTHIN

# also by victor mcglothin

SCHEMERS

First Printing, 2015

Victor McGlothin Publishing
P.O. Box 867482
Plano, TX. 75086

www.VictorMcGlothin.com

## special thanks to

My Father, who gives me strength and brings me joy.

Dr. Terre McGlothin, MD

Dr. Jenifer Broderick-Thomas, MD

Dr. Katrina Lee, MD

Cindy Noble-Funderburgh

Angela Ransome-Jones

Lisa Renee Johnson

Latoya Smith

Brian W. Smith

"The twists and surprises are both plausible and unbelievable, the novel both engrossing and entertaining."
—*Booklist* on *What's a Woman to Do*

"4 Stars... Victor McGlothin has written a superb, true-to-life book. With a masterfully created plot, it explores the turbulent lives of three courageous women. This book offers a gripping, emotional glimpse into the dark world of the unknown."
—*Romantic Times BookClub* on *What's a Woman to Do*

"A fast-paced, soulful, dramatic story."
—*The Sunday Oklahoman* on *What's a Woman to Do*

"An absolute page-turner...intriguing and thought-provoking"
— Kimberla Lawson Roby,
*New York Times* Bestselling Author, on *Autumn Leaves*

"Credible, honest." —*Kirkus Reviews* on *Autumn Leaves*

"The pacing of the story and the storyline itself ought to keep the reader interested until the last page is turned since there's plenty of drama and secrets to keep you wondering and guessing until the end. Victor McGlothin has told a story that is sure to satisfy fans of his first novel, AUTUMN LEAVES, as well as new readers."
—Book-remarks.com on *Autumn Leaves*

"McGlothin creates a sizzling slice of life in 1947. McGlothin weaves convincing historical elements into a fast-moving caper, and Baltimore Floyd is a delightful scoundrel."
—*Publishers Weekly* on *Ms. Etta's Fast House*

# chapter one
# FOR THE MONEY

Love is conceived in the eyes. Joy, lust, sadness and pain are the mere side effects of the things we see. What we encounter visually is a monumental component in what we become. However, murder is quite different altogether. It begins in the heart and seeks refuge in the mind. Once the thought of murder settles in, there's nothing left to do but see it through.

Such was the case for Lena Harmon, M.D. Committing murder in cold blood was the furthest thing from her mind as she hid in her office, anxiously thumbing through the latest issue of *OB/GYN Today*. There it was, a top of page twenty-three, her first published article in a national magazine. In spite of an unflattering head shot that emphasized her full cheeks and a second chin she hadn't noticed before, the article was a resounding hit.

"New Sex" was the title for Lena's composition which discussed her adamant stance in regards to the necessity of women protecting themselves during interludes with new sex partners. While building a successful medical practice over the past seven years, Lena heard more than her share of wild sexcapades. She'd been apprised of countless indiscretions from women ill-suited to deal with the pitfalls of newfound sexual freedom. She'd listened to horror stories from repentant cheating wives who took home more than they bargained for after sharing what was already vowed to their spouses. Now that the doctor's two cents on hot and heavy love affairs was properly documented, Lena felt compelled to get back to reality. She sighed regretfully while studying the photo, admitting that her smooth, honey-bronze complexion wasn't nearly as radiant after neglecting her monthly facial appointments and a personalized fitness program at the gym.

Before she closed the magazine, Lena read her name in print once more. Tracing the letters written in large bold type forced a prideful smile between her full, perfect lips. She'd overcome a fear of failure and it resulted in a popular editorial read by millions of women throughout the country. What started out as a fleeting idea became a reality. Dr. Lena Harmon was published and loving it.

Lena's reality also included a busy waiting room overflowing with expecting mothers, who scheduled wellness appointments weeks in advance and a collection of urgent-care patients, whose irresponsible sexual conduct warranted necessary and immediate consultations.

At 9:00 sharp, Margo fanned herself with the daily patient schedule as she approached the doctor's private office. Margo Stewart, office manager and medical assistant, was a chocolate shade of brown. She appeared younger than forty-eight and never owned up to her age if asked, not once. Although petite, she more than made up for her size with titanic proportions of attitude and experience. Her rigorous duties required training as an administrator and lion tamer.

"I hope you took your vitamins today, Dr. Harmon," Margo said evenly. "We've got a real traffic jam out there. I was careful not to saddle your mornings with new patients. I know it takes a while to sort out things but we have two referrals from the Uptown Women's Center. And, from what I gather, this situation is a sin and a shame." Margo flipped through pages of notes and reeled them off one by one while explaining further details. "It's a basketball player's wife and his sidepiece. Uh, I mean, his mistress." She corrected herself when Lena peered up disapprovingly from a stack of charts. "Uh-huh, both of 'em pregnant by the same point guard and due to deliver on the same day," Margo continued. "Yep, and probably got the same itchy issues down there too. Listen Doctor, they rode in together. Now if that isn't a hot mess in a top hat, I don't know what is." Margo took a breath to compose herself. "Now then. Mrs. Ellen Kirkpatrick's condition hasn't changed since last month so I put her in room three. Trina Wilson is in room two with her usual problem except this go around she got the heebie jeebies from her building superintendent. Guess she found herself a real maintenance man and finally stopped picking up ex-cons at the bus stop."

Lena snickered softly. "I'm sure she'll start filling me in as soon as her feet hit the stirrups."

"Whether you want to hear all about it or not," Margo added, as she held a chart against her chest like a favorite photograph. When Margo noticed there was a break in the conversation she realized the doctor was waiting on her to wrap it up.

"Oh, and lastly and because I like you, I thought I'd start the day off with a bang."

Lena tilted her head but still couldn't see the name typed on the label so she peered up from the stack charts. "What are you up to Margo?"

"Not me. It's your favorite patient kicking back in exam room one. Dane Tolliver has herself a new attitude and brand-new everything else. It's got to be the most extreme makeover I've ever seen. They say money can't buy you love but I'll bet she paid enough to double her odds." Margo spun on her heels then paused. "By the way, don't think I forgot. I want my copy of the magazine article autographed. Thank you, Dr. Lena Harmon," she said pleasantly. Before Lena had a chance to reply, Margo dashed off down the hall to squash a heated argument in the waiting room. It was lion-taming time.

Lena stood just outside of the examination room, flipping through her first patient's chart. She studied a sentence which appeared to be purposely scrawled in a way that made it difficult to understand then she casually pushed the examination room door open.

"Mrs. Tolliver, it's always good to see you," she said, just before her eyes drifted up from the hand-written notes jotted on the information sheet. Her eyes widened when the older white woman, wearing nothing but a satiny, plum-colored thong, twirled around slowly to show off her spanking new breast augmentation. Lena surveyed what appeared to be thirty-year old goods wrapped around a woman who had grown children that age. Mrs. Tolliver had obviously undergone plastic surgery and a litany of liposuction in several areas. Her stunning appearance was overwhelming.

The doctor couldn't help but gawk at her patient's new body. "Mrs. Tolliver, what's with all this? Aren't you supposed to be the grieving widow?"

"Honey, I gave up on that grieving crap eight months ago. Of course I mourned Clint's passing. Shoot, I even find myself missing him every now and again but our marriage was dead and buried long before they lowered my husband's remains into the ground... may he rest in peace. It was high time for me to get out of the house

Dr. Harmon, do some shopping and enjoy life instead of living for the dead." Mrs. Tolliver rested both hands on her narrowed hips like a swimsuit model flirting with a camera lens. "So, what do you think of the stuff I bought?"

Grasping the sassy socialite's transformation was more difficult than Lena cared to admit. She was a smidge envious that the sixty-year-old widow had it so well put together. Mrs. Tolliver's previously outdated, gruesomely gray hairstyle was tapered and trimmed into a silvered salon masterpiece; which took at least ten years off of her age. Ear and nose reconfigurations set off her other nip and tuck beautifully.

"Mrs. Tolliver, I just can't say enough about your new look. It's simply amazing. Honestly, I think I'm a bit envious," Lena answered, still somewhat astonished. "But, I know you didn't book an appointment with me just so you could show off."

"Well, thank you and I didn't as a matter of fact," Mrs. Tolliver replied, in a more reserved tone than before. "You'll have to cut out the Mrs. stuff from now on. I'm single for the first time since I can remember and that's one of the reasons I need to see you." Lena remembered reading the comment section on Dane Tolliver's sign-in card. The words, *vaginal irritation*, were scrawled so small they could hardly be understood, so she knew the patient was embarrassed, and very likely worried.

"Doc, I'm afraid I may have gotten myself into some trouble while making up for lost time and years of terrible sex with Clint. Now don't get me wrong, he was a good man but a horrible lover. I do mean simply awful, bless his soul. Sure Clint put his heart into it but that wasn't the problem. He was all thumbs although I never knew how to tell him just how bad he sucked. Yes, I do mean that literally. He sucked so bad that I faked it from the time he flopped down on top of me until he rolled over and fell asleep. For over thirty-two years I spared that man's feelings when I should have been focusing more on my own. Well, I was in a big hurry to run out there and experience what I'd heard so many women carrying on about in that *Cosmo* and *Vogue*. Guess now that I've enjoyed the fellas beating down my door, among other things, I'll have to pay the piper." All of the jubilation that lifted her voice had vanished. Almost instantly, Dane appeared older than the woman who'd paid handsomely to push back the hands of time.

While tactfully avoiding eye contact, Lena cleared her throat. "I see," she replied softly. When her patient seemed to run out of words, Lena motioned toward the cloth gown still neatly folded on the examination table. Dane Tolliver eased on the proper attire as Lena snapped into physician mode. She pulled on a pair of latex gloves then offered a congenial smile. "Hopefully your condition is nothing serious, perhaps a minor bacterial infection caused by your body getting acquainted with all of the action you're getting with *the fellas.* We'll take a look, run some tests and talk about it once the cultures come back. Meanwhile, remember that times have changed and it's up to us women to look out for ourselves. Men would slip and slide right in every time without protection if they could, which reminds me. I'll need a urine sample before you go."

After Lena collected vaginal swabs for the lab, she collected the chart and headed toward the door.

"Oh, Doctor. Will I get an answer back by Thursday?" Dane asked, innocently. "I have a hot date Friday night and two more on Saturday."

"I should know something by then but there's no rule that every date has to land on a mattress," Lena joked.

"Damned if it don't, Doc. I got new boobs and a lot of catching

14

up to do," the woman replied smartly. "Hell, I deserve a whole slew of happy endings. They beat the snot out of pretending."

Despite her impending diagnosis, Dane eagerly anticipated more of the new sex that called for a wellness examination. Lena was certain she would see her favorite patient again soon, likely under the same circumstances if the test results returned negative for Sexually Transmitted Diseases. Lena was also sure the older woman was getting tuned up more than a concert piano, which caused her to stare into green eyes of envy for the second time that morning.

Later that day, nearly all thoughts of famous athletes' mistresses and forgiving wives were gone from Lena's mind as she pushed her shopping cart toward the checkout counter at the neighborhood grocery store. Although she wasn't a frequent reader of gossip and entertainment magazines, there she was a number of them in her cart. *Vanity Fair* and *Essence* were shoved beneath a loaf of wheat bread and breakfast croissants. She scanned the magazine covers to see which of them had the kinds of articles that convinced Dane Tolliver to run the streets in search of what she'd faked far too long with her deceased husband. Lena's own sex life was listless. It paled miserably in comparison to most of her patients and teetered somewhere between barely and boring. So, there she stood in the checkout line pondering all the bad sex she'd faked with her husband, Ledger. Although faithfully married to an older man who continually thought less of making love and more about making his conglomerate double in size, Lena always viewed her relationship as solid.

While dashing home to get dinner started, Lena was optimistic about an evening of intimacy. She looked forward to sharing a mouthwatering meal and perhaps a sensual rendezvous afterwards, even if it required a little faking.

As soon as the shopping bags hit the granite counter top, Lena eased over to the kitchen desk to check the message on the LAN line. She prayed silently that there wouldn't be an apology from her husband begging forgiveness and breaking yet another date. Suddenly, a delightful smile spread across her lips when there was no such message. Lena was still smiling after she placed a tray of glazed pork chops and bread stuffing into the oven then set the timer on the asparagus spears and candied yams. "Everything is just about ready," she said to herself, then tossed a naughty leer at the bottle of Chardonnay she'd selected from their wine cellar. There was still plenty of time to grab a quick shower then slip into something more revealing. A black silk negligee with a daring slit rising up past her mid-thigh was a suitable seduction accessory, one she wouldn't be wearing shortly after dessert if Ledger knew what was good for him.

After setting the scene for satisfaction, Lena's strapless four-inch heels barely touched the marble floor when she sauntered down the back staircase. To pass time, she watched "Wheel of Fortune" until the popular game show ended. Lena checked her watch repeatedly as the national news concluded, realizing her perfect plans were anything but that. She put off the inevitable as long as possible then dialed Ledger's cellphone number while picking at the limp asparagus spears and stiffening stuffing. Lena was about to leave a voice message until she heard the door close, leading from the garage. "Fix your face," she told herself, as heavy footsteps drew nearer to the kitchen. "Life doesn't always have to be about you."

"Good, good. We can wrap it up tomorrow," Ledger said into his telephone headset. He casually strolled into the dining room, wearing an exquisite gray houndstooth suit. He nodded hello to Lena with a New York Times in one hand and a soft brown, leather satchel in the other then returned to his phone call. "I'll expect a car to meet me at LAX. Good. All right then."

The manufactured expression Lena put on scarcely concealed the disappointment running just beneath the surface. She composed herself to handle whatever lame excuse Ledger was certain to offer, followed by a somewhat sincere apology. Unfortunately, he had the audacity to begin gloating how well his day went. "Lena, you won't believe how easily I had Cartwright Brooks eating out of my hands. Closing the deal on the movie theater in Portland is a cinch now that I've unloaded two service stations on a foreign group at twice what I paid for them last year."

Ledger was a good man, who loved his wife. Unfortunately, he thought it should have been enough to satisfy her. He believed everything could be accomplished with a sound agreement in which both parties held up their end. Ledger's first marriage fell apart due to irreconcilable differences, resulting from his extended business trips and unrelenting drive to build his empire. Lena quickly discovered how it felt being a distant second to her husband's enormous pride and that her love was no match for his infatuation with success.

Still, Lena worked hard at being supportive while Ledger continued his grandstanding for several minutes, as if he were making a pitch to a prospective buyer. She smiled politely, understanding how proud he was of his latest accomplishments. There was a time when she would have been very impressed with his distinguished and stately appearance. For a man of fifty-nine, he still had most of his hair, although silvering at the temples and much thinner than when Lena first ran her fingers through it. He was then a good looking forty-seven-year old adjunct professor of business at the University of Texas Consolidated, a position he filled for one term as a favor to the Dean. In return, Ledger received an overwhelming endorsement that put his name on the lips of every alumnus with venture capital connections. He was a slave to his precious legacy, a monument to himself. When Ledger finished patting himself on the back, he completely summed up their relationship in three words. "What I do?" he asked, with widening brown eyes.

She inhaled deeply to bridle her tongue before something unintended came flying out. "Good evening, honey," Lena answered eventually. "I'm glad you had a great day. I'm glad you're home. I also think it's interesting that you didn't think to call me and say that you might be running ninety minutes late. Dinner was delicious by the way, an hour and a half ago."

"Is that the reason for the blank stare?" Ledger questioned. "Business ran over and the west coast firm didn't want to close negotiations. With the time zone difference, I had to keep my team working overtime so I had dinner brought in for the entire group. I am very sorry."

Lena closed her eyes briefly then exhaled. "A genuine apology usually comes at the beginning, rather than the end of a sorry-ass excuse. They tend to be better received that way."

"But I didn't think you were really serious the other day, expecting me home for dinner." He extended his arms wide like a politician extolling self-importance. "I guess I could warm up a plate if that helps the situation any."

"No. Don't trouble yourself. A simple phone call would have helped the situation. You have priorities and I know that. I'm just silly enough to think I'm still number one on that list."

Ledger crossed his long arms, obviously bothered by having his priorities challenged. "Look, it's late. Apparently, I screwed up."

"Apparently," Lena agreed.

"Why don't we relax and—." When nothing came to mind, he repeated himself. "Why don't we just relax?"

"I didn't mean to drag this out or belabor the point but…" she offered.

"That's never stopped you before," he interrupted.

"Ledger, if I'm wasting your time or getting in your way, just let me know and I'm sure I can find something creative to do with myself." Finally, Lena's sexy lingerie caught his eye.

"If I didn't know better, Mrs. Harmon, I'd think you were threatening me." Ledger chuckled as he poured himself a glass of cognac. "I've apologized Lena. I'm busting my behind to secure our future; and I'm not stepping out on you. Although you might be a little upset tonight, don't forget how good you have it."

He was grandstanding again, pointing out original oil paintings, articles of fine china and distinctive crystal pieces throughout the vast dining room. "You have several expensive homes. You take the most exotic trips and are blessed with a caring husband. I can't count the number of black women who would love to be in your shoes. Hell, plenty of white ones too. Most of the men I know would take advantage of that."

Lena stood up from the dinner table, wobbled back on her heels then drew a sip of wine into her mouth. She swallowed then smiled soberly.

"I can see this evening has no chance of turning out right. All I wanted was a quiet evening with my man. Despite a full day at my office, I rushed home and prepared dinner then threw on something inviting. I hoped it would lead to something naughty and nice but I was aiming high. Honey, look, I would never threaten you and I'm glad that you're not seeing other women but I'm not going to live out my marriage with the saving grace, 'at least he doesn't cheat'."

He shook his head disapprovingly. "Humph. You get it all out yet?"

"No. Not quite. You said something else." Lena's eyes narrowed when recalling exactly how he'd phrased it.

"Something about homes, trips, black women and oh yeah, white ones, too. Ledger, I've never wanted more than the one house I'm standing in. The trips we take usually result in you leaving early or you being strapped to that ridiculous cell phone headset. As for the other women who'd love to be in my shoes, if this is the best we can do," referring to her spoiled entrée and Ledger's bulging annoyance, "that number of bitches who want this shit, can have all my goddamned shoes. They might fit those ratchet heifers better anyway."

After a glint of silence floated between them, Ledger burst out laughing. Lena stared straight through him as if he'd lost his mind.

"What the hell are you laughing at?"

"You're drunk."

"It doesn't mean I'm wrong."

"No, baby, not at all. Actually, it's rather sad that we're at each other's throats like this. I'll find a way to make it up to you. I wouldn't want you to consider giving up your shoes or *your husband*, so easily."

She almost managed a smile... almost. With nothing to add, she repeated the obvious while approaching the staircase railing.

"I just wanted to have a nice quiet evening with my man."

After drinking three glasses of wine, Lena was quite tipsy and she was also right back where she'd started, wanting some quality time and wondering if her marriage was as solid as she pretended.

At three o'clock in the morning, Lena staggered out of bed toward the bathroom. When she didn't find Ledger lying beside her, she wandered downstairs. There he was, sitting on the sofa, still dressed in his tailored suit with a *Newsweek* straddling his lap instead of her. She contemplated begging him to join her in bed but decided instead to toss a blanket over the entire situation and share her disappointment with a whole pint of cookie-dough ice cream. At least then, the night wouldn't be a total loss.

# chapter two
# FOR THE SHOW

Tuesday was hectic. Lena's waiting room swarmed with antsy patients throughout the entire day. Most of the women had read the New Sex article and immediately sought out her opinions on the social aspects of dating as well. Lena was not prepared for the unintended consequences. She had no interest in playing the psychologist or mating advisor but worked at a dizzying clip to keep pace with the demand for her medical expertise. Margo juggled the doctor's schedule and both of them skipped lunch to accommodate two new patients. While obstetrics was a great way to make a living, providing gynecological-only services had crossed Lena's mind.

The rising cost of malpractice insurance had recently forced several of her contemporaries out of the baby delivery business. They complained about the losses in revenue but none of them missed the absurdly long hours they walked away from. Lena fully understood finances and the constraints of running a medical practice while maintaining some semblance of a normal life, regular dinners with her husband, small talk, pillow talk, and of course, the ever elusive happy endings. Scaling back her practice to offer solely women's health amenities would have provided all the *normal life* she could hope for. On the other hand, as soon as she envisioned Ledger fast asleep on the sofa in his business suit, that thought was quickly dashed away. Lena had her fill of eating and sleeping alone so she closed the book on normal then plunged back into the here and now, where seeing to the needs of patients made her feel worthwhile.

Margo sauntered in the small break room, which adjoined the doctor's private office. She laid two charts on the counter. "Catch your breath yet?"

Lena sipped from a water bottle then nodded. "Barely. Who's up next?"

"Well," Margo answered, too casually. She floated a lengthy pause then cut her eyes at Lena in a way that suggested a number of other things were up for discussion. "Katy Abernathy and Caroline Dumas are ready for pap smears in exam rooms one and two."

Lena shifted her weight while eyeing her assistant suspiciously. "Is this the part where I'm supposed to guess what else you're not telling me?"

"There's just one other thing. A man, a very handsome man, is in the reception room."

"So. What's he want?"

"Seeing as how his business card paints him as a pill pusher, I'd have to guess he wants a meet and greet with the doctor." Once again, Margo was playing coy and intentionally vague.

"Are you blushing, Margo? You *are* blushing," Lena teased. "He can't be that fine. Anyway, tell him I only visit with pharmaceutical sales reps after four o'clock on Tuesdays and Thursdays." Lena began to flip through the charts Margo placed on the counter. When it was clear that the office manager was stalling, the doctor glanced up momentarily from a dated ultra sound reading.

"What is with you today?"

"It's 4:30 and today is Tuesday," Margo answered, with an impish grin.

Slightly embarrassed, Lena chuckled. "Okay, you got me but tell that man I'll get to him when I get to him."

"Yes'm. I'll run tell him now," Margo sang playfully. She strolled away humming a carefree tune.

Over the next forty minutes, Lena performed two routine cervix exams followed by brief consultations with long-term patients. Afterwards, she collapsed behind her desk to attack a daunting stack of paperwork.

Margo peeked into the office to check on Lena's availability then she primped her hair before striking out towards the waiting area. An anxious smile stretched across her lips when she returned with good news. "The doctor is available now," Margo announced, just this side of flirty.

Sitting and waiting, until doctors had nothing better to do than meet with pharmaceutical sales representatives, was par for the course so the man seemed to take no offense. He stood graciously and thanked Margo for her hospitality while he waited. She'd given him a thorough once over, from his polished leather lace ups and athletic-cut suit to his broad shoulders. Margo took her time appreciating his charming smile, male fitness-model build and the most beautiful hazel bedroom eyes she'd ever seen. Margo had a thing for the tall, dark and handsome type. She knew he was probably out of her league but that didn't stop her from wishing. *Oomph, I knew I should have gone to medical school*, Margo thought jokingly, as he followed closely behind her to Lena's office.

"Dr. Harmon," Margo whispered. "This is the gentleman who's been waiting to meet with you."

When Lena neglected to look up from an opened letter lying on her desk, Margo cleared her throat. "Uhhmm. You know, the one I was telling you about."

"Yes, send him in," she said, although her eyes remained focused on the tri-fold correspondence from a referring physician.

Margo smiled uncomfortably then tossed an indulgent smile at the handsome salesman. "She'll see you now. Good luck." She turned on a dime, humming the same mellow tune as before. "Hmmm-hmm-hmmm! Now, I know what I want for Christmas."

Lena gathered brochures, daily mail and a folder on her desk then she opened a desk drawer to store the items temporarily. She was tired and it was evident in her standoffish behavior. "Thanks for waiting. What can I do for you?"

"A better question is will you allow me to help your patients?" Aries said softly, so as not to alter Lena's relaxed demeanor.

The doctor seemed passively interested to hear yet another industry pitch. Adding insult to injury, Lena snickered out loud in the man's face. She couldn't help it when imagining that Margo was listening attentively on the other side of the door, with her ear pressed firmly against it.

Margo was right, however, regarding the salesman's attractive appearance. The six-foot-two inch tower of chocolate with a chiseled jaw line and dreamy eyes was really something to see. His exquisite taste in men's apparel and designer shoes was a bonus. Yes, Margo had correctly rendered a very astute evaluation. This sales rep was *that* fine.

"Please excuse my manners. Have a seat," she offered eventually. He wasn't the first exceedingly handsome man to cross Lena's path so she gathered her thoughts. *Composure*, she told herself. *He's probably easy on the eyes but dumber than a box of rocks.*

"Before we continue, Dr. Harmon, allow me to formally introduce myself. I'm Aries Dupree and I'd like to thank you for taking time out of your busy day. I know you're bombarded with droves of sales people like me beating down your door."

*At least he's well-mannered,* Lena thought as her demeanor softened. "Yes. At times it can be difficult to carve out time after a challenging day. However, as you aptly stated, I do expect a certain quality of care for my patients so it comes with the territory. I hope your products are as effective as your introduction."

Aries nodded his thanks for her cleverly embedded compliment. "Actually, I'm the new area sales manager for Veritas Pharmaceuticals. We're a small company but aggressive. Within the next two months, you'll be hearing a lot about us as we roll out our product line that includes prenatal vitamins, contraceptives, vaginal creams and an array of cutting edge testing equipment. I'm sure you'll find our customer service comparable to industry leaders and our strategy beneficial to a medical practice your size."

"Your strategy?" Lena asked curiously.

"Yes, Doctor. While it's not sexy, our strategy is an indefatigable commitment to making our physicians' lives easier and their patients' lives better by offering alternative products that are superior to those currently on the market."

*Indefatigable,* she thought. *He has the vocabulary to match his charm.* Lena looked at his business card. "That sounds more like a mission than a strategy, Aries Dupree. Okay, I'll bite. Leave your brochures and some more business cards. You said you'd be up and running in a couple of months?" When he nodded, she said, "Good, get back to me when you've got something to sample."

Aries smiled amiably. "You can count on that, Doctor."

"Thanks for stopping by." Lena looked away casually as if not impressed by his smooth delivery and calm assurance. When Aries extended his hand across her desk, Lena shook it then waved good-bye dismissively.

"Oh, by the way." Aries reached into his leather satchel. "I hope you won't mind autographing this—." He pulled out a copy of the *OB/GYN Today* featuring Lena's article. "If I'm not being too presumptuous?"

Lena blushed. "I'll be happy to sign it. Did you read the article?"

"You kidding me? "New Sex", that's a very provocative title. Besides, this makes you a national celeb. Much respect is due for all the hard work."

When Margo returned, it appeared the two of them were getting along like old friends. She cut her eyes at Lena, leering jokingly while Aries placed the magazine back inside his leather bag.

"Margo will see you out. Have a good day," Lena said, finally.

As Margo watched Aries exit from the doctor's office, she also watched the doctor sneak a passing glance at him. "Who's blushing now?" Margo whispered. "I told you he was fine."

Lena smiled agreeably. "Yes indeed."

When Aries Dupree walked off the elevator on the ground floor of the hospital, he raised a cellphone to his ear.

"Hey, it's all good. Everything went off without a hitch. I even got the doc's signature. After tracking her for five weeks, it felt good to step up and touch the merchandise. See you in a minute." Aries sped out of the visitor parking lot. He plotted his next move as he hit the Dallas Tollway heading south.

Fifteen minutes later, his shiny black Porsche SUV merged onto Interstate 635 going west. As a precaution, Aries checked his rear view mirror before exiting at Webb Chapel Road. The truck shipping district provided perfect cover for a business which would rather stay off the police radar and away from unwanted foot traffic.

Several single-story buildings aligned the industrial park, one identical to the next. All of the non-threatening brick and mortar beige-colored office units were equipped with oversized garages, warehouses and storage facilities. Aries pressed an alarm code on the keypad to gain entry. The buzzer sounded. He checked his teeth in the reflective glass before opening the door. "Damn, I'm smooth," he said, arrogantly.

The receptionist seated at the front desk smirked.

"Obviously one doctor in particular doesn't think so," Cherry Bella said, smacking heartily on a wad of gum then giggled. "At least not yet anyways."

The leggy blonde flashed a knowing grin as Christopher Denmark entered through the service doors leading from the warehouse. Cherry stared at him longingly; finger-combed her short cropped hair then blew an impressive chewing-gum bubble the size of her face.

Christopher was fit and drop-dead gorgeous. He was also the brains behind Men of M.O.E.T. Corp., listed as a global investment firm. He shook his head regretfully as Cherry picked bubble gum residue from her salon-styled coif.

"That's not a good look, Cherry. And extremely unprofessional," he added, referring back to Aries' over-confidence. "Why do the newbies always get so full of themselves the first time off the leash?"

"What'd I do wrong?" Aries asked, with both hands raised defensively. "After being on the leash for months, I dug up everything I needed on the doctor. I know her schedule, shopping habits, manicure dates and hell, even the name of that fruity champagne she likes." He scoffed at what he considered an unnecessary reprimand from Christopher. Actually, it was his first coaching session.

"And you did well keeping her under surveillance," Christopher answered. He offered a reassuring pat on the back to temper the criticism. "But remember, Tony, we created Aries Dupree. He's suave, understated and confident without being cocky. We also created the perfect setup then schooled and rehearsed you in a manner that's sure to payoff for all of us." Christopher, as tall as Aries, stood nose to nose with his newest protégé.

"Cocky gets you the drunk skank at the end of the bar. Cocky also gets a certain doctor concerned about making a mistake she'd rather not. Dr. Lena Harmon is not the mark," Christopher shrieked, his voice rising sharply. "Her greedy, fat, husband is!" Aries bit his tongue. Cherry's eyes turned away from their conversation when Christopher assumed his role as the alpha dog to yank on Aries' chain. "You are a part of M.O.E.T. Corp because I recruited you, trained you, and put these expensive clothes on your back."

"I had good clothes," Aries challenged. "I had a couple of things working."

"You had shit!" Christopher argued. "You were running snatch and grab scams in Atlanta hotel bars when I discovered you. How many times did you get busted on petty larceny beefs? Six! How much money did you have when I bailed you out? None!" Christopher composed himself then straightened his silk necktie. "This is a business. No room for screw ups or show offs. Need I remind you, Ledger Harmon is worth 170 million. If you do as instructed, it will be impossible for him to refuse when we demand a hefty five-million dollar donation to M.O.E.T. Corp." A devilish grin parted his lips. "Now, do we understand each other, Mr Aries Dupree?"

Aries exhaled heartily then nodded. "You are right Christopher and the best at what you do. I've stepped out of line. I'm sorry."

"You'll be very rich if you stay focused. Raphael just snagged four million from an old lady's children who wanted her legacy to remain intact instead of seeing their dear mother getting her kicks in a three-way on YouTube. Raphael put in three months of hard labor and it was worth it. Now, he's vacationing on a private island that we own. You wanted in. I thought you were ready or I wouldn't have unlocked your cage."

Aries flashed a crooked smile at Christopher. "Yeah. We've worked too hard to get crossways now. Here's a bit of news, though. If you bark that loud at me again, I just might have to get in your ass."

"Whatever it takes to get your attention, Aries," Christopher replied calmly. "Whatever it takes. I've thrown down with lots of M.O.E.T. crew in one score city or another. We'll tussle a time or two, me and you, but putting *Money Over Every Thing* is how we roll at M.O.E.T. and make lots of money. Oh yes, my friend, it does make the world go around."

Aries slid both hands in his pockets. "And all this time I thought it was love."

"You are half right. The love of money is one hell of a motivator," Christopher answered. "Let's join the conference in the back. Chaz and Tanner are reviewing hidden audio from two prospective donors that they're already tired of banging. Nobody wants to give it up for the team these days." Laughter followed Aries and Christopher into the air-conditioned warehouse.

Both of the men went back to work as if they hadn't just gone chest to chest like snarling mutts. Christopher had made the same speech many times before, when blasting new Assets to the organization back into his reality, the one where money poured in or blood poured out. There was no room for errors, pretensions, mistakes or mishaps. It was an all or nothing proposition. Men either became a M.O.E.T. money maker, who pulled his own weight or risked being put down like an insignificant stray.

# chapter three

# TO GET READY

Towers of expensive office furniture were wrapped in thick plastic in the medium-built 20,000 square-foot warehouse. Leather sofas, custom-made desks and chairs were strategically arranged in a way that muffled discussions held in the makeshift meeting room. Owners of the building and all of its contents were conveniently being held under investigation for tax fraud. Christopher learned about the available space during a card game with the property supervisor at the Dallas County real estate office. Christopher's name was on a six-month sublease contract, at pennies on the dollar, before the last hand was dealt. The location was an excellent temporary headquarters for a score city. It was far away from the beaten path, offered a great deal of privacy and a slick cover in plain sight. Leaving things to chance took matters out of Christopher's hands so each step was well conceived, from beginning to end.

When the meeting started, Christopher approached the imported mahogany conference table, which sat on the far left side. After he took a seat at the head of the rectangular-shaped table, four men standing near him began to applaud. "Atta Boys" and "Congratulations" rang out into the still air.

Although uncertain of the reasons behind the cheers, Aries chimed in as well.

"Okay-okay. That's enough sucking up," said Christopher, eventually. "Everyone have a seat. Aries, why don't you watch the door?"

Joining Christopher at the conference table was a big deal. Only money makers were allowed to have a say in money matters. "We have a lot to discuss and divvy up this evening," said Christopher, once a small projector threw images onto the adjacent wall.

Aries backed away from the table in as slow reluctant manner. He tried to hide his embarrassment but it was pointless. Each of the men seated with Christopher had endured the same slight, being told to excuse themselves while business was being discussed. Aries loitered inside of the warehouse near the doorway leading to Cherry's desk. He was within ear shot but couldn't hear a single word because of all the thoughts swarming around in his head. "Why ask me here if I'm going to be put out?" he mumbled sorely. "That was not cool, Christopher."

"Pushed aside," Cherry said quietly. She'd walked into the warehouse to find Aries, knowing he'd have bad feelings about what happened.

"It's nothing, Cherry. I was just talking to myself."

"I know and I said you got pushed aside, not put out."

"What?"

"Christopher Denmark is the alpha dog and that's how it has to be. Maintaining order is very important in our business. No detours and no deviations, otherwise anarchy and all sorts of mutiny would take place. We can't have our Assets turning on us, now can we?" She smiled when Aries tossed a questioning glance her way.

"So he pushed you aside like the runt of the litter. Don't go getting all out of sorts over it. He's done it to all the other Assets before you. Remember, you were brought in to earn your keep and supply this enterprise with capital. No one pulls up a chair to eat unless they understand two things first. One, Christopher is the boss and the only boss. Two, in order to get a seat at the table, you have to contribute to the take."

"Then why invite me here today? To see this?" he added jokingly.

"Exactly."

"You're kidding me?"

"No, sir. This is also part of the plan."

Aries smiled. Suddenly, he was more intrigued than angry. "The plan? Okay, I've bumped into Robert and Tanner in the parking lot before and they never have two words to say. Are the three other guys part of the plan? They don't look like Assets."

Cherry nodded and gestured for Aries to follow her. "Step over here. I'll fill you in." Aries accompanied her to a small room, hidden behind a mountain of maple wood roll-top desks from Norway. Inside, were three flat-screen monitors keeping a watchful eye over the property and offered a closer look at the activities going on at the conference table. "You're right. The others are not Assets but just as important to our success."

"It takes a village to make Money Over Every Thing operate?"

"No. A well-oiled machine and dedicated operators. Take a look at Tanner, for instance. He's the one in the tan blazer, with the perfect salon-styled hair and designer teeth." Cherry's gaze fell on the sleekly-built stunner seated two chairs from Christopher's right.

Tanner Gregg was a former quarterback at USC, a golden boy from Malibu, California. Even though he was a college bust who rode the bench for three years, he'd managed to sleep with most of the cheerleaders and A-List actresses in Hollywood by the time he flunked out during his junior year.

"Tanner is beautiful, tall and well… tanned. He's eye candy, strapping and blessed with the right amount of wow."

"Is there a reason your tongue is hanging out?" Aries asked. "Other than the obvious, I mean?"

"Sorry, got carried away but Tanner is so damned cute he barely keeps his pants zipped long enough to take his targets to dinner."

"Good for him."

"Yes, very good and the company pulls in eight-million dollars for our troubles, that's eighty percent of his take. He'll walk away with two million after his first deal gets closed this weekend."

Aries liked what he heard but something didn't sound right. "M.O.E.T. sets the guy up with a nice back-story, impressive clothes and, by the looks of it, some very expensive dental work. After the company finds a rich target for new Assets, we're only allowed to keep one million of our first take, not two."

Cherry let a playful smile dance around on her lips. "What if you're nailing a high profile lady Governor and her rock star daughter?"

"Wow," he whispered, in amazement.

"Exactly. However, the Governor's oil-tycoon-hubby is paying us so our video of his wife and daughter's greatest tricks have no chance of going viral."

When one of the men seated across from Christopher laughed aloud, Cherry chuckled. Robert Tate, son of a laundromat owner from Flagstaff, Arizona, was fanning himself with a stack of 100 bills from the briefcase placed in the center of the table. With looks like his, it was no wonder he hopped on the first thing smoking when his father began grooming him to run the family business. One of the most attractive Assets ever recruited by Christopher, Robert's dark hair was tapered close around the ears, which accentuated his firm jaw line and was an ideal complement to his steel-gray eyes. From humble beginnings, he was bred to wed a local girl, fall in love by twenty-one then settle down with a house full of cute-as-kitten kids. On the other hand, his love of the fast lane and high class swagger were custom made for pulling in the kind of loot that made kings of small countries blush.

After closing their first deal, company Assets were awarded one million dollars, 2.5 million for the next three and then a five-million dollar windfall after their fifth scheme paid off.

"He's a real charmer, that one," Cherry added, "and he's pretty enough to stand atop a Neiman Marcus wedding cake if you ask me. Robert is looking into buying a private island after his deal closes next week, his fifth in a row." Cherry laughed when Aries swallowed hard once realizing the implication.

Considering all of the money at stake, Aries was even more interested. "Okay, now you really have my attention. Tanner's having a ball and that goes without saying. Robert racked up five consecutive scores and just hit the lottery, so I know why he's here but who are those other three?"

Seated at the table across from Robert, Tanner and Christopher were three very intricate parts of the M.O.E.T. brain trust and although they looked exceedingly average, the team wouldn't have remained three steps ahead of law enforcement in the score cities they fleeced.

Take Raja Wayne, a twenty-six-year-old statistician from India; who was orphaned at birth and a peculiar shade of raisin-brown. He's a pint-sized computer genius," Cherry said, regarding the man who was naïve about the rules of romance. "Raja knows far less about love than any man with his intellect and bank balance.

36

"Who's the middle-aged banker in the sweaty business suit next to him?"

"That's Walter Shulman. He's far from a banker. You might call him a fixer with some strong ties to several organized crime families.

Walter was connected and more than capable of taking matters into his own hands if an Asset failed to live up to his contract. Christopher ran the show but Walter was the wrangler. Next to him was Myron Maroni, a mousy-brown haired photographer with a frail build, an olive complexion and a host of acne scars.

"Flea is the nickname Christopher gave Myron and he wears it like a badge of honor," Cherry added. "They threw in together over ten years ago when running illegal poker games in Boston. Yeah, they catered to those rich Harvard malcontents with more trust fund money than they knew what to do with."

Flea, ever the loyal pet by Christopher's side, was skillful with a camera and other various recording equipment but suffered from hypochondria and the distasteful habit of gnawing on his fingernails whenever a bad case of nerves got the better of him.

Whether by circumstance or design, Christopher had assembled an exceptionally gifted team. Cherry, Walter, Raja and Flea were all top-notch in their fields, which made for easy setups and smooth take downs. The time in between was allocated for the Assets who Christopher recruited and trained to make the magic happen. As crews of takers go, Men of M.O.E.T. was a proven entity with a list of disgruntled former clients a mile long. When a scheme worked according to plan, it was a thing of beauty. On the flip side, very ugly things resulted when it didn't.

It was early Thursday morning when Aries awakened to a high-pitched stripper squealing that emanated from the first floor of his loft apartment. He sat up and stared at the vacant side of the platform bed where his late night guest had slept.

"And stay out!" someone demanded, gruffly.

Aries rolled off the mattress and onto the slick cement floor. "What the hell is going on!" he shouted. He was still half asleep while pulling on a pair of white linen lounging pants over his bare behind. "Hold on Pandora!"

As he approached the staircase leading to the first floor, he ran into Christopher. Flea followed so closely behind him that Aries actually looked for a leash. "Tina," Christopher said, eventually.

"Who?"

"That sweet piece of tail who just flew out of here in her panties. Her name was Tina, not Pandora."

While fondly reminiscing on his wild night of debauchery with a very limber performer, Aries tossed Christopher a puzzled smirk. "I call her Pandora because she has this freaky little black box with a mirror and an electronic tongue inside of it."

Flea glanced at the pants and silk shirt that Aries had apparently strewn on the floor the night before. He aimed a small digital camera at the clothing then pressed the shutter release button to snap two quick pictures. "Just how wild did it get in here last night?"

Christopher grinned at the thought of Aries' fuzzy recollection. "Black box, huh? I'd pay to see that."

"I did and it was worth every dime," Aries replied quickly. "Wait, what are you doing here and at six in the morning, Christopher?"

"It's 9:00 and you were supposed to be at the Coffee Café on Preston Road at 8:15."

"Yep, I was there at 8:15," said Flea. He threw a smug wink at Aries.

Christopher sniffed at a can of scented spray he found on the dresser. "And your target was there at 8:15, just like she is every Thursday morning *by 8:15*. If I hadn't just discovered why you failed to meet your target as planned, I might be concerned." He sprayed a tiny puff of mist then bristled at the spicy aroma. "Why does every stripper have a thing for cinnamon?" he said, to no one in particular.

Flea glanced at pictures he'd taken of Lena at the coffee shop earlier as Christopher leaned against the dresser to settle into a conversation he did not want to have.

"Aries look. We've invested a lot in you. If what we do is too demanding then maybe you should write me a check for the sixty-grand MOET contributed to this score so far and we'll call it even."

"You know I don't have sixty thousand dollars and I wouldn't fork it over if I did." Aries lowered his head to collect his thoughts. "I am determined to make good on everything you've put in. Last night was a mistake. I went in too hard with Pandora."

"Tina," Flea said, to correct him.

"Man, whatever. Fact is, I was a little bored from all the waiting, after weeks of reading up on Dr. Lena Harmon, studying her habits, her background and her bra size."

While wagging his index finger at Aries, Christopher shook his head disapprovingly. "See there, if you actually had put in enough time to discover her bra size instead of romancing pole dancers then I wouldn't even be here and having second thoughts about bringing you in on this saucy deal."

Flea pointed his camera lens at Aries and snapped off three more images. He nodded his approval at the pictures of the well-built man, who had committed himself to staying fit while waiting for the go ahead to move in on his target. "He's been working out, that's for sure. Look at the guns on this guy." Flea extended his arm to show Christopher the impressive photos on the camera.

"Flea, please step out for a minute so I can speak to Aries," said Christopher. His gaze remained locked on the floor until Flea was out of earshot. "Now then, let's get something straight. You're an Asset. You're in my pocket. You will bust your hump getting to know your target's bra size, how she likes her coffee, her favorite sexual position and how many times you can make her cum before she taps out. Now, am I crystal clear or are you a slow learner who needs to be convinced just how serious I am about my money?"

"I got it," Aries answered, after brooding silently.

"And just so we're on the same page. No more skanks. Not here at the loft, not anywhere, until we take down the mark. You can't take the chance of Dr. Harmon seeing you with another woman unless that becomes part of our strategy." Christopher started off toward the staircase then stopped suddenly. "Disinfect this place and trash everything your stripper touched. It smells like a cinnamon-scented ass factory in here."

Aries knew he'd disappointed his handler. Christopher not only invested in his future but selected him over thirty other candidates for this particular score and he bet on Aries to come through. Lena's husband was arrogant, more in love with his legacy than his own wife. While it made him very rich, it left her extremely vulnerable to falling for another man. Aries possessed a talent for pleasing women and the time had come to employ his specific skill set. He had grown tired of hustling female corporate executives for extravagant trips and expensive toys. This was his shot at a big time money grab and he earned it. Failure was not an option. Aries was into MOET for a stack of money that put him squarely in the game.

He had something to prove and even more to lose.

# chapter four
# LET'S GO!

5 Star Laundry, an affluent dry cleaners, located in the trendy upscale section of Uptown was just on the fringe of the wealthiest community in Dallas. It was Thursday evening and busy as usual. The line of customers stretched out of the front door and onto the sidewalk. Although overpriced, 5 Star offered same-day service and the best eye candy north of downtown. Hipsters, fashionistas, metrosexuals, hot soccer moms and various beautiful people all waited patiently while thumbing through their cell-phones to pass the time. Picking up freshly laundered pieces of their weekend wardrobe on Thursday meant not having to deal with it on Friday night and that made it well worth the wait.

It was 6:30 when Lena pulled into the parking lot. She stepped down from her Mercedes SUV, wearing surgical scrubs and a bad attitude after a difficult day in the operating room. When she saw the line of customers, she shook her head disappointedly.

"This is ridiculous," said Lena, into the cell phone pressed against her ear. "No, I can't do it tomorrow Margo. I need to pick up my lab coats this evening. I'll just tough it out." Suddenly, the Yummy Yogurt sign next door caught her attention. Lena sighed hard, the moment she gave into her weakness for cold sweet treats. "The yogurt shop is empty. I'll stop in there for a minute and let some of these skinny minnies clear out first. Yeah, I know I said I would start working out so I don't need reminding from you."

Lena stopped in the middle of the sidewalk when a tall model approached from the opposite direction. The lanky red head sauntered with a casual stroll, expecting Lena to step aside so she could pass. Lena had seen this before from other photo shoot goddess types. "I have to go Margo but put Mrs. Childers' chart on my desk in the morning. I think she might be due for a hysterectomy."

After ending the call, Lena tossed the phone into her green leather Michael Kors bag hanging over her shoulder.

"Uhh, excuse me," the woman huffed.

"You're excused. Now, walk around."

The woman sneered down her nose and whispered something under her breath in a foreign language. Lena didn't understand a word of it as her nemesis angrily stepped off the curb to continue on her way. The following insult, uttered in broken English, hit Lena squarely in the ego. "*You* should be in street... fat-silly-nurse."

Lena whipped her head around with a stiffened neck. "I heard that! I'm a doctor, thank you, and unless you want a hysterectomy too, you'd better keep it moving Red!" Lena backed away slowly to keep an eye on her sidewalk adversary. "I'm tired of Euro-tramps trying to walk over everybody. I was born here, you're just visiting." Lena was not typically the confrontational type but an increasing number of foreigners acting as if they were entitled to everything on a platter, including the entire sidewalk, had gotten the best of her.

A few minutes later, Lena exited the yogurt shop with an ounce of satisfaction and single scoop of frozen yogurt to calm her nerves. The line at the dry cleaners was substantially shorter so she opened the door and joined on at the end. Lena licked at the fruity goodness without a care in the world. She had completely dismissed thoughts of the tall red head and verbal sparring on the cement outside. All was good in her view and about to improve.

Lena's eyes were trained on her cellphone screen when the cute Asian cashier called for the next customer. Instinctively, Lena moved forward as three people ahead shuffled a few steps closer to the counter. When a stream of pink-colored yogurt ran down onto the waffle cone in her hand, she raised it closer to her lips and licked at it. Suddenly, she felt a pair of eyes boring a hole into her forehead.

"Pinkberry Paradise, huh?" she heard someone whisper.

Realizing that question was aimed at her, Lena lifted her eyes to find a petite blond-haired man wearing a black leotard and soft-sole dance shoes. He had additional black clothing in the thin plastic cover draped over his long skinny arm. Lena followed his eyes and smiled back to her half-eaten scoop.

"Yes it is," she answered. "And they sure named it right. This is sinful."

"I remember the affair I had with Pink Paradise very fondly." He smiled then pointed at his lips to indicate that Lena had something on hers. She quickly pulled a small mirror from her purse.

"Ohhh. Thanks." After sharing a giggle between them, he nodded *you're welcome* then headed toward the door.

In the mirror's reflection, Lena found a pink yogurt ring circling her lips. She wiped at them with a napkin then checked the mirror again. This time, she discovered the physique of a professional athlete standing in line two places behind her. Lena raised the small compact then angled it to get a broader view. Above his gray and blue running shoes, she saw his long, hairy, muscular legs that disappeared into a pair of navy athletic shorts. Someone cleared their throat to insist she inch up along with the line. Lena quickly measured her steps then held the mirror out to the side again, wanting to get another glimpse. His gray tank top was fitted, clinging to ripped arms and broad, strong shoulders.

After the gentleman standing directly behind Lena cleared his throat again, she finally heard the cashier summoning her. "Ma'am. Next customer, please."

The woman smiled as Lena worked feverishly to get the yogurt cone droplets under control. She licked at the cone until realizing it would turn into a complete mess unless she devoured it in front of everyone, including the guy whose face she couldn't wait to see.

"Sorry. Can I throw this cone away," Lena asked quietly.

As if on cue, the young women with a fashionably spiked haircut held up a small lined trashcan. "No problem. Happens all the time." After the melted cone was disposed, she handed Lena four neatly pressed white lab coats, covered in clear plastic.

The moment Lena turned from the counter to exit, a strong but subtle voice called her name.

"Dr. Harmon? I thought that was you," he said.

There was a hint of familiarity in his voice. Lena scanned the line until she found a perfect set of dimples and a warm pair of hazel eyes smiling back at her. He extended his hand like an old colleague but drew it back slowly when Lena didn't reciprocate the gesture.

She was a slightly embarrassed for not immediately recognizing the man's face and even more because of their audience. It felt as if everyone was looking at her, knowing full well she couldn't stop looking at him.

"Heyyy, uh… good to see you. I was on my way out." She took off like a frightened rabbit towards the door.

"Hey, wait a minute," Aries said, following her out onto the sidewalk. "As hard as it is to get a meeting with you, Dr. Harmon, you're just going to roll out on me." Built like a gladiator, Aries' lean frame towered over hers, casting a long shadow down the pavement.

"I'm sorry. You do look familiar but I can't place you," Lena offered. She looked him over head to toe for another appraisal, just to be sure.

"I'm Aries… Dupree," he added, hoping that would stir her memory. "We met at your office last week." When she searched the recesses of her mind but came up empty, he chuckled.

"You're married to one of my patients?" she asked.

"Unfortunately, still single. I'm the pharmaceutical sales rep from Veritas."

"Ohhhh, yes-yes-yes," she answered, extending her hand finally. "I didn't recognize you without your clothes on. I mean, half dressed like that. I mean…"

"I was out for a run. I live a couple of blocks from here."

"Well, it was good seeing you Aries."

She turned and walked away. Aries stood there, statuesque and dumbfounded. In the blink of an eye, Lena stepped into her luxury vehicle and disappeared into traffic. Aries spotted Flea shooting pictures with a long telephoto lens and laughing hysterically from a sandwich shop across the street. To make matters worse, Aries lost a hundred-dollar bet that Lena would at least look back at him for one lasting glance but she left him standing alone with his good looks and what was left of his pride. Flea, having been on dozens of stakeouts with other Assets, knew a thing or two about women; and especially rich ones who were accustomed to having their way. He warned Aries how fickle they were and that nothing worth taking came without a healthy dose of grit. Aries was learning to listen to people who were more experienced dealing with the rich, powerful, and privileged.

Aries returned to his loft apartment to study his target's file that Christopher assembled. To perform his tasks effectively required thorough knowledge of his target and committing himself to taking the assignment more serious. Trained in the lost art of Courtship by professional romance experts that Christopher had flown in from London, Aries was well-suited on the nuances of attraction and companionship. His street pedigree was respectable but Lena was not merely some cinnamon-scented stripper with a freaky bag of tricks. She was more of a gem than he could have imagined.

"When your target spun on a dime and marched off, you should have seen your face," Flea teased. "It would have been worth a thousand dollars to watch you squirm like that." He cleaned the lens on his camera with a microfiber cloth then pointed it at the large bay window.

Standing directly in front of an eight-foot mirror, anchored to the wall in the den, Aries brushed at the waves in his hair then shot a playful look at Flea. "It was that funny, huh?"

"I have to say it was. She left you standing there with your mouth opened. I got pictures."

Aries wrapped the bow tie around the collar of his pristine white dress shirt then orchestrated it with long nimble fingers until it was a perfectly constructed knot. "Ha ha ha. I'll bet you do, Flea. I'll bet you do. See, the thing is, I learned my lesson. Never underestimate any woman who doesn't need a man to pay her bills, especially one that whips out a Platinum Amex card for her dry cleaning."

He slid a tailored black tuxedo jacket over his shoulders and primped at his thin mustache with his finger, glad to have another shot to make up for his last mistake. "I'm going to watch my steps from now on and let the game come to me instead."

"Now you're talking. I might not look like much but I'm a good seer. Christopher has me tracking your interactions with the target because I'm the best. Remember, you won't always spot me but I'll see things you need to make her husband pay." Flea went back to cleaning his camera lens then he said, "If I'm on top of my job, and I'm always on top of my job, I'll see things you can't from your vantage point. I'll text you if something comes up that requires immediate attention. I got your back and that's what I'm responsible for."

Aries turned away from his reflection in the mirror with a questioning look on his face. "What happens if my Seer gets out of position when I really need another set of eyes?"

"Let's make sure that never happens." Flea aimed his camera at Aries. He snapped a candid shot of Aries in a flawless Hugo Boss tuxedo. "Just make sure you stay on point and it'll never be an issue." Flea tossed a solemn look at Aries then punctuated it with a bright camera flash. "Wow, dude, you look like a million bucks."

"Thanks. Let's get to it then."

Cars stretched along the boulevard as valet parking attendants pulled away from the curb with one luxury vehicle after the next. Dallas Police and private security teams stood guard as special invitees strolled through the gates of Doug Nielson's fairytale mansion.

Doug's home was a hidden jewel in the midst of garage nightclubs and eclectic eateries. A thirteen bedroom fortress known as The Ellum Place, was a stone's throw from downtown and tucked behind a row of modest split-level office buildings. The king of prefabricated military housing was once a homeless failure until he convinced the federal government to give him a $25,000 grant to design a prototype for snap-to military barracks in Afghanistan. Once he completed a scaled model that successfully snapped together like Lego pieces, the Pentagon hand delivered a contract for $417,000,000 because Doug Nielson had no known physical address. With nearly a half billion dollars, he opened a checking account, bought the entire side of Elm Street where he'd previously slept in a cardboard box, then built his mansion on the exact spot.

The annual Ellum Place Fundraiser was the hottest ticket in town. The grand ballroom was packed with an assortment of old money and newly minted opportunists. Some of the guests had hands in building Dallas while others benefited from the technology necessary to sustain its growth. Others, like Lena's husband, were on the VIP list because of their connections to both old and new money-makers.

A twelve-piece orchestra played a classical music piece as Lena entered the foyer wearing a long midnight blue dress with rhinestone embellishments on the banded shoulder straps. Although her hair didn't quite turn out like she'd hoped and she was squeezed into a shape gear undergarment, Lena knew she looked gorgeous.

She scanned the vast room to see who she knew and if another women happened to be wearing the same gown. During her surveillance, she noted several pieces of exquisite artwork, new tapestries and a forty-foot velvet painting of *Dogs Playing Poker*. While most people viewed it as a monstrosity and giant waste of space, Lena raised a glass to salute what it stood for. The owner had merely surrounded himself with a number of things that brought him joy before the riches came.

After a respectful toast to the host's eclectic taste, Lena casually skirted along the dark marble floors and soaked in the grandeur of the room then waited on a call from Ledger. He was at a business meeting in Phoenix that ran over but he'd assured her of making the event. He always assured her but often faltered on those promises. Lena hadn't been there thirty minutes when the cellphone buzzed inside of her strapless purse. She stepped out onto the veranda to answer it. "Hello. Hey, I was wondering when you'd call."

"Honey, the meeting went late. The Japanese investors spoke very little English and someone sent a Chinese interpreter by mistake."

"I can see how that might draw things out," she reasoned. Waiting on the other shoe to fall, she tempered her words. "So, what does that mean for tonight? You are still coming?" Lena smiled at a silver-haired couple promenading throughout the backyard, arm in arm, obviously very much in love.

"You're not going to like this but I can't catch a flight out tonight. It was unavoidable," he said, his words trailing off at the end.

Lena flagged down a young waiter who circled the broad patio area with champagne flutes on a silver tray. She gestured for him to come over. "Ledger, I got dressed up and curled my hair hoping we would at least get a chance to dance and be together like a real couple." She grabbed a glass of champagne and took a sip. "What should I tell Doug Nielson if he asks, where's his favorite homeboy is like he always does?"

"Just explain that I was hung up on business and that I'm sorry."

"Oh, I don't get a sorry but your goofy golfing buddy does? I have to go, dear. I'm thirsty."

Lena ended the call then slid the phone back into her small satin pocketbook. She remained there for a few minutes, peeking up at the stars and humming along with the soothing orchestra music. Coming to the real conclusion that she'd gotten dressed up fornothing, she sighed then set the glass down on the nearest table.

"Nice night, doctor," Aries said, from the arched doorway. He was rather dashing and the way he brimmed with charm made his presence welcome. "You mind if I join you or is this area reserved for someone else?"

"Aries, right?" she asked, casually.

"You remembered this time."

"I usually catch on," she joked.

"I saw you out here but didn't want to intrude."

She looked him over and made a poor attempt at hiding the fact that she was impressed. "You're very spiffy this evening."

"Thanks and royal blue really dances off your eyes."

Flattered by his compliment, Lena looked away. "I'm guessing you're not out for another run?"

"No. Not tonight," he replied. "Actually, thought I'd drop by Ellum Place and see what all the fuss was about. This house is as majestic as they say but I don't get the name. I Googled it but Ellum isn't even a word, not a real one anyway."

"Where are you from?"

"Springfield."

"Missouri?"

"Illinois."

Lena chuckled to herself then placed her hand on his forearm. "Oh that explains it. You're not from around here," she said, with an overplayed drawl. "But you're right, though. We southerners tend to draw out our syllables at times. That's how you get Ellum from Elm."

"Really? That's what it stands for?"

"More than stands for it. That's what it is." Lena flagged down the waiter then relieved him of two glasses of champagne. "Here, take this *Aries*, I'm about to school you on a thang or two about this

50

here neighborhood." She took a quick sip then laughed when some of the effervescent bubbles tickled her nose. "Whew, that kind of tickled. Okay, listen. This area, Deep Ellum, is for Deep Elm or as Henry Ford used to say, Down on Deep Elm."

"I thought Ford was a Michigan man."

"That might be so but he opened one of his first plants right across the street. Over there where that two-story taco stand is now. In the 20's, this area was rocking non-stop. Every blues singer of that era you can name performed on this street. Bessie Smith, Jelly Roll Morton and Robert Johnson all came played Deep Ellum. Blind Lemon Jefferson even had an apartment not far from here and he paid a small boy named T. Bone Walker to lead him around by the arm."

Aries wrinkled his brow and scratched his head. "Now I'll give you Bessie Smith and I did hear that Jelly Roll spent some time this far south but T. Bone is from California."

Lena was in her element now. She cocked her head back as if she was being challenged. "Pull out your phone and go to Googling then. Look up Aaron Thibeaux Walker's bio and tell me where he was born. I'll wait." She glanced at her watch then began humming the tune of "Westside Baby," one of T. Bone's biggest hits.

"Okay. It says the Grammy Hall of Fame Award recipient died in Los Angeles in 1975."

"Doesn't it say on that overpriced gadget where he was born?"

"Yes, doctor. I was getting to that. It says the famous blues guitarist was born in Linden, Texas."

"Uh-huh, that's about 140 miles due east from here, off of interstate 30," she heckled playfully. "Keep reading."

When it became very clear that Aries was no match for Lena in the blues legends category, it was too late. "Well, if I must continue, let's see where this goes. In 1929, he began recording acoustic blues under the name of Oak Cliff T. Bone."

"That sounds awfully familiar. Where is Oak Cliff?" she asked, knowingly.

"Right over the Trinity River Bridge about three miles away," he answered, begrudgingly.

Lena placed her drink on the table and took a slight bow. "And that concludes our history lesson for his evening. That think I drank... I mean, I think I drank that champagne too fast."

"My favorite doctor," Doug Nielson howled, gleefully as he approached Lena and Aries. Lena gathered herself, put on a straight face then shook off the buzz running just beneath her surface. She hugged the unusually tall millionaire with naturally white hair, wearing a 1970's style powder blue tux with a matching ruffled shirt. "While he's a grand looking man Lena, he's no Ledger."

"Doug Nielson, this is Aries. He's a drug rep, not my date." She didn't care how it sounded to Aries but she wanted no parts of a scandal.

"I was in no way implying that but you could do worse." Doug shook hands with Aries, who expressed genuine displeasure. "So, where is my *favorite homeboy*?"

"Ledger is hung up on business. He sends his apologies."

The eccentric inventor nodded that he understood. "Did Ledger tell you to say that? You think he's really sorry for ditching me?"

"His absence was unavoidable and besides he is your *favorite homeboy*, right?"

Doug was satisfied with her answer. "Well, maybe he can stop by when he's not so busy." He pecked Lena on the cheek then nodded to Aries. "Nice to meet you, Aquarius. I hope you enjoy the festivities."

After the party host eased back inside of the ballroom as peculiarly as he appeared, Aries buttoned his jacket. "I know some doctors look down their noses at *us poor little drug reps* but I thought we were having a good time. It appears I've overstayed my welcome."

"Don't be so dramatic. It wasn't that bad. Was it?"

Aries lowered his tone so as not to bring any more attention to an embarrassing situation. "Not that I was foolish enough to pretend I was your peer but a modicum of respect would have been nice, Dr. Harmon. Have a good night." Lena watched silently as Aries entered the house and faded into a crowd.

"Go on then, *Aquarius*! I was only being honest," she said. "It couldn't have sounded *that* bad."

# chapter five
# BUSINESS, BABIES AND BITCHES

Sunday morning rolled in cool as the other side of the pillow. Whole Foods was absent of the young families and senior citizens who flooded the aisles the day before. It was relatively empty and Lena enjoyed having sections of the store to herself without fussy infants in strollers and overindulgent parents bribing them with handfuls of sugary snacks. Alone time was very relaxing to Lena because no one was asking for her professional opinion or thoughts on her husband's latest business venture. A quiet store made it ideal for selecting freshly restocked fruit and vegetables, and Lena took advantage of it. She picked through bright red tomatoes, sniffed the cantaloupes and squeezed her share of avocados. Her mother always advised to pick your friends like you do your fruit, carefully every time. In doing so, Lena was never one to keep a number of close associates and her produce selections rarely disappointed.

Moments later, she stopped by the butcher for prime cuts of steak and fresh water rainbow trout to provide options for dinner. Ledger was due to catch a late flight out and she wanted to cook a gourmet meal before he left. Lena had just about everything she needed, so she headed toward the front of the store.

Suddenly, she heard someone singing one of her favorite blues songs in a slow soulful tone that made her smile. She pushed the cart to the end of the aisle then stopped to listen. Lena poked her head around the corner, expecting to find an old man who shared a fondness for the blues, and perhaps a better time in his life. Aries glanced up from a box of dry cereal before she had a chance to retreat and get out of her own way.

*"And when I'm with my baby,"* he sang sweetly, *"I don't want a soul around."*

"Sorry, I didn't mean to interrupt."

"You didn't, Dr. Harmon," he replied flatly. "Good morning." His salutation lacked the warmth she was accustomed, making it obvious that he was no longer impressed by her presence.

"You have a very nice voice Aries. I like that song, 'West Side Baby.'"

"Thanks. I went out and bought every T. Bone Walker CD I could find after my history lesson the other night. I'm not too big to admit when I was schooled."

"I wouldn't go that far," she joked, though half-heartedly. "Any way, it was good bumping into you." Lena backed away then headed toward her full cart, feeling out of place and very much the intruder in his world instead of the other way around.

When she began to push the cart, he called out to her. "Dr. Harmon!" Lena turned back in his direction with a high dose of anxiety simmering just beneath her calm demeanor. "In the chance that we bump into each other again, I'd rather it not be awkward."

"Kind of like this?"

His brilliant smile peeked through a sexy sideways smirk.

"Yeah."

"Then let me apologize for the way things ended the other night," she offered.

"I'm a grown up, so that won't be necessary."

"Oh, I believe it is," she insisted. "After you left, I replayed the words I chose; which is something I seldom do because I'm usually on point."

"Okay."

"I did not purposely belittle your profession. Your career must be difficult. Most physicians go out of their way to avoid meeting with—"

"Drug reps?" he said, behind a chuckle. "It's not illegal and it's a good gig. Besides, I get to meet good people, sometimes," he added, to keep her off balance. When Lena laughed, Aries knew she was interested and not merely apologetic. "Well, I hope we're cool again. I still plan on getting your business."

Lena's disposition improved instantly. She smiled and blushed openly. "We'll have to see about that. Maybe you could put a call into my office manager. She can set up some talk time for me and the staff."

"Thanks. I'll call Margo next week."

"I'm sure you call on hundreds of medical offices. How can you remember my manager's name?"

"Margo is a real sweetheart," Aries replied. He let the comment hang in midair for a moment with hopes of striking a cord of jealousy.

"If she thinks the same about you, there won't be any problem booking a meeting then."

"Hope to see you soon, Doctor."

As Lena sauntered off, she pushed her groceries with a great deal more rhythmic sway to her stride than before. She felt good about being back on even footing with a thoughtful and well-mannered pharmaceutical drug representative, whose silky singing voice still resonated in her ears long after she left the market.

By 9:00 on Tuesday, Lena was up to her elbows in newborn babies and a waiting room full of patients. She dashed into her office through the back door then shed her medical scrubs. Margo tapped on the door twice.

"Yes, Margo, come in." The office manager opened the door just enough to slip inside then locked it behind her. "I know I'm late. I know there are tons of angry women waiting to be seen. And by the way you're avoiding eye contact, I've put on a lot of weight since the last time you've seen me half-dressed like this."

Margo was surprised to see cellulite, dimples and bulges in places there hadn't been before. She wanted to lie to Lena about the shocking expression but couldn't pull it off so she did the next best thing, changed the subject. "Good morning, Dr. Harmon. These ladies are accustomed to you running behind because that's the nature of the OB/GYN business. The operating room nurse emailed this report and said Mrs. Johnson and her new baby girl are doing fine."

Fully dressed in a blue designer pantsuit, Lena sat down at her desk. The button on her slacks popped off when she plopped into the leather chair.

"Damn it. There goes another pair of pants. Margo, hand me that black belt from inside the armoire." Margo did what she was asked and kept her mouth shut. Lena whipped the belt around her waist, tightened it and then exhaled.

"Somebody keeps getting in my closet and shrinking all of my pants," she joked uncomfortably. When her office manager snickered, Lena burst out in a big laugh. "Oomph, okay. I'm ready now. What am I walking into?"

Five charts landed on the desk. Lena picked up the first colored folder then flipped through it as Margo recited notes from the summary sheet she made the day before. While reading off the last detail from file number five, Margo studied Lena's face. There was something going on in the doctor's eyes. It was a smile. Lena's eyes were smiling and there was no mistaking it. "Dr. Harmon, you alright?"

"What? Oh yeah. I just remembered a song I liked? Do we have any drug rep talks coming up?"

"No, Ma'am. You told us to pause on that because we were only booking them to eat those catered lunches then ditching once the discussions began."

"That's right. Let's revisit that decision after hours today."

"Yes, Ma'am," answered Margo. "I'll dip into the room and tell the patients you're on the way."

Margo was a real customer serviced jewel. She prided herself on making patients feel important when they had to wait for long periods of time. Since Lena often had several things going on at once. It was important for someone from her staff to peep into the examination rooms every fifteen minutes to provide updates on the doctor's whereabouts. Margo found that it helped to apprise patients when Dr. Harmon was leaving the hospital, was in route, had just arrived on campus or was finally in the office. For most Obstetricians, life was fast paced and on the edge. Lena always argued that she wasn't paid for doctoring nearly as much as she was for hustling and handling. The medical part was easy. Making sure all of those patients were seen and served in a reasonable time-frame was the real accomplishment.

Lena hurried down the hall with a chart in her hand and a gray stethoscope dangling down the front of her lab coat. She stopped right outside of exam room number two, took a deep breath to calm herself then stepped into the room wearing a pleasant smile.

"Mrs. Petrie. How are you today?"

Shonda Petrie slowly lifted her head off of the elevated exam table, as if she had the weight of the world on her shoulders. With a perfectly styled weave, ashy swollen and darkened skin, she was a walking contradiction. Shonda was a successful executive at Dash Cola who paid too much attention to style and not hardly enough to substance. Her 250 pound girth and inability to quit smoking should have worried her half to death.

"Hey Doctor Harmon," she wheezed. "I've been waiting for thirty minutes and almost fell asleep." The forty-one year old shifted her weight on the table to get more comfortable.

Listening to patients complain was par for the course, especially when they carried around another human inside of themselves all day so Lena smiled heartily and turned on the charm. "I am 100 percent sorry for keeping you waiting Shonda. Your time is very valuable to me." Lena pumped two squirts of anti-bacterial sanitizer on her hands then spread it on thoroughly. "I would ask how you're feeling but I can see you're having one of those challenging days."

"Challenging hell, everything on my body hurts." She grunted as Lena felt the baby's position and probed for the child's heartbeat with her stethoscope. "That office manager of yours can be a bitch too. I'm just saying."

"Shhh. Quiet now. I'm listening for my friend." She glanced at Mrs. Petrie to see if her comment made an impact. When Lena saw her patient grinning softly, she knew it had. "There is my little drummer boy. His heart is beating just fine." She pulled the rubber ear pieces out then let the stethoscope fall around her neck, before flipping through the patient's chart. "252 pounds. Shonda that's too much."

"Margo made a mistake. She probably had the scale set wrong. I don't know why but she hates me."

"We both know the best answer to that. Roll over." Lena felt on Shonda's side then checked the records again. "Okay, relax." Dr. Harmon heard a knock at the door. Cathy, the youngest member of the office staff, stepped in. She apologized for interrupting then asked if the doctor would have time to squeeze in lunch with her husband. Mrs. Petrie sneered at the thin brown-skinned woman with a short butch haircut. The ornery patient would have blown her stack if she'd known the intrusion was a cleverly timed rouse to move Dr. Harmon on to the next patient. Fifteen minutes was all the time she had to spend in order to remain on schedule. "Yes, I can," Lena answered. "That'll be fine." Cathy eased out of the room quietly as if she were never there.

"Lunch with the husband, huh Doctor? Don't they call that a nooner?"

"I wish," Lena replied. "Let's talk about your current situation for a minute. Shonda, I don't like the way you're handling this pregnancy. You've gained a lot of weight and stink like a pack of Newports."

"Wait a minute, Doc!"

"Sorry, but I don't have that long. Look, you almost lost the last child and I'm not about to let you harm this little boy." Lena bit down on her bottom lip then huffed. "Smoking is tough to kick, I get that, but you're over eating and neglecting exercise. Now, your high blood pressure pregnancy is putting my Little Drummer Boy at risk. He needs all the oxygen he can get. I'm prescribing Chloropine."

"You know I don't like pills."

"You're a good person, a good mom and probably one hell of a vice-president of whatever department you manage at Dash Cola. But, I run all this up in here Shonda. You will figure out a way to stop smoking long enough to deliver or walk off about twenty pounds so your baby can breathe."

Shonda rolled her eyes to avoid eye contact. "Michael left me."

"What?"

"He said I ate too much, fussed too much and worked all the time."

"What are you going to do about it?" asked Lena.

"Excuse me?"

"Do you want him back or do you care?"

Mrs. Petrie pondered a while then wiped at the tears running down her cheeks. "I hadn't thought about it. Since I work sixty hours a week and pay most of the bills, I can't say that I miss him all that much." She raised her eyes to see why the doctor was laughing. Lena was doubled over, rolling hysterically. "What's the deal with you, Dr. Harmon?"

"You're a real piece of work, too bullheaded for your own good. Hmmm, I have something to say and I hope you do take it the wrong way and get mad enough to prove me wrong." Lena ignored the taps on the door, which often occurred when laughter emanated from a room after the doctor overstayed her time limit. "I'll be right there!" she shouted. "Now back to you, Mrs. Petrie. I like you. I always have but I will do my best to whip your ass if I continue to care more than you for my patient you're carrying."

"You're wrong for that doctor!" she yelled.

"Prove me wrong then! Or, I'll transfer your care to another doctor who may not give a damn." Lena stared the larger woman down until Mrs. Petrie blinked first.

"I'll show you and Michael. I'm a good mother! A good person!"

"Wipe your nose and get dressed. I'll send Margo in to help you." Lena reached for the door knob then turned towards Shonda.

"Oh and one more thing, I don't appreciate the way you talk about Margo. She's the best I've ever seen at putting up with difficult patients who bully people where they work, so you will be sweet as cherry pie to her from now on. Are we clear, Mrs. Petrie."

"Ooh, sometimes I can't stand you."

"Then I'll take that as a yes. Have a good day." When Lena exited the room, Shonda was sniveling like a beached whale.

Margo met Lena in the hallway. She wanted to laugh but managed to compose herself. "Is Mrs. Petrie still a patient?" she whispered. Dr. Harmon exhaled and nodded. "Then you gave her the... *and I'm not about to let you, yes let you, harm this little boy speech.*"

"Yes and as good as I could give it, too."

"Is that why she's in there blubbering? With her mean self," Margo added, to rub it in.

"She's not mean, Margo. Shonda recently watched her man walk out the door and she's just realizing he's gone, maybe for good."

"Wow. She's not my favorite but I'd better get in there and try to calm her down."

"And I expect nothing but the best attentiveness you've got. She really needs some pampering."

"I understand, Doctor, and I will put on my best face." Margo opened the examination room door wearing an assuring expression and the best intentions to match. "Oh, Mrs. Petrie, let me help you with that. You just relax a minute."

Lena hoped her patient was either angry or fearful enough to heed the advice given but she wouldn't have put any money on it. Corporate women in charge of a lot of money and man power, were known for being the most defiant when prescribed medical advice they didn't like. Shonda Petrie was no exception and dependency on cigarettes made it more likely for a pre-term delivery.

Lena pushed Shonda hard, with an expectation that she would rise up to meet the challenge. Failure to comply was not a viable option.

## chapter six
# REP WRECK

After the last patient checked out, Lena joined her team in the break room. Cathy collected dishes and coffee cups then sat them near a rising pool of hot water in the sink. Valerie pushed long, fiery, red hair away from her freckled cheeks then eased off her shoes. She worked with Lena the longest but had been passed over for office manager because she bolted for the door every day at 5:00 sharp, regardless of how many patients were still left to see. She was responsible for taking copays, scheduling patients, handling cash and making bank deposits. Valerie's duties were expanded when she demanded more money. Margo didn't go along with Lena's agreement to raise Valerie's salary but she was a firm believer in earning every cent.

"Dr. Harmon, do you want to order more of that gourmet coffee?" asked Margo. "We're just about out of it."

"I could do without that peculiar aftertaste but the price wasn't bad," Lena answered.

"It gave Cathy gas. Huh, Cat?" Cathy turned off the water faucet then gave Margo a terrifying look. "It's okay Cathy, you're new around here but we all poot from time to time." Valerie leaned back in the chair and laughed. Suddenly she ripped off a high pitched squealer that surprised everyone, including her. "See, there. We're all human."

"Some more than others," Lena spat, behind a stern side-eye expression.

Valerie grinned apologetically. "Sorry, Dr. Harmon. I had some of that gourmet stuff too."

"That settles it, no more expensive coffee for this group," Margo announced. "It's not worth the aftertaste or aftershock."

Cathy laughed as she washed the remaining coffee cups.

"If there's not anything else, I'd like to catch a boot camp work-out session. It's down the street but really gets busy after 5:30."

"That's fine but let me share this before y'all take off," Lena answered. "There have been a number of requests for pharmaceutical companies to schedule with us. I know y'all love to have them cater lunch, fix your plates then disappear on me. Rep Wrecks are not only huge wastes of my time because doctors typically get nothing out of the meeting, it's also a bad reflection on me when y'all book them and bounce. Try displaying some scientific curiosity every now and then. So, until further notice, there will only be one rep-wreck a month so choose wisely and plan to stick around for the whole boring spiel while eating the free meal."

Valerie frowned miserably over the new edict from the boss.

"Then I'm not sure it'll ever be worth it."

"That's my point," said Lena. She kept a watchful eye on Margo, who seemed unaffected. "Have a good workout, Cathy. I should be at somebody's boot camp too but I'm too tired." She flipped on the small TV then channel-surfed for the local news station she liked. "Margo, see about setting up a Rep Wreck with that Veritas Pharmaceuticals guy. You know the one."

"Yes, Doctor," she replied knowingly. "I'll look into it."

The following Wednesday, Margo unlocked the office back door after Aries text that he was on his way up. She primped her hair and straightened the reception area until hearing a soft knock. When she pulled the door open, he greeted her with a warm business-like handshake. Aries' charming smile put Margo at ease immediately but she didn't know what to make of the cute white woman, standing behind him, with the metal pushcart loaded with food.

"What's all this?" she asked.

"You expect me to dazzle and serve you all at the same time?"

"No. Usually, it's done the other way around," she teased. "Come on in, everyone is in the break room."

Margo walked into the break room with Aries following closely behind. "Girls, we have a visitor today from Veritas Pharmaceuticals so be on your best behavior. Aries Dupree has catered lunch so be sure to thank him before he leaves."

Pin-drop quiet was an understatement. Cathy looked him over as if she was not quite sure about being a lesbian. Valerie crossed her thick thighs in a hurried manner, like she was afraid her vagina would call out Aries' name if she didn't. Margo helped the food server open several warm containers of catfish, blackened shrimp with dirty rice. Lena leaned back and took it all in.

She was prepared to sit and listen attentively, ask a few questions and thank Aries for the food but he was even more appealing than she remembered.

Aries had a pair of roving eyes in the room as well. Cherry Bella played the role of waitress to the hilt. She moved about seamlessly, being helpful and invisible while Aries introduced himself and handed out pamphlets about Ansure, a new permanent birth control product. Even though he never had access to the revolutionary invention, thorough knowledge of its process and effectiveness was enough to captivate his audience.

"Thanks again for making the time to learn about Ansure and a few other offers which will be available from Veritas shortly. It is an effective option for a variety of reasons which includes; decreasing heavy menstrual cycles, it's non-hormonal and has a short 45-minute recovery time."

"And has this received FDA approval?" Lena asked. She picked at the end of a catfish fillet while secretly wondering what it might be like to nibble on Aries' neck.

"Yes, Dr. Harmon, all of our products are approved by the Federal Food and Drug Administration. We don't come to market until we know we're ready to take it over."

"Hee-hee-hee," Valerie laughed, flirting shamelessly.

Cathy snickered at her co-worker's goofy attempt to win Aries' approval. "How old do you have to be for this Ansure thing?"

"Eighteen," he answered plainly. "But it should only be considered for women who are certain they don't want any more children and desire a permanent method of birth control."

Margo looked at the pamphlet's front and back cover. "Is it reversible, Aries?"

*Aries*, Lena thought. Somehow it felt odd to hear another woman call his name but she pretended to be unaffected by it. Aries swallowed before answering.

"Unfortunately not, Margo. The procedure forms a natural barrier that prevents sperm from traveling through the fallopian tubes to a woman's eggs and it's intended to do the job until, well, post menopause."

As Cherry cleared the counter tops and sealed containers of uneaten food, Lena quickly sorted through the other material Aries brought in to discuss. She was familiar with the science and research behind the procedure for hormone therapy but other questions began to gnaw at her. "Why don't y'all finish lunch at your desks," she said to her staff, seemingly out of the blue. "I'd like to ask Mr. Dupree some pointed questions regarding his instructional insertion techniques."

Margo flashed a playful smirk then chased it away before anyone caught a glimpse of it. She knew Lena's was very married but wondered if her boss was merely window shopping. Cherry was the only one quick enough to pick up on it but acted none the wiser.

"Hmmm-hmm," Valerie hummed. "I'd rather hang back and quiz Mr. Aries, too. Chalk it up to scientific curiosity."

Cathy snickered again then skirted out as ordered. Margo glared at Valerie in response to her blatant insubordination.

"Val, you need to quit. Come on and help me prepare exam rooms for the afternoon rush."

Valerie exited the break room with a plate of seafood in hand, although, not fooled at all by Lena's casual dismissal. "I'm just saying, why I can't stick around for some instructional insertion techniques?" she joked.

Once Aries and Lena were seated across from one another, their knees almost touching, Cherry cleared her throat.

"Uhhh-hmmm. Will that be it then, sir?"

"Yes, thank you. Excellent job," he answered. His eyes refused to turn away from Lena's.

Once the caterer departed, Lena realized they were in a closed room alone. Her mouth became uncomfortably dry. "I think I need a drink of water." She stood up then walked toward the refrigerator. "Thank you for coming by today. I think my staff really liked the discussion and your grasp of the literature." She sipped from a bottle of water, swallowing slowly to stall her return to the chair she wisely abandoned.

"I agree. Hopefully, you'll be on board when our Texas charter goes through next month."

"I'm in and I believe Margo was even thinking about a procedure for herself. Otherwise, you might have been cut off and shown the door shortly after that delicious catfish hit the plate." Aries cast his eyes toward the floor until Lena turned toward him to investigate the silence. "A penny for your thoughts?"

"I'd better go before I say something that has no business coming out of my mouth." He arose to his feet then walked closer to Lena in a slow, deliberate manner. She watched his every step anxiously, as he approached her with a handshake. "Maybe after we're in business, a friendly hug would be appropriate?"

"Thanks again for coming. The food selection was a hit." After she cleverly dodged his innuendo, Aries backed away from Lena and the situation gracefully.

"It has been a pleasure speaking with your team, Dr. Harmon," he added, innocently. "My office and cell numbers are both on the card."

"Leave some literature on your way out." That was her way of saying, *this isn't happening dude.* Lena had no idea that her eyes and mouth had betrayed her. They were communicating something altogether different.

When Aries arrived at Men of M.O.E.T. Corp, he found Cherry, Flea and Raja seated at a small table in the warehouse. They were feasting on catfish, shrimp and dirty rice.

"Hey Mr. Duuupree," Cherry teased soulfully. "What took you so long?"

Flea bit into a fish fillet then chomped heartily. "The way I heard it... hmm-mmm-mmm, this is so good, he was closing the deal."

Utterly disgusted, Cherry raised her hand angrily. "Could you please stop talking with lunch hanging out of your pie hole?"

"He always does that. Always!" Raja added, with a condescending scowl. "Flea is incorrigible."

Aries leaned back in the folding chair. "I think it went well but you can never tell."

"You can always tell if you know what to look for," said Raja. "Life is ninety percent probability, four-point-five percent chance, and five percent certainty."

Listening with an ounce of uncertainty, Aries shook his head at Raja. "Is this cat for real?"

Cherry nodded as she sipped from a tall cup of peach tea with a straw. "Yep, that's what Raja does. He's the second foremost statistician in the country."

"I'll be number one soon. Stanislaus Fonderlin doesn't have long to live. He contracted Ebola." Raja smiled gratuitously then devoured a piece of blackened shrimp.

Christopher walked into the warehouse from the other side. He spoke quietly into a cell phone with single-word replies.

"Yes. Yes. Seven. No. Seven. Absolutely. Bye." He put the phone away then observed members of his team eating a late lunch. "It looks good. Aries and Cherry, could you join me in the office when you're finished?" Cherry swallowed then wiped her mouth with a folded napkin. She understood that a request from Christopher was usually immediate so she stood up and followed him as he turned to walk away. Aries searched the tin container for something to eat until he found Flea and Raja's eyes insisting that he join Christopher's impromptu meeting straightaway.

"Now? Really? I should have stopped at Taco Town on the way back," Aries huffed.

Flea shrugged nonchalantly. "Just don't eat their Nacho Surprise."

"It's not real meat," added Raja. "That's the surprise."

Aries still heard Flea's howling laughter when he stepped into Christopher's office to discuss the status of Asset #29's case. The room was a basic twelve-by-twelve box with antiquated lighting and off-white paint covering every imaginable inch of the walls. There were no pastel paintings, artistic metal artwork or framed posters of poorly crafted mission statements. Nothing in the room displayed a personal touch, nothing.

As soon as Aries sat next to Cherry on the opposite side of the rectangular solid oak desk, Christopher cast an anxious expression towards them. "Well, let's hear it. How did the Rep Wreck go today? You know doctors really despise the whole *'drop in and do nothing but eat'* meetings."

"You wouldn't have known that by the reactions today," Cherry responded. "Aries knew his stuff and the ladies loved his delivery."

"Aries, what did you think? Is it time to mix things up a bit?"

"I was prepared, even made personal connections with a couple of the ladies. Dr. Harmon though, she's a hard one to read."

Christopher leaned back in the leather chair then cast his eyes on Cherry. "What's the report from your perspective?"

"Our man was confident and quick on his feet. If this doesn't work out, he has a bright future pushing pills and vajay-jay products. But seriously, Dr. Harmon was careful not to show her cards. She watched everything and everybody in that break room, except me. I was just a fly on the wall, a non-existent white girl serving seafood. It was kind of cool being invisible."

"Anything else?"

"Yeah, Dr. Harmon was irritated when one of her staff flirted openly with Aries but she handled it. The doc likes to remain in control and prides herself on it. She didn't blink when the young lesbian receptionist seemed somewhat bi-curious all of a sudden and probably didn't even understand why."

"Then what happened?" asked Christopher, as he grew more intrigued by the minute.

Playing the scene back in his head, Aries laid things out as he saw them. "Well, Dr. Harmon asked her staff to take their lunches so we could discuss instructional insertion techniques." Cherry blushed when she remembered hearing that first hand.

"Really? She said that with a straight face?" Christopher asked.

"Sure did," answered Aries. "Didn't even blink. I thought, okay she's feisty and doesn't mind her people knowing. Then, she iced me with a cold stare and an empty goodbye. She said, *have a good day and leave some literature on your way out.*"

"Wait, she sent her staff out of the room then sent you packing a few moments later?" Christopher said, in the way of a reprimand. "What exactly did you say before the ice storm blew in?"

"I mentioned how I'd better go before saying something I shouldn't have then offered a handshake and..."

"And what else?" Cherry asked. She was hanging on the edge of her seat.

"I said maybe once we're better acquainted, a friendly hug might be more appropriate?"

Embarrassed for Aries, Cherry turned her head away. Christopher shook his head in disbelief. "You didn't. Please tell me you didn't fumbled on the one yard line?"

"What'd I do wrong?" Aries asked.

"You talked too much," answered Cherry.

Christopher sighed hard then chuckled. "I should have sent

Raja. At least he might have stumbled onto an algorithm that told him when to shut up!"

Aries was confused. He didn't understand how the others were so sure of the mistake he made, when neither was there to witness it. "Okay, since I have two romance experts in my midst, maybe you should tell me how I could have done things differently."

"You want to know what you could have done differently." Christopher said. "Shut the hell up and left. Be more mysterious, not more professorial. I've seen you pick up the hottest woman at the bar without saying a word. Just do more of that."

"But she's really intelligent, a damned medical doctor," Aries argued.

"She's a woman," Cherry quipped. "She's a married woman who doesn't usually allow stray men in her personal space. And, she sure isn't interested in talking about the prospects of cheating in her own place of business."

Aries fought back a smile that pushed between his lips but he lost the battle when a loud burst of laughter roared from his mouth. "Ha ha ha ha. You're right. I should have shut the hell up. During all of this preparation and watching my every step, I forgot the most important thing. Beneath that large brain of hers, she's still just a woman."

"Ding ding ding. We have a winner," Christopher cheered. "Now we can calculate the next set of moves and lay out a strategy that'll knock the Ice Queen off her pedestal."

Cherry swept her hair aside and threw a come hither leer at Christopher, like a lioness in heat. "And get the good doctor in a compromising position, on her back."

In an inept attempt to disguise his affection for her, Christopher looked away awkwardly.

Aries' eyes pinged back and forth on them. "Y'all need to cut out all this playing around and get a room."

"Business first, Mr. Dupree," was Christopher's answer. "Business *always* comes first.

## chapter seven
# BACK AND FORTH

The trio spent an entire afternoon discussing Lena's shopping schedule and other potential habits to exploit. Christopher pulled a camera-size projector from the top draw then casted a slew of images onto the wall. Aries took mental notes as the slide show of photos and points of interest played like a scene from a spy thriller. He left the meeting with strict marching orders to play it close to the vest as agreed, without deviation, then soon become a necessary evil in Lena's life; one she couldn't imagine herself doing without. First order of business was using Dr. Harmon's schedule to create a void she didn't even realize existed. Aries wasted little time getting right down to it.

| Mon. | Tues. | Wed. | Thurs. | Fri. | Sat. | Sun. |
|------|-------|------|--------|------|------|------|
| Work Late | Mani/ Pedi | Morning Off | Dry Cleaning | | Boutique Shopping | Groceries/ Cleaning |
| Work Late | Gym Spin & Sip | Morning Off | Hair Salon | Dinner w/ Husband | Coffee Shop read/relax | Groceries/ Cleaning |
| Work Late | Mani/ Pedi | Morning Off | Dry Cleaning | Dinner w/ Husband | House-wares Shopping | Groceries/ Cleaning |
| Work Late | Gym Spin & Sip | Morning Off | Hair Salon | Dinner w/ Husband | Coffee Shop read/relax | Groceries/ Cleaning |

He walked into the sandwich shop in the garage level of the hospital. While looking over the layout, he noted the angularly shaped room that narrowed near the back. He also counted the number of people in earshot of the two unoccupied tables. He noticed a white, middle-aged male, dressed in surgical scrubs, lean in closely to whisper his affections to a young operating room nurse across a small circular table. He seemed unsure if she felt the same about him. Aries ordered a chicken-salad sandwich and baked chips then claimed a table against the wall. He knew Lena frequented the tiny eatery for lunch when she was too busy to leave the building. With any luck, he would casually run into her for a calculated conversation.

Nurses passed through the narrow hallway near the sandwich shop, groups at a time. Aries also drew attention from female hospital employees flirting with the good looking single guy who periodically glanced up from a stack of documents that appeared very official. After two hours, he'd had enough of looking busy and unapproachable. He tossed the uneaten sandwich in the trash and then cleaned off the table before going about his way.

For three days Aries made his way to the sandwich shop and waited, figuring it only had to be a matter of time before Lena happened by. At the end of another lunch rush, he closed his sports magazine and prepared to find another avenue to coincidentally bump into Lena. He had nothing against the limited menu but a steady diet of soup and picnic food left much to be desired. He squared away his table then walked down the long corridor toward the parking garage. He thought he was imagining things until he heard a woman call his name for a second time.

"Aries, I thought that was you," Tina insisted. "Damn, man you're wearing that suit."

The stripper from his previous wild night out had resurfaced. She was honey brown and wore long hair pulled back into a fluffy pony tail. Tina was a stunner, dressed in dark gray fitted jeggings that hugged her round behind. Nearly five-nine in her heels and fit as a trained dancer, Tina was an exotic beauty who was used to men falling over themselves to catch her eye. She was upset when Aries recognized her without a hint of interest.

"What, you can't speak now?"

"Hey, Pandora, I mean Tina. What are you doing here?"

"I'm just stopping by to see a friend but what's been up with you? I ain't got a call or nothing." Aries saw her mouth continue to move but he couldn't stop thinking about Christopher's rules about unnecessary women, when working on a score.

"Look, it was good seeing you again but I have to go. Take care, Tina." He felt good about being disciplined enough to pull himself away from one of the best rolls in the sack he could remember. Something felt wrong about leaving her pissed off in the middle of the hallway but he couldn't take the chance of Lena walking up.

"Whew, that was close," he said, under his breath.

"You're wrong for walking off like that, Aries!" she shouted. He wanted to pretend she wasn't yelling at him when Margo and Lena opened the door to walk in from the parking garage. "Hey! At least you could let me come by and get the earrings I left at your apartment."

"Hi Aries," Margo said, coolly. She giggled when peering down the long hallway to see who was loud-talking him.

Lena looked past him to check out the woman with both hands parked insistently on her shapely hips. "Hello, Mr. Dupree," Lena offered plainly. "She's really pretty."

"Hey, Margo. Dr. Harmon, it's nothing like that," he responded in his own defense.

Margo looked up at Aries then down the hall again. "Maybe your girl doesn't know it's not like that." She laughed at the embarrassing situation Aries found himself in then headed toward the elevator.

"Dr. Harmon, let me explain," he said, shifting his weight uncomfortably.

"What you do is your business, Mr. Dupree." She sidestepped him to jump on the elevator going up with Margo. Before the doors closed, she turned towards him wearing a disappointed expression. Aries caught a glimpse of it but vowed never to share any of the unfortunate misstep with Christopher.

"So, can I come through and get my stuff or not!" Tina asked, louder than necessary.

"Not!" Aries answered, in a huff. "Absolutely not!" He shoved the exit door open and strode out angrily. "Damn it. That did not just happen." His cellphone rang once he pulled out of the parking structure. It was a number he recognized. "What is it Flea?"

"Dude, you can't get out of your own way," Flea heckled. "Talk about worlds colliding."

"Where were you? That was a catastrophe."

"I was watching just outside the glass doors. You were coming towards me then that fine-ass Pandora chick stepped off the elevator."

"You should have told me the doctor was coming in!" Aries grunted.

"I texted you but cell phones don't work in lower level parking."

Aries was seething at the thought of a badly timed meeting between a casual screw and a pile of money he'd yet to nab. "Don't mention that to anyone, Flea. I'm hanging up now."

"Wait! What are you going to do to fix this?" he said quickly.

The look of displeasure shown on Lena's face flashed into

Aries' mind. "I'll figure out something. In the meanwhile, just plant the tracker on the doctor's truck and keep your mouth shut!" Aries tossed the cell phone on the passenger seat and made an immediate left onto the freeway. He ran a number of scenarios in his head all at once. "If Lena was mine, and she walked up on me and Tina like that," he thought aloud, "What would I do to convince her that none of it mattered?" Suddenly a sinister grin danced on his lips. "Yeah, that just might work."

For the next thirty minutes, Flea hung around the hospital parking lot, in the area designated for physicians. Doctors came and went for several minutes. When the coast was clear, he walked past Lena's SUV then dropped to the ground. He wrestled a tracker from his front pocket then slapped the magnetic sensor in the bottom of her muffler. Moments later, he vanished from the parking structure like a ghost. With a foolproof method of keeping up with her whereabouts, Aries could execute his plan more effectively. Flea was ecstatic at the thought of ending his lengthy stakeouts in a hot car, while waiting on Lena to make a move.

Later that evening, Aries threw on runner's gear and waited. He sipped iced coffee while waiting anxiously on the patio of a salad shop across the street from 5 Star Cleaners. He peered down at the digital readout on his smart-phone when it beeped. The tracking device Flea planted was signaling that Lena was drawing near his location. He watched the red blinking dot move slowly down the small screen until it stopped. Aries looked toward the cleaners as Lena stepped out of her vehicle while talking on the phone, totally oblivious to being watched.

A text message flashed on Aries' phone:

FLEA: Get into position. No line today.
She'll be in and out fast.

Knowing that Flea was a seasoned pro at his game of watch-and-wait, Aries didn't hesitate. He stood from the table then headed for the exit with both eyes peeled on that dry cleaner's door. In the time it took to secure his cell phone in the plastic runner's sleeve strapped to his arm, Lena was back onto the sidewalk with lab coats in hand. Aries was losing time. He had to move quickly.

Cars zoomed past as he hesitated on the sidewalk hoping for a chance to dart into the street. When a sportscar zigzagged in and out of lanes to make the green light, it nearly clipped Aries at the knee.

"Watch it!" he growled, as Lena's SUV pulled into traffic in the opposite direction. He waved two taxis to hurry out of his way once their traffic light turned green. "Come on, go! Go!" Aries grunted.

When the next light caught Lena, he took off like a rocket down the sidewalk after her. Bystanders whistled and marveled at his speed as he flew through the intersection like his shoes were on fire.

Aries kept his gaze locked on the white Mercedes SUV as the light changed. He had little chance of catching it so he began to slow down. Then, without notice, a small miracle happened. A moving truck pulled out in front of Lena and blocked the road. Car horns blared unmercifully as the passenger of the giant diesel hopped out and waved orange flags as if he was a matador attempting to calm a heard of raging bulls.

Aries couldn't believe his eyes. The only person smiling through the ordeal, he slowed his pace to a comfortable jog then casually crossed directly in front of Lena's vehicle. She captured an eyeful of him sailing by with sweat streaming down his face and neck. Lena was still watching him when the moving truck pulled forward and drove off.

While it took some doing and a great deal of luck to pull it off, Lena had an unexpected Aries citing and couldn't look away.

He returned to the loft apartment for a long shower after that intense stunt. Even though it was all part of the game, Aries was glad his next move wouldn't require half the energy or risking his life.

Sunday morning came and Lena headed to the Whole Foods store as usual. When she collected a shopping cart, Aries made his way to the checkout stand. Cleverly as planned, Lena looked his way after he sneezed loudly into a handkerchief. She stopped at his lane to say hello but he politely smiled and nodded instead. Lena looked dazed and confused when he said, "Hello Doctor," then non-chalantly strolled by with two bags under his arms.

She whipped her head around to see if her eyes were lying. It was Aries in comfortable jeans, a faded maroon V-neck tee and brown leather sandals. *Damn, he looks amazing*, she thought. But what was that about? Lena made a U-turn with the shopping cart then crept closer to the tinted store windows. She saw Aries get into a black Porsche SUV alone before she continued her grocery shopping. The thought of seeing him and being moved in a peculiar way each time, bothered her. He'd seemingly dropped out of the sky without warning. Nonetheless, she found herself greatly welcoming his arrival.

Coincidentally, two full weeks passed without a glimpse of Aries or a mere word from him. Lena told herself it was for the best and believed she was over the harmless attraction. Pushing him out of her mind became easier when a beautiful bouquet of yellow roses arrived at her office. The long stemmed flowers came in a slender white box with a red bow. Lena assumed the gift was just another of Ledger's ploys to ask forgiveness without actually having to say the words. Although she wasn't clear of what he was apologizing for, it still felt good to know her husband cared enough to stay out of her doghouse.

She sneaked into her office several times throughout the day to stare at the gorgeous flowers between examinations. Lena was floating on a cloud by the time her last patient left. She clipped a single rose then held it to her nose, imagining all of the salacious acts she imagined performing for Ledger later that night. Her moment of quiet contemplation was interrupted by a light tap on the door.

"Yes, come in," she said, still buzzing with elation.

Margo opened the door and stepped into the office. She flipped a patient's chart opened then started in. "Tomorrow is another doozy, Dr. Harmon. Dane Tolliver called so I put her on and we got more babies having babies. Yep, two teen pregnancies back to back. One of them got..." she said, with her words trailing off. "On my goodness, those roses are breathtaking."

"I know and just the perfect timing, too. I haven't seen too much of Ledger since he decided to take his company public. It's like we're ships passing in the night lately." Lena held the rose beneath her nose again and inhaled the refreshing scent. "He's going to have to dock that boat tonight, though."

"Oooooh weee! So you actually get to play doctor, huh?"

"I might even be the naughty head nurse too," Lena said playfully.

"Ha ha ha. I got that one down. Let me know if you need some pointers."

When Lena placed the rose back in the box with the others, Margo picked up the small unopened envelope that accompanied the flowers then handed it to Lena. "Mr. Harmon is a very busy man but he's still on his A game. We can talk about these files in the morning."

"Thanks. You know I haven't stopped admiring the flowers long enough to read this card." Lena opened the white envelope and slid it out. "Roses are red and sometimes yellow, I'm really an awesome fellow," she read. "Signed, T. Bone Walker?" Her mouth dropped wide open as her mind flitted all over the place.

"Kind of corny but very sweet," said Margo. "Who's T. Bone?"

"Uhhh, it's just Ledger playing around," Lena answered, somewhat flabbergasted. "That's the name of an old blues singer I like. Ha ha ha, Ledger is such a kidder."

"Well, isn't that clever. I hope he never loses his sense of humor."

"Yeah, me too," was her stoic reply. "I'll see you in the morning, Margo. Thanks."

Margo gave Lena a reassuring smile and laughed on her way out. "Head nurse. That's a good one."

Lena leapt to her feet then hurried to lock the door. She spun on her heels, stared at the flowers then picked up the card again. "Oh my God. Aries?" There was no doubting it. Those flowers had to be from Aries. Ledger never went in for sappy poems or clever prose. He barely took the time to send roses on Valentine's Day and always signed his name. Lena sat down and eased back into her leather executive chair. "Not cool Aries!" she thought aloud. "You're going to hear about this."

After sorting through stacks of medical pamphlets and assorted drug literature, she found his card. Lena punched in the first six digits of his number when her cell phone buzzed with a text notification. She touched on the message icon and nearly dropped the phone. Reading five little words slapped a smile across her face before there was any way to stop it.

ARIES: Did they make u smile?

Yes, indeed they did. Lena loved the flowers and basked over them all day. To play it cool, she acted clueless.

"Who is this?" she mouthed, while typing her response.

ARIES: Aries... T Bone Walker Dupree
wants to see u

Lena chuckled sweetly then looked at the door, hoping no one heard her.

LENA: *I think that can be arranged. When?*

ARIES: Tonight for coffee.

Coffee was noncommittal and safe, she reasoned.

LENA: *Sure. I know a place.*

ARIES: Thank u. It'll be good to see u and talk

LENA: *Just talk...*

ARIES: Yes, Ma'am.

LENA: *No monkey business...*

ARIES: Not even a little? LOL Understood

LENA: *Very funny, T. Bone...*

After sending the address, she collected her things and headed out the door. Seeing another man for coffee was an easy decision because there wasn't any ill will or scandalous motive behind it. Lena was merely meeting a potential vendor for products beneficial to her patients. If, by chance, Ledger asked where she'd been Lena was prepared to tell him the truth of her whereabouts as she parked at Mocha 'n More, a chic coffee bar on Carlisle Street.

When she reached the small building, Lena grew increasingly nervous with every step toward the entrance. The coffee bar was a quiet place off the beaten path and almost secluded within a sea of busy restaurants. It offered the subtle ambiance perfect for a meaningless meeting with an attractive pharmaceutical drug representative that no one ever had to know about.

While she looked around the room, a mountain of questions filled her head but she was too curious to turn and walk away. *Why did he send a delivery in the first place? What are his intentions? Wait, what will he think of me for showing up? Lena, it's just coffee,* she told herself. *He's not trying to get you naked.* She peered down at her rounded hips then sighed miserably. *God, at least I hope not.*

## chapter eight
# MOMENTS LIKE THIS

It was difficult to detect but Aries was almost as nervous as his target. Flea was seated at the rear table snapping photos and reporting to Cherry behind a laptop he pretended to be working from. This was either the beginning of a relationship which netted millions of dollars or the end of everything Aries worked so hard to accomplish.

Raja warned him that the coffee and chat meeting was known as "The Keep." At this point in the game, women either showed up to see what was in store or demand their pursuer keep his distance before she called the cops. Targets rarely changed their minds after The Keep. Raja calculated Aries' chances at 35% if Lena never cheated on her husband before and 68% if she had.

Cherry's opinion was altogether different. What it lacked in scientific probability, her two cents was arguably the closest thing to an absolute there ever was concerning women and sex. She told Aries that 90% of women knew whether they're going to let a man lay her down within the first ten minutes of saying hello. The other 10% decided in the first five minutes just how far they were willing to go.

Aries weighed his odds while watching tentatively from his table along the far wall. When Lena walked in, he exhaled then smiled.

"Hello, Dr. Harmon," he said nervously. "Please have a seat."

Lena continued standing for a moment. She looked the place over as if she hadn't been there before then gave Aries a suspicious look before taking the seat he offered at his small rounded table.

"I can only stay for a minute," she said, quietly.

There was no way to hide the panic spreading throughout Aries so he used it for to his advantage. "I'm sorry, Dr. Harmon. All of a sudden I feel like a clumsy sixteen-year-old stumbling over an extremely pretty girl."

Lena blushed right on cue. "That's flattering although I haven't been a *girl* in quite some time." The waiter stopped by to take her order. Lena glanced at her watch then asked for a latte, before sending the waiter away. "Aries, I think it's time you called me Lena. I mean, you did send me roses. They're beautiful by the way."

"I didn't know what to do after that run-in with what's her name at the hospital."

"She left her earrings at your place but you can't remember her name?" Lena said, sarcastically. "Quit tripping."

"Yes, of course I remember her name. Well, kind of," he added, jokingly.

"You're a dog. A dog." The way she leaned back and sneered playfully suggested she didn't mean it as an insult.

"Not hardly. I moved here, didn't know anyone so all I did was work."

"And hook up with beautiful women."

"Ol' girl was fun so we hung out."

"Is that what they're calling it now, hanging out?"

Aries flirted with his eyes then stared into Lena's. "Is this an interrogation? You're coming at me straight with no chaser."

The waiter returned with a tall white cup of mocha and a shot of Grand Marnier. Lena thanked him with a pleasant smile but kept her gaze locked on Aries as if she still didn't know whether to trust him. Lena held the cup below her lips then sipped from the plastic lid. "Hmmm, that's nice. I love orange liqueur. It's smooth, sweet."

"Yes, I agree."

"So, why did you send roses to my office and what makes you think I want them from you?" Her tenor was more serious than before.

Caught off guard, Aries bristled slightly. "I didn't know what else to do. I wanted to remain cordial with you because I like you and want your business. Look, my grandfather was a gambler but terrible at cards. Whenever he lost his paycheck in a poker game and came home flat broke, my grandma would toss him out. The next day he'd show up with a handful of flowers to help her get over it. It worked, every time."

"What are you bribing me with flowers to get over? Are you bad at cards too?"

"That look on your face when you saw me with…"

"Oh, what's her name, again?"

"Yeah," he said, repentantly.

"You represent a reputable company with quality products. I plan on prescribing some of them to my patients. It wouldn't matter if you had a dozen groupies."

"Thanks, that means a lot. I value your opinion, Doctor, uhhh, Lena."

"Good, then gifts and meetings like this won't be necessary. Besides, I assumed that your box of flowers was from my husband. What if I had taken roses from another man home with me?"

"Point taken," Aries said, with a blank expression. "It won't happen again." In reality, his stunt had gone incredibly well. Lena was there, sharing his space and enjoying the view.

"Well, thanks for the latte. It's been a long day. I'd better be going." When she reached for the car keys on the table, Aries softly placed his hand on top of hers.

"Wait, Lena."

"Yes, what is it?"

"I would be lying if I said I wasn't attracted to you and have been since I walked into your office that first time."

She snatched her hand away. "Whoa, hold on. You know I'm married, as in I have a man, and I've never once thought about cheating on him."

Aries felt deflated. All he could think of was Raja's statistics based on women who never cheated. He felt the full weight of his 35% odds crashing down on him. Aries needed Lena to be open to seeing him again. "Sorry, I really didn't mean anything by it."

Lena glanced around their immediate area before leaning in closer to whisper further objections. "Aries, you are intriguing and very nice to look at. I'm probably ten years older than you and not built like those fine young things you're used to. The flowers were a nice gesture but it stops here. I don't do this."

When Lena stood up and headed for the door, Aries followed behind her. "Let me walk you to your car?"

They exited the building, walking side by side, both quiet and uncertain of what had transpired a moment ago; and neither prepared to relinquish the thought of what might have been. When they reached her SUV, Lena turned to say goodbye. Aries reached for her hand, again. This time, she didn't pull away.

"Seven Years," he said. "You're only seven years older. I read your bio. I'm thirty-five," he lied.

"Still, I don't step out on my husband."

Aries pulled Lena against his chest and kissed her on the mouth. She wanted to stop him but her mouth wouldn't cooperate. His soft lips brushed against hers as the tip of his tongue slow-danced against them. "I know you usually don't do this. But, I just had to know."

Lena enjoyed the weight of his toned body leaning into hers. She loved the way it made her feel, delicate and secure. She moaned breathlessly when Aries caressed her face and gently stroked her cheeks with his fingers. Her head swam with vision of Aries licking the rest of her body the way he tasted her eager lips.

"Oooh-Oooh. You feel good but I can't Aries." She felt his penis stiffen against her like a steel baton. "Oh hell, I got to go." Lena pushed him away and jumped into her Mercedes as fast as she could. Aries watched her fasten the seatbelt. There was nothing else for him to say. This was "The Keep," after all, and he had done his best to get her on the hook. When it seemed as if she was more on it than off, she flung a stinging glare directly at him then lowered the window. "This is not me. I'm not this kind of woman!"

Aries didn't respond to her rejection, so she backed her truck out of the parking lot and sped away in a huff. He was left standing in the same spot, wondering what his next move would be, if any. Flea joined him outside the coffee bar.

"Did you get that?" Aries asked.

"Yeah. The camera loves your work but will Dr. Naughty come back for more? That's the question."

Lena drove towards her subdivision then parked near a grocery store to collect her thoughts. She felt guilty as sin yet sensually charged at the same time, failing to understand why a woman filled with regret also wanted to satisfy urges rifling between her thighs. She shook her head angrily during the drive home. Lena was forced to snap out of it before pulling into the exclusive community.

She rounded the turn onto Salt Grass Lane then pulled onto the long driveway leading to the garage. As the wooden doors raised, Lena looked at the seven-bedroom home. The 10,000 square-foot mansion seemed smaller somehow even though the landscape lights illuminated the dark-red bricked building. What Lena had always viewed as her bright and shining fortress seemed lifeless and cold as she pulled into the three-car garage and shut off the engine. Unfortunately, she couldn't calm the angst she carried into her house.

The tide of mixed emotions caused Lena's knees to weaken. She was ashamed of the way Aries' kiss made her feel. She loved it from start to finish. Nothing would change that but she was determined to try.

"Hey, Lena!" Ledger called out. "I'm in the kitchen."

She put on a brave face then picked up her pace as if it were an ordinary evening. "Hey, honey," she replied, while walking over to Ledger. When she bent over to kiss him on the cheek, at the granite dinner table, she realized Aries was still on her lips as well as her mind. She cut the pleasantries short and sat her purse on the counter.

"I see you started dinner without me," she joked. There were three metal to-go containers stacked on the stove top. Ledger was half finished with a second one.

"I called to see what you wanted to order from that Italian place. When you didn't answer, I made an executive decision. There's some stuffed eggplant over there, penne pasta with chicken and that marsala dish we always fight over." He laughed before shoving another forkful of salmon into his mouth. When she did not budge an inch, Ledger waved a glass of white wine at the containers.

"If you're in the mood for pasta, let me taste it. I had a hard time choosing between that one and this fish."

"I stopped for coffee on the way home. I'm afraid it ruined my appetite. I'm going up for a shower. Maybe you could come up and wash my back," she offered, with the hopes of screwing her way out of the guilt bag she fell in. "Bring your little blue friend, if you like."

"Sounds tempting. I just got the prescription filled but it's not advisable to take my blue buddy on a full stomach. Give me a minute. I'm sure we can work something out."

Lena had marched half the steps up the back staircase before it occurred how commonplace it was to give Ledger a heads up so he'd have time to get his head up. For a man his age who was not in the best shape, full-on erections weren't guaranteed when called upon so the aid of performance enhancing drugs became a way of life. The thought of making love to a fifty-nine-year old man who couldn't get it up at a moment's notice meant giving into some concessions not previously considered. Lena wondered how it never occurred to her before as she peeled off her clothes in the master bathroom and stared at her reflection in the full-length mirror. It was evident that her youth was fleeting but their love had always been enough so nothing else mattered. Lena dimmed the lights and climbed into the shower alone, praying that it would continue to be.

An hour later, Ledger tip-toed into the bedroom and stripped off every stitch of clothing. Lena was fast asleep until awakened, suddenly.

"Baby, wake up," Ledger whispered. He eased into the bed alongside of Lena. "Looks like I'm too late to scrub your back but I can still scratch that itch if you're interested."

She squinted at the digital alarm clock on the nightstand. "What time is it?"

"Prime time," he answered, sliding his hands beneath her satin teal negligée. "You don't even have to stir. Let me handle this. Yeah, I know what you like." Ledger fumbled with her breasts, pecking here and there then sucking on his favorite one. Lena moaned as she guided his head to the left breast as well.

"It was feeling neglected," she mused. "I've missed you waking me up with that bad boy attitude."

"A woman as fine as you needs a little reminding every now and then of what she's got at home." He ran his tongue up her neck them along both shoulders.

Lena slipped her arms out of the spaghetti straps. She wiggled from underneath Ledger's protruding belly to free herself from the sheer nightgown.

"Don't keep me waiting too long," she cooed in his ear.

The potency of the erection meds varied from time to time so Lena couldn't take any chances. She placed her hands around his waist and shoved her tongue inside his mouth in a blind effort to shake off all remnants of Aries. Ledger seemed surprised by Lena's naked aggression.

"Ooh, you're ready to get it on. Go ahead and put it where you want it, then."

She felt around below his stomach until locating it. Ledger's slightly erect penis felt like a pitiful facsimile compared to Aries' swollen tool, but Aries was not her man. The deep penetration Lena craved was literally at hand. It just required a little effort and a lot of lubricant.

"Hold on. Looks like a flat tire. I think I have the solution. Lay down," she ordered.

Ledger frowned at his penis as if it betrayed him on purpose. "How could you do this to me?" he clamored. "Can't you see I'm looking out for you?" He rolled onto his back then propped a pillow under his head. Lena crouched down on her knees then took his rod in her hands. She shook it then licked from the base to tip and back again until it responded. When Ledger's penis hardened, Lena closed her eyes and slid the head into her mouth.

"I'll pump it up." Lena inhaled and took in as much of his shaft as she could then peered up at him. She enjoyed making Ledger squirm and groan with pure delight, while she satisfied her husband. When he reached for her arm to pull her on top of him, Lena eagerly obliged his command. She straddled him and began grinding heartily. Writhing back and forth, she planted her outstretched hands on his chest for leverage. "Is it good, Ledger?"

"Oomph," he grunted. "Uh-uh, wait-wait-wait. I can't breathe."

"What?" she asked, in mid-thrust. "You okay?"

"Climb off for a minute."

"You're serious?"

"Hell yes, I'm serious."

Highly pissed off, she froze momentarily then hopped off to check him out.

"Whew, my chest," he huffed. "Your hands pushing down on it like that shortened my breath." Ledger was in complete denial that his soft midsection his lack of exercise or eating right had anything to do with his breathing. "Okay, I think it's better now. Maybe you could sit up and rock back on it."

Suddenly, Lena felt as if she was making love to an old man. Fifty-nine was by no means elderly but lately it had been always something different with Ledger. A few weeks ago it was his bad knee then days later an ornery hip acted up. "Alright, let's try this again," she said, halfheartedly. "I'll take it easy on you."

"Only in the beginning then it's smooth sailing," he responded, with a load of optimism.

Lena took matters into her own hands for a second time when Ledger's manhood refused to comply. Regardless of the degree of sucking and stroking she applied to the situation, the south did not rise again. Ledger apologized, fixed himself a nightcap then fell asleep downstairs with the television on.

Feeling lonely and unsatisfied, Lena opened the top drawer of the nightstand and pulled out a shiny, black battery-operated dildo she lovingly referred to as Zeus. She spread her legs, cranked the toy on high and worked out every ounce of frustration. Thoughts of Aries slipped in and out of her mind while the pleasure stick throttled magnificently in her wet chasm. After she climaxed for a third time, Lena moaned aloud. It was the first time she dared to whip out Zeus when Ledger was home. He detested it, viewed the vibrator as a threat to his manhood and threatened to throw it out. As a result, Lena lost some respect for her husband's lack of sexual prowess; whether she was ready to admit it. Everyone grew older and so did their body parts, she reasoned, but dealing with it introduced another host of issues altogether.

# chapter nine
# YOUNG AND FOOLISH

Lena spent the weekend thinking about life, love making with her husband and the battery-operated backup. Suddenly, she found herself looking at her current situation differently. Lena was bothered by the way her clothes hadn't fit properly in months, how the puffiness beneath her chin made her look older than she felt, and why so many people were trying their luck with one weight loss plan or another. Her life was medicine and marriage, yet both had been insufficient to that point. Spending the rest of it helping patients maintain healthy sexual organs while tremendously dissatisfied with lackluster sex in her own bedroom, was a larger issue. Lena wanted to convince herself that a steamy kiss with Aries had nothing to do with her new reevaluations. She wanted to continue on through life without faulting Ledger for growing older. She also wanted to feel totally unaffected about her pudgy neck fat and jiggles in more places than she would have thought possible at her age.

Monday morning came with a lot of considerations. However, seeing Aries again was not one of them, so Lena walked into the office trying to get a handle on how much she hated the "M" word.

"Hey, Dr. Harmon. Happy Monday," Margo said, as softly as she knew how.

"I know. Me and Mondays don't get along, either." Lena looked at the snipped single yellow rose sitting on the desk. She cast a frown while tossing it into the trash. "Wait a minute. You're even bluer than usual for a Monday."

Margo sat in a chair on the opposite side of Lena's desk.

"Guess I'll never get used to young girls coming in here with stupid looks on their faces when they realize they're pregnant after that stupid thing they did with a stupid boy was just plain…"

"Stupid?" Lena answered. She understood Margo's angst with teen girls who jumped in bed with boys who had nothing in mind but scratching a primal itch. "It's not all the boys' faults, Margo. Never is, never was."

After the office manager snapped out of her saddened state that began when two sixteen- year-old girls arrived with positive home pregnancy test results, she handed Lena their charts. "One of the patients doesn't know just how stupid she is and the other is too scared to tell her momma how stupid she was." After saying her peace, Margo exited the room without as much as another whisper.

Lena reviewed the charts thoroughly and scribbled notes on the patient interview sheets. She picked up both files then checked her watch before entering exam room number one at nine o'clock on the nose. She had a distinct feeling that a family's dynamic was about to change forever.

"Hi, I'm Dr. Harmon and Happy Monday morning. So who is my patient today?" Lena's lighthearted intro fell flat as the thin blonde girl seated on the exam table in a printed gown refused to raise her head. The patient's mother, an older copy of the cute and fair skinned child, cleared her throat to hasten a salutation from her daughter.

"Huh-hmmm! Didn't you hear the doctor, Becca?"

The woman was mid-forties, fit and rocking highlights in her thick, shoulder-length hair. Beige riding pants clung closely to her toned legs and buns of steel, which made it glaringly obvious that the woman was dedicated to working out, if nothing else.

"Yeah, Mom, I heard her. God!"

"Don't you use His name like that!" Mrs. Hollingsworth shouted.

Lena stepped in before it became a shouting match, not to mention she wasn't interested in starting her day with words bouncing off the walls in the small room. "It's okay, Mrs. Hollingsworth. Rebecca is a little nervous I'm sure."

"Well, she sure in hell should be after missing her period for two months in a row *without telling me!*"

"Because you're so freaking judgmental!" screamed Rebecca.

"Rebecca, calm down!" Lena warned. "And Mrs. Hollingsworth, the same goes for you. I have other patients and they can hear your raised voices, which suggests I don't have control of my office."

"She shouldn't pop off like that," the mother spat, in her child's direction.

"If I can't contain what goes on in my exam rooms, you'll find yourselves in someone else's." There was a brief stare down between Rebecca and her mom.

"Can we call a truce and get on with this or should I tell my staff to delete you from my patient list?" Mrs. Hollingsworth exhaled angrily. She was weighing her options when Lena made it clear that her level of perception exceeded what it had been given credit for. "You've never come to see me before, yet I'm sure Rebecca has a regular gynecologist. I'm guessing you didn't set an appointment at your usual doctor's office because a number of the girls in Highland Park are patients there as well. My being an African American physician helps to limit the chances of bumping into Becca's classmates and their parents, right?"

Mrs. Hollingsworth's face softened. "It's not like that, Doctor. Well, not really."

Margo tapped on the door then stepped inside just far enough to hand off the urinalysis report. Lena read it then laid the results on the small work desk, positioned to the left of the examination table. "Either way you're here now and it's confirmed that Rebecca is pregnant."

Rebecca raised her eyes to meet Lena's. "How pregnant?"

"At least ten weeks."

The mother began do the math in her head then she became livid. "Ten weeks ago, you went skiing with the church group to Colorado. Becca, you were having sex on a spiritual retreat? Good Lord, this is shameful. Where were the chaperones when you and Bradly were sneaking off and doing God knows what?"

"Just like you Mom, they were too busy to watch us."

"This isn't the time, Becca."

"It never is for you, Mom." Rebecca was resolute and angry, far more than Lena reasoned she should have been.

"Look, ladies, there's a lot to discuss but this isn't the place. I'll explain what to expect going forward then schedule another appointment in a month or so."

"Oh, that won't be necessary," Mrs. Hollingsworth huffed, with her eyes fixed or Rebecca. "I'm telling your father and we're meeting with Bradly's parents tonight to discuss terminating this thing."

"Maybe you should think about it before making a rash decision," Lena suggested.

"Get your clothes on Rebecca, we've got to tell your dad before calling the Bentons for a meeting." When the girl sat still and defiant, her mother yanked on her arm. Becca pulled away like an unruly toddler.

"No! You will not be calling Bradly's parents because he doesn't have anything to do with this."

Lena watched quietly, like a fly on the wall as the plot thickened. Every now and then Lena thoroughly enjoyed her vocation. Paternity revelations were one of the best parts.

"What do you mean, Bradly isn't the father of this baby? Why would you cover for him after dating for two years?"

"I've done nothing but cover for him the whole time. Bradly is gay, Mom!" Lena's eyes grew wider than Mrs. Hollingsworth's as Rebecca folded her arms in a 'so there' fashion.

"We'll just see about that. I'm calling Helen now." She whipped out her phone to dial but Rebecca snatched it out of her hands.

"Don't! Bradly hasn't told them yet and this is no way to out him." Rebecca was terrified for her friend and fearful of the secret she'd kept, being exposed by her own undoing. "Please, Mother, don't." Tears began to stream down her flat cheeks. "I'm so sorry, I messed up bad, Mom. The three of us used condoms but they kept slipping off."

Mrs. Hollingsworth stood from the stool then threw a questioning glare at her daughter. "A threesome? With who?"

Lena pretended that she wasn't just as interested as the mother to find out but she was hanging on every word.

"The Tunstall twins, Derrick and Erick," Rebecca announced, sorrowfully. "We played a drinking game and I lost— twice." She lowered her head again and sobbed uncontrollably.

Lena had heard it all then. She looked at the patient's mother to see if she needed to save the girl from a sound thrashing. Lena was slightly confused when she discovered a calculating grin stretching onto Mrs. Hollingsworth's face.

"Mayor Tunstall's sons? Oh myyyy God," she sang.

"Oh my goodness," Lena seconded. "You two have a whole bunch to talk about and I have another patient waiting on me, so can I trust you all to be civil when I leave?" Rebecca sniffled with a rosy red nose, swollen eyes, and a blank stare parked on her face.

"Oh you bet your ass, we're going to be just fine," was Mrs. Hollingsworth's smug reply. "I'll be in touch about the next appointment, Doctor. You've been a great help."

Lena exited the room more perplexed by Mrs. Hollingsworth's sudden change of heart. She felt sorry for Rebecca and even worse for whatever laid in store for those Tunstall Twins and their father, The Mayor.

In the room across the hall, Lena discovered a mother crying over her daughter's plight, as well as her own. "Dr. Harmon, thanks for seeing us on such short notice," said Clara Sampson. The mid-forties single mother was tall and attractive, despite runny mascara. She straightened out her green jacket and fitted skirt then wiped her nose on a cotton handkerchief, printed with a floral design. Ms. Sampson's lower lip trembled when she tried to speak.

"Whewww. I can't believe we're here."

"Hi Dr. Harmon," said Patrice, finally. She was afraid and ashamed when her mother gave a fearful look then turned away, as if she couldn't stand the sight of her child.

"It's good to see you too, Patrice," Lena offered, sincerely. She smiled softly at the thin, chocolaty brown girl who sat on the examination table with her long legs crossed at the ankles. Patrice was a tenth-grade honor student with sights on medical school after college. A favorite patient of Lena's and well-liked by the entire staff, the thought of Patrice carrying a child was a difficult mental leap to make. There are two things an Obstetrician never gets used to, sixteen year old girls in desperate need of birth control and those who show up too late for it to do them any good.

"How can I help you today?" Lena said. She allowed her words to fill the room and touch whoever wanted to accept the question and respond accordingly.

"She needs some birth control pills, Dr. Harmon," Ms. Sampson said, with an air of indignation. "Patrice has been trolling porn sites, so I know it won't be long before she's letting these mannish boys stick their fingers in her and Lord knows what else."

"Momma," Patrice whimpered, just above a whisper. She was embarrassed but couldn't argue against her mother's assessment.

"Young ladies are interested in the human form Ms. Sampson but I do understand your objection to online adult sites. Patrice, how do you feel about birth control pills?" Lena asked. When the girl shrugged her shoulders, Lena tilted her head slightly. "Patrice, is there more to this, more than just curiosity?"

Patrice's mother rolled her eyes. "I know there'd better not be."

Lena placed her hand on the girl's shoulder and made sure to keep an eye on the mother. "Patrice, are you sexually active?"

"Why-why did you ask me that?" she stuttered. Lena stood back on her legs because she had seen this scenario play out too many times to count; mothers learning of their daughters' sexual experience while in the doctor's office, was a common occurrence.

"I can speak with you alone then bring your mom back in afterwards, if you'd like."

"And talk about what?" Clara Sampson queried. "Patrice is only sixteen, so I'm staying."

"It doesn't matter, Dr. Harmon. My mom is going to find out everything, anyway. She always does." Patrice turned her face towards her mother then let out a woman-sized sigh. "Yes, I had sex one time but it wasn't anything like on those movies I saw. There was blood everywhere and it hurt real bad."

Ms. Sampson was speechless. She placed an opened palm over her opened mouth. Lena stepped in with a few kind words to bridge the silence between them as she pulled on a pair of latex gloves. "It always shocks moms when their daughters get involved sexually. Lay back Patrice and I'll check things out." She glanced at Patrice's mother, who was still shuddering against the wall quietly with terror-filled eyes. During the entire pelvic examination, Patrice looked away. Her expression was still and vacant. Lena had suspicions but kept them to herself. "When was your last period?"

"A month ago."

"So, you've missed one?"

"No, Ma'am. It's due any day now," she replied. Ms. Sampson looked on and held her breath as Patrice squirmed uncomfortably on the padded table.

"Okay. Sit up," Lena said, once the exam was completed. She pulled off the gloves then tossed them in the trash receptacle. Like clockwork, Margo tapped on the door and opened it with results from a urine sample. Margo gave the doctor a lifeless expression before leaving the way she came, straight-faced and struggling to hide her true feelings.

"What's that, Dr. Harmon?" Ms. Sampson questioned.

"It's the preliminary results from a pregnancy test."

Patrice sat up taller, as if to buffer herself from a harmful reaction. "Don't they send those out with blood tests?"

"Yes. However, I like to check for hCG pregnancy hormone before patients leave the office. If there is no hCG, there is no fertilized egg. This test is likened to a home pregnancy kit. While blood tests are the most precise, it can rule out pregnancy at this time." Lena read the report, checked the name and date of birth twice before addressing her patient.

"Well, it appears that you are pregnant, Patrice."

"Ohhhhh, I'm sorry momma!" she wailed aloud. "I'm so sorry!" Before Lena knew what happened, Clara Sampson leapt over the stool and slapped the taste out of her daughter's mouth.

"Stop hitting her, Clara!" Lena yelled. "I'll have to report this."

"Dammit, you do that then!" Ms. Sampson retorted viciously. "All I've done was pray over this girl and try to do the best for her. Now she goes and ruins her life over some boy." She staggered out of the room slowly as if the soul had been ripped out of her body.

Margo and Cathy dashed into the room to see what happened. When they found Patrice holding the entire left side of her face, it was clear. "Let me get some ice for that," Cathy said. Her words were steeped with compassion.

Amid uncontrollable sobs, Patrice pulled herself together and uttered five troubling words, "She doesn't love me anymore."

Cathy returned with a bag of ice then held it against the girl's swollen cheek. "It's gonna be okay, Patrice. Your mother is hurting right now. She'll get over it, I hope."

Hospital protocol required all doctors and their staff to report child abuse and physical assault. Reluctantly, Lena made a call then filled out the police report. It added insult to injury and then some. During the two-hour wait for Patrice's father to arrive, Lena learned that the only boy she'd been with had also impregnated two other girls at her high school.

Lena was torn between obeying her motherly instincts, which suggested she coddle Patrice and offer reassuring words to help cope with her dilemma, and double down on Ms. Sampson's natural reaction. However, when learning of the potentially harmful position the girl put herself in, Lena felt compelled to drop the hammer of common sense.

"Patrice, no one is perfect. Mistakes come with life and that's the way it is but you are a smart young lady. Don't put your life at risk by lying down with any boy who doesn't use protection. And how do I know he didn't? He can't get all three girls pregnant unless he's sleeping around without condoms. That's reckless Patrice, it's irresponsible and nasty. Don't you ever fall for that level of foolishness again. You're better than that."

Margo walked Patrice to her father's waiting arms in the reception area. He hugged her tightly but could scarcely make eye contact. This scene was becoming all too familiar. Within minutes, Lena went back to treating patients while trying to get passed the pain and brutality she had witnessed. It felt like something heavy stepped on her heart with both feet. Lena may not have minded so much but it was only Monday morning.

# chapter ten
# SWEET SENSATIONS

Aries sat on his hands for a week. Waiting on Lena to reach out and acknowledge her interest was getting the best of him. He ran several miles each morning and busied himself by studying the photos of him and Lena together. Every picture that Flea had taken privately was tacked up on the bulletin board in his spare bedroom. He stared at each one closely, wondering if he could have done anything differently or if Lena was already in deep enough to sink the hook. Aries felt caught in a Catch 22. He wanted to contact her, apologize profusely for invading her personal space then worm his way back into her good graces; to go even harder the next time. Unfortunately, Christopher's demands to stay away from Lena forced Aries to wait and watch.

After a long boring day, he turned on the television, channel-surfed, caught a couple of daytime court TV shows, and a very entertaining episode of "Starsky & Hutch." It wasn't until a poorly made commercial, hawking cheap pedicure tools that Aries came up with a novel idea to get back in the game; without acting against Christopher's wishes. A naughty smile tickled at the corners of his mouth as he turned off the TV.

The nail shop on McKinney Avenue was adjacent to a small grocery store and tanning salon. Three of the fourteen booths were taken by housewife types. It was a Tuesday evening, so the mood was relaxed and tranquil. Aries selected the booth nearest to the middle of the room so he'd have the best vantage point if Lena came in according to her schedule. He was in no mood to hang out there for almost a week like he'd done to catch Lena at the hospital sandwich shop. The best-case scenario involved her dropping by, stumbling into him and then the fireworks resuming where they left off. Worst case, Lena would have skipped her bi-monthly pampering session. Aries needed her to be the creature of habit she'd been while Flea tracked her.

Mindy, the lead nail tech, was a naturalized citizen from Taiwan. Although petite, she was wiry. Nearly five-feet tall and only 115 pounds, she handled Aries' size fourteen feet with ease. He avoided her attempts at chatty conversation by placing headphones over his ears but it did not stifle her child-like attempts to make conversation. Aries tried hard to appear preoccupied while listening to a soothing jazz-fusion compilation.

Mindy worked her magical hands on Aries' right foot as she nestled it snugly in her lap. After nodding off more than once, he sat up in the leather spa chair to shake off the tender loving care Mindy applied during his foot massage. When he arched his back and stretched, the nail tech giggled, so did the woman sitting directly across from him on the opposite row of chairs. Aries lowered his headphones then gestured hello, after recognizing her. He was so pleasantly surprised to see Lena, sitting comfortably in a lime-colored sun-dress with spaghetti straps over the shoulders. There was a subtle difference in her smile, it beamed brighter than before. Aries wanted to see if there was anything he could do to help Lena sustain it.

"Get him, Mindy," she said, jokingly.

"I try, doctor Lena," she cooed excitedly, without taking her eyes off her client. "He big. Strong muscle but I don't mind."

Lena smirked and rolled her eyes in an 'I'll bet you don't mind' fashion then shut her mouth before those exact words came flying out.

"Doctor, Harmon," Aries responded, amicably. His manner of speaking was purposefully businesslike.

Mindy's eyes widened then she whipped her head around and shot a questioning glare. Caught completely by surprise, Lena met Mindy's peculiar expression with a parental leer that said, mind your business. When the nail tech trained her gaze on Aries, he was scrolling through a list of numbers on his cell phone, which suggested he wasn't at all interested in carrying on further conversations with Lena.

"You and Doctor Lena close friends?" Mindy asked. It was obvious she hoped they weren't; at least not too close. Aries shook his head then covered his ears with the headphones.

Pretending to be deeply enthralled in the pages of a fashion magazine, Lena did her best to keep both eyes cast downward. Fighting the urge to steal glances across the aisle was a losing proposition as Mindy rubbed oil up and down Aries' long, dark legs as if she was stroking something more personal. Lena was relieved when a cell phone buzzed inside of her purse. It gave her something else to concentrate on. Aries was leaning all the way back and biting his bottom lip when she managed to steal a glance of Mindy's handiwork. *I know she is not rubbing his thighs*, Lena thought as Mindy squeezed his legs just above the knee. *I'll be damned, she sure is*. Lena fumbled her phone when Aries' mouth popped open and a guttural moan rolled out. She was sexually aroused and slightly embarrassed about it.

SCHEMERS

"Oooh-ooh! Whoa-whoa-whoa, hold up Mindy," he stammered. "That's all I can take on this one. Maybe you should start on the left leg."

Several ladies in the shop had taken notice of Mindy's small hands had danced dangerously underneath his tan cargo shorts.

"Okay, Aries," she replied. "You feel like king?"

"I do have a *royal* feeling right now, thanks."

Lena shook her head disapprovingly again then tapped at her cell phone screen. She felt like a voyeur into Mindy's foot fetish fantasy until reading a new text message which put her onto the sexiest secret in town.

> ARIES: Can't believe ur this close to me after
> I intentionally avoided your office.

She raised her eyes from the text message then delivered a questioning leer to Aries, asking if he was actually waging a covert texting campaign in the same room. When he returned her stare with a smooth side-eyed head tilt, she gave a noncommittal shrug then fired back a response.

> LENA: *I didn't expect u 2 turn down*
> *good business.*

> ARIES: But u wanted me to take my kiss back?

Lena hesitated before typing a reply.

> LENA: *Well...yes! No! I don't know...*

Aries wasn't sure what expression to wear once she read that message but he was certain she would think twice about it.

> ARIES: I'm not giving that up.
> Still makes me feel invincible,
> when I think about it.

He put on the most humbling expression and waited. Aries smiled casually at Mindy to throw her off, when her expression seemed to harden.

The effects of his last text hit Lena like a slow bullet. The second her eyes scanned those words, her life begun to change. She was frozen by the thoughts zigzagging through her mind. After weeks of pushing Aries out of her head, he returned in mere moments as if he'd never left. She reread the message before typing what she thought was a safe answer.

> LENA: *We've been thru this.*
> *I'm not going back there with u.*

Lena sneered at the phone sensually as another nail tech sat down in front of her and gestured to take her feet out of the soaker.

"You want full Pedi, today?" the older woman said, while inspecting her feet like salmon at a meat market. Lena nodded then turned her eyes to the phone screen again. "Foot scrub is five-dollar extra. Your feet rough, need scrub. Really rough heel, you got. Maybe ten-dollar extra," the lady added. When she scrunched up her face as if she smelled something disagreeable, Lena pulled her feet away angrily then dunked them back into the water.

*I know she didn't just put my business out there like that*, Lena thought, then looked at her with a stinging glare that missed the mark. As her phone buzzed again, she waved off the aging foot critic like a bothersome house fly.

> ARIES: If your feet still need some attention
> after she's done, I got u.

Lena chucked like a young girl who was being smiled at by the cutest boy in school.

> LENA: *So you heard that?*

LENA: *LOL This woman is bananas.*
*And I told u to STOP!*

ARIES: Just teasing since ur not into me.
I met someone new 2 help me get over u.

Lena bit her bottom lip, while typing her concerns.

LENA: *I didn't say that. Well... not really.*
*This someone new... Is she pretty?*

ARIES: Very. Reminds me of someone else
who loves the blues.

LENA: *Whatever... Where'd u 2 meet?*

ARIES: Ok, now ur getting in my business.
Meet u in the courtyard in 1 hour.

Aries was ready this time with a clever grin as he climbed out of the spa chair, handed the manager a wad of cash and strolled out of the door before Lena had a chance to object.

She watched him leave and considered showing up until the nail tech wrestled her right foot out of the tub. "Not another word from you," Lena hissed. "Loud talking me. My heels don't even look that bad." When the woman scrunched up her nose again, Lena conceded the point. "Okay but you didn't have to broadcast it. Just hurry up and get to scraping. I have things to do, in about an hour." Lena glanced at the time displayed on her phone then studied every text message exchanged between her and Aries.

Aries did the same thing from the front seat of his Porsche SUV, parked a block away as Cherry deliberated over each one carefully from the screen-shot Aries forwarded to her phone.

"Yes, Aries. Now, that's how you make the magic happen," she said. "Looks like you're enjoying yourself. If she shows up, just do your thing."

"My thing?"

"Yes, your swagger-man thing."

Aries laughed, while keeping an eye on the courtyard. "The last time I went all in, Lena burned rubber out of the parking lot. I'm putting swagger-man back in the box."

"Don't you dare. I saw the pictures of you two together, Aries. She let you kiss her. *Let you.* It may not have led to anything yet but your tongue went into her mouth and she didn't slap you or call the cops. I say let swagger-man roam."

"She did moan a little bit when I squeezed her ass," he said, as an afterthought.

"Uh yeah, what woman wouldn't? With a big, strong, pretty boy all up in her grill, likely for the first time, I'm surprised you two didn't get jiggy in the back seat."

"Jiggy?" he said, laughing at her choice of words. "I don't think Lena's gotten jiggy in this millennium."

Cherry sighed then pointed to something that jumped out at her from the text train. "Maybe that's what she needs and just doesn't know it. Look at the message she sent after you wrote, 'Just teasing since ur not into me.' Her response is very revealing. She wrote back, 'I didn't say that.' Every woman has a tell, Aries. We can say what we think serves us best but we all do that one thing that gives our true intentions away. Dr. Harmon may think she'd be better off without you living in her head but she wants you there. Maybe she's bored and wants a wild fling before her vajay-jay dries up and rusts shut."

"That is not a good visual, Cherry. You're supposed to be helping."

"And I am. You'll see. Play the available jock next door who women can't stand but all want to mount. Then, show your

SCHEMERS

intelligent side and hit her with the four-touch program like we trained you. Be irresistible yet unavailable, she'll want what she can't have and be butt-ass naked in no time."

"Ha ha ha. No doubt, that's a helluva plan. Girl, how do you know so much about this kind of stuff?"

"This is what I do. I've seen scores fall apart when it looked like a done deal and others that came together like a happy ending without any significant warning. Christopher is counting on you. Don't say anything but he bet a million dollars of his own money on you to succeed."

"Dayyyum, Cherry, a million?"

"American dollars."

"This just got real, huh?"

"Don't freak out. He's lost more than that on an Asset before and didn't blink. You're hand-picked by Christopher so it probably would piss him off if you screwed up, so good luck." She hung up the phone and smiled, knowing a man like Aries would concentrate on not losing Christopher's money instead of banking on his.

Aries was determined to roll out all the charm and show Lena what she'd been missing. Almost to the minute, she walked into the courtyard with a careful and curious saunter. She wiggled her toes as Aries approached, wearing a grateful expression. "Thanks for meeting me," he said, then looked down at her feet. "Very nice. What color is that?"

"Brazilian Bronze. You like it?"

"I do. It looks good next to your skin."

"Thanks, I was obviously long overdue for some foot maintenance and distracted by a handsome man sitting directly in my view."

"He's glad you showed up."

"Yeah, about that."

"No way, you're backing out? I need you to help with something. It's important."

"I'm almost afraid to ask," Lena said, nervously. She hoped Aries' dilemma wouldn't lead to another steamy kiss that she would most certainly be kicking herself for later.

"Come into this shop with me. I need a woman's opinion." He reached for her elbow and tugged playfully. "Who knows, you may even find something for yourself."

The M Street Perfumery was an exclusive fragrance house known to wealthy customers who preferred an authentic scent unlike the multitude of others. The small store catered to individuals who refused to shop at department stores. Depending on the chemicals and their accessibility, very distinct fragrances were procured at $500 to $3,000 an ounce. Each bottle was delivered with a letter of authenticity validating its exclusivity. Aries figured this to be the most comfortable place to have a date that didn't feel like one until after it ended.

When Lena walked into the perfumery with him, she was impressed by the associate's professionalism and immediate acknowledgment of her presence. She was greeted at the door with warm hellos and a silver tray stacked with white, neatly folded hot towels. Lena looked at Aries for an explanation.

"It's for the removal of scented lotions and oils from your hands," he said. "Go ahead. It eliminates aromas that might be confusing after a few selections."

Lena accepted a damp towel from a tall woman with perfect makeup, immaculate hair in an attractive black dress. "Oh, I like this," she said. "I need one of these wonderful ladies in my office to follow me around from room to room."

"I'm sure that can be arranged," Aries jested. "Let's head to the back, my perfumer is waiting."

"Perfumer?"

After they were seated closely together at a fragrance counter near the rear of the long, shotgun styled room, a thinly-built man who looked to be around fifty-years-old walked towards them. Aries nodded hello to the gentleman, moving at a reserved pace.

"Bonjour, Monsieur Dupree," he announced, with a thick French accent. "So glad to see you're on the schedule for today."

"Lena, this is Nicolas Pierre. He's one of three master perfumers in Dallas and perhaps the best nose in Texas."

"Madame Lena, it is my pleasure to make your acquaintance."

"Aries, this is exciting," Lena whispered. "I feel under-dressed."

"It's not stuffy like that. Nicolas will make you feel at home. Right, Nick?"

"But to be sure, Monsieur Dupree." Nicolas held out his hands, palms up, to suggest he wanted to inspect Lena's. She giggled again then happily obliged. He placed her hands in his and squeezed them softly. "Your pores are almost prepared," he murmured, signaling for another hot towel. The attractive woman arrived with her silver tray and stood beside him. Nicolas wrapped Lena's arms with the towels up to her elbows. She watched closely while he carefully cleansed her skin.

"Man, I could get used to this," she told Aries. "When do you get your pores prepared?"

"I don't need it because I'm selecting a sexy woman's fragrance today. That's why I needed you, an exceedingly sexy woman."

"You look real cozy in here, Aries. How often do you bring dates to impress them? Yeah, I know what you're doing."

"You're the first and it isn't a date, remember. I do want to impress a special someone but it has to be a surprise. I can't very well surprise her if she picks out her own special fragrance. That's where you come in." He looked for it and then suppressed his knowing grin when Lena's forehead wrinkled. She was taken aback the moment she thought Aries had moved on to another love interest after she rebuffed his advances.

"So, what do I do?" she asked, somewhat less tickled about the situation then.

"Nicolas, please explain the process for Madame Lena."

"It would be my pleasure," he said causally. "Madame, I would hate to insult your knowledge of fragrance design, so please stop me if you already know these things I am about to say."

"Fragrance design? I thought this was only a high end perfumer shop."

Arise winked at Nicolas. "I think you should take it from the top Nicolas. I never get tired of learning at the feet of a master."

"Merci. Then to begin at the beginning. I am an expert in fine fragrances. I have studied chemistry and pharmacy at major French and American universities to become a foremost professional in olfactory composition. My successes include a number of colognes for English royalty, Chinese dignitary and the current president."

"You designed a scent for President Obama?" Lena inquired quietly.

"And a perfect blend slated for a winning brief in Paris later this year." Nicolas took a bow to celebrate his accomplishments by lowering his head towards Aries for an extended moment.

"Nicolas, I thought we talked about this," he said, in a pleading manner.

Lena eyed both men when it became clear she was omitted from their private understanding. "What did I miss," she asked.

"What the Madame does not know and it is not my place to answer," said Nicolas, in a serious and buttoned-up tone.

Aries was left without a way out. "Guess I'd better tell her then?"

"Yes, because I'm feeling like something is stuck in my teeth and you two are trying to figure out which one is going to tell me."

"Lena, it's nothing like that. Nicolas has won several national awards in perfumery but hasn't qualified for international recognition."

"Until now," added Nicolas.

"Yes, now he's in the final rounds with something I helped him with."

"*You* studied perfume?"

"*You studied perfume?*" he repeated jokingly, using the shocked tenor that traced Lena's voice. "Why did you have to say it like that?"

"I just meant, it's so specialized," she said, when the words she searched for wouldn't readily appear.

"Don't be startled. I plan to own a fragrance company in a few years. It's currently a hobby but with a lot of large sales accounts from the pharmaceutical group and some luck with Nicolas, who knows."

Lena looked at Aries with an air of astonishment. "I am thoroughly impressed. Now, what?"

Aries rubbed his hands together as Nicolas opened a large wooden box aligned with several rows of small glass bottles. Each of them was filled with various popular scents and topped with a rubber eyedropper.

"These are scents you may not recognize individually but when layered together, they will become more familiar."

Nicolas opened several bottles and made sure to keep them out of the Lena's sensory zone. "Please observe," he said, holding a tiny paper strip under her nose. She sniffed then nodded.

"That's orange blossom."

Nicolas drew a small measure of liquid from another bottle then dropped in on the same paper strip. "Correct. Now, try this."

"It's woodsy but there's something else," she said, while searching the recesses of her mind. She handed the test strip to Aries, when she couldn't identify the scent.

"Yes, wood and leather, I think. Wait, and a musty spice?" Aries guessed correctly.

"You are getting quite good at this, Monsieur Dupree. And let's see how you do with this one." Nicolas handed Aries a cylinder-shaped container with coffee beans inside of it.

"Thanks, Nick." Aries took the salt-shaker sized bottle and rattled the contents. He sniffed at holes in the lid then handed it to Lena; who copied his movements.

Nicolas handed Lena a paper strip and then passed one to Aries. "You may know this scent from a premium department store's counter."

Lena sniffed and sniffed and sniffed until she sneezed. "Whooo, I like this, Nicolas. It smells just like my Gucci Premiere."

"You have a very good nose. Those are some of the major scents in your Gucci fragrance."

"That's clean, refreshing," Aries agreed. "I'm looking for something sexy but understated. Nicolas, let's work a quartet of scents and see if we can find something original." As directed, the perfumer set several groups of bottles on the bar then placed three strips in front of each group.

"Please tell me about the woman for which this fragrance will be designed."

Aries closed his eyes and concentrated. "These combinations describe her best. Light-hearted vanilla musk, caraway spice and bitter almond." Lena watched attentively as Nicolas rearranged the bottles to match Aries' recipe. "Seductive cinnamon, cedar wood and cloves with a dash of black tulips. Then she's gardenia, sensual amber notes and a bursting bouquet of jasmine."

"Only one more. This is her in springtime. I smell sweet Brazilian rosewood, lemon citrus, ginger and a splash of peach."

Suddenly, Lena wanted to be somewhere else, anywhere else. She felt like a third wheel in a private discussion about Aries' new woman, who she was suddenly jealous of. She tried to shake it off but the feelings lingered. "She sounds like a sweet girl," Lena said, once Aries opened his eyes. "And would be lucky to have a man go through all of this for her. You're very thoughtful."

Nicolas stood at attention, awaiting further instructions. "Will this be all, Monsieur Dupree?"

"I think so. Thank you."

"Before we go, I should look for something my husband might like," she said, as an afterthought. Lena looked over her shoulder to view several rows of premixed scents. "Nicolas, do you have anything already prepared, that I could purchase today?"

"Of course, Madame. Come this way, please."

They left Aries at the back counter, alone. He watched Lena squirt and sniff from several bottles. After sampling a number of masculine fragrances, she was ready to leave without making a selection for Ledger. Aries paid close attention while keeping his distance. When Lena looked frustrated and dispirited, he placed the palm of his hand in the center of her back then escorted her to the courtyard.

VICTOR McGLOTHIN

The sun tilted over the horizon just as they reached the cobble-stone square.  The mood was set for a smooth departure if Aries handled it right.  "Thank you Lena.  Having your opinion meant a lot," he said, looking directly into her eyes.  He brushed a few renegade strands of hair from her face after a gust of wind blew, as if on cue.

"I enjoyed it, Aries, really.  It's interesting that so much science goes into composing perfume."

"Then, why the sad face?  You look defeated."

"After you and Nicolas went on about unique scents and perfect-ing a special fragrance, I became excited.  I wanted to find some-thing for my husband."  Aries placed both hands inside of his deep cargo pockets then tossed a sincere expression at Lena that begged to be questioned.  "What?" she asked.  Her gaze was locked on his.

"What if I let you test our fragrance?  Your man might go for it."

Lena's eyes lit up like Time Square.  "Oh no, I couldn't do that.  It's yours."

He studied Lena for a moment.  "Here, take this," Aries said, as he placed a tiny glass spray bottle in her palm.  "No guarantees.  It's still in the development stage."

She opened her hand to look at it and marveled at the thought of creating something.  "I don't feel right."

"Okay, at least take a whiff.  Maybe you'll change your mind."  Lena was elated.  She pulled his large hand toward her, preparing to spray his wrist.  "No, not there.  A man's heat emanates from his neck and head," he explained.

"Oh, sorry."

He tilted his head to the left then guided her hand up to his chest.  "Go, ahead.  Hit me right on the carotid artery doctor."

Lena couldn't deny enjoying their exchange.  She was giddy.  "Alright close your eyes, in case I miss."

Aries squinted cautiously. He laughed aloud when seeing her aim was slightly off. "Closer, Lena. Don't get it in my mouth."

"Then close your eyes *and* your mouth," she teased. "Ready? Hold still." She pressed the metal top down. A faint mist landed on Aries' neck. Lena leaned in anxiously. "I don't smell anything."

"Now it's your turn to hold still," he commanded. "And close your eyes." Aries circled her slowly, creating a fragrant vortex of chemical intoxication. "Using your nose, tell me what you recognize."

"Oomph!" she cooed. "That smells so good!"

"I agree but *what* do you smell?"

Lena leaned her head back then inhaled. Her nostrils flared as she breathed him in. "Earth, I smell an earthy scent. Like a sandal-wood candle I had once. Nice. I'm getting a burst of nutmeg and it's making me hungry."

Aries laughed as he stood a few inches from her face. "Right, so far. Now keep your eyes closed tight and inhale like a kid at a bakery.

"You're going to make me pass out Aries, stop playing."

"Just tell me what your senses convey," he whispered, against her ear. She shuddered helplessly before offering a reply.

"You smell incredible," she answered faintly, before regaining her senses. "It's not overpowering but bold and masculine."

"What else?"

"It's light. Crisp. Erotic."

"You're good at assessments," he said, fully enjoying their give and take. "Is that all?"

"Fire," she concluded, sensually. "I'm getting some serious heat."

Lena opened her eyes to a dimly lit walkway and the most irresistible man she'd encountered in years. "It's perfect. For you, that is." Lena pulled back to collect herself. "Ledger wouldn't wear it this well." She quickly handed the small capsule back to Aries.

"No worries. Glad I could share it with you though. I haven't felt that comfortable with anyone else."

"I do feel special but I think it's getting late." An awkward moment stood between them when neither reacted to the obvious chemistry they shared.

"Well, I would walk you to the car but the last time things got kind of, you know."

Lena noticed a genuine glint of vulnerability in his eyes. "You don't trust yourself with me since you have a new girl?" Before he came up with an answer, she leaned in and cupped both of his shoulders with outstretched hands then pulled him close. Suddenly, she pushed him away playfully.

"What was that for?" he asked.

"I wish I knew." Lena turned and walked away as the sun dipped into eve of night.

Aries watched her until she reached the valet stand. He headed in the other direction a few seconds before she looked back over her shoulder, for a lasting glimpse of him. Aries had no idea how well he'd pulled off his tasks successfully, orchestrating a date that wasn't. He was adequately irresistible yet unavailable and worked Cherry's four-touch program to perfection. Lena climbed into her Mercedes wondering if Aries was falling for another woman and if he could possibly see her, with the same hopeful gleam in his eyes that pierced her defenses. Subsequently, she almost felt silly for being so concerned about losing a man that wasn't even hers.

# chapter eleven
# CLOSER

Aries received a call to come into headquarters as soon as possible. Remembering how hungry he'd gotten during the last meeting, he rolled into the drive-thru window at Taco Town. He ordered beef quesadillas when Raja's warning about the chicken taco surprise came to mind. There was far too much at stake to battle food poisoning while navigating through dangerous waters.

The Men of M.O.E.T Corp. conference table was littered with stacks of photos and charts. Christopher was seated at the end with Raja and Cherry on either side of him. Walter Shulman, the quiet project manager whose presence scared Raja to death, stood slightly behind Christopher. He cast a discerning leer as Aries entered the warehouse and never broke his gaze until the Asset took a seat at the table.

"Good evening Aries," said Christopher. "Cherry tells me you're close to cracking this thing wide open, so to speak." Cherry blushed at his choice of words. Raja pressed his lips together to strangle a sophomoric giggle that Walter surely would not have approved of. "Now that we're all here, let's discuss exactly where we are in this project." Everyone around the table lent their attention to the top page of their respective stack of materials. It was the latest pictures taken by Flea at the courtyard and chronicled the sensual foreplay between Aires and Lena's playfully indulgence just an hour before.

"I think you captured a point in time very well, Flea," said Christopher. "Despite my strict orders, Aries took it upon himself to draw his target in even after 'The Keep' occurred." He looked to the Asset for an explanation.

"I got tired of sitting around waiting on Lena, Dr. Harmon, to make up her mind so I decided to work the four-touch program and push the envelope." Aries glanced at Cherry, who pretended to have no idea what he was talking about.

"You think it worked?" asked Christopher.

"Lena couldn't stop smiling when we were together and hugged me before I left," Aries answered, with an air of humility.

"What about you, Cherry," Christopher said. "You think Aries got closer to nailing this deal down?" When she didn't respond, he slapped his open palm on the table. Although Cherry knew it was coming, she still flinched.

"If you want my honest opinion, then yes," she said, hesitantly. "I also think Aries should have stepped up sooner and tried to close the circle faster. Our other two Assets have already scored and are vacationing in the French Riviera, for God sake."

"Leave God out of this," said Christopher. "We've got enough problems. Ledger Harmon just doubled his life insurance after announcing that he's going public with his Ontario-based Yummy Yogurt franchises. Disneyland Resorts put in a decent bid and the sly dog turned down the 120 million dollar offer, flat."

"It'll be worth twice that once he presents the initial public offerings," said Raja, with a lift in his voice.

"I'd buy a thousand shares, myself," Aries added confidently.

"That would be a wise investment," Christopher agreed.

"And to make sure you're in the best position to do that Aries, let's button down this project then use his money to buy his stock with."

Flea held his cell phone underneath the table while checking his bank balance. "Wouldn't that be something, to fleece Ledger Harmon and use his money to buy millions in stock from his company? That's genius and I want in."

All eyes were fixed on Aries as he sat up taller in the black leather chair. Christopher chuckled and flipped through the remaining pages in the stack in front of him.

"This is usually the place in the meeting where I map out the best case scenario for getting the target in a compromising position with a seer on location to provide the proof. However, Aries, you have seen fit to break protocol and have it your way!" His voice rose as his discontent became more evident. "What next! Since you're obviously better qualified to manage this project than me and Walter here, what do we do now?" Christopher noticed Walter's frustration growing when he took a subtle, deliberate step in Aries' direction. "No-no, Walter. It's alright. Our Asset got creative and pitched a ditch that we're all currently staring into the bottom of. I'm sure he's got a bright idea how to climb out of it with, let's say, eight million."

"I'd put money on it," said Flea, before cowering under the weight of Walter's heavy stare.

"Me too," said Cherry. "I've seen the pictures of Aries and Lena together. He can pull it off."

"Predicting human behavior is so unpredictable," Raja explained. "But, I think he can do it also."

Walter scowled at Aries. "What about you? What are you willing to bet?"

Aries knew of Walter's connections to organized crime and his reputation for making bodies disappear, yet he was undeterred.

"My life!" he answered emphatically. "I'm willing to bet my life on this. Just give me a little more time before you pull the plug."

Cherry smiled at the way he stood up to Walter. Raja shot Aries a prideful wide-eyed expression then he swallowed hard. Christopher looked at the bottom page of the stack. It was a life insurance policy for two-million dollars, purchased by M.O.E.T. Corp. under the name of Anthony Mitchell, Aries' real name. Christopher slid it across the table then casually raised his eyes to get a long look at Aries. "Good, then sign it so we can get on with our business, to be concluded, in one way or another."

Aries settled back into the leather chair after signing the policy. Unless he found a way to sleep with Lena and screw over her husband with embarrassing photos as proof, Aries was worth more dead than alive. It was a haunting proposition but Aries had to forge ahead and play out the hand he was dealt.

Only four miles away, Lena's house was dark and quiet. She'd arrived to find a hand-written note from the pool service, attached to the garage door, in regards to scheduling a cleaning for the following week. Other than that, it was apparent no one had come or gone since she left for work earlier that morning. Ledger was in Bali or Barcelona, Lena couldn't remember which. It didn't matter though, because gone was gone regardless of where.

She drew a hot bath in the handmade cast iron tub, manufactured with satin nickel claw feet. While the water ran, Lena puttered about in her bathroom wearing only a black sheer kimono that Ledger had shipped from Japan some months ago. She flicked at her hair, which was admittedly between styles and frowned at a chorus of split ends in need of taming. While the water rose, Lena studied her reflection in the full-length mirror. She poked at the bags beneath both eyes and pulled on her fluffy cheeks. After stretching her neck to get a closer look at loose skin she hadn't noticed before, sadness filled her chest. Lena eased the gown off of her shoulders then dropped it on the floor. She turned to the side and pinched at the flab covering what had once been a marvelous behind. Lena stood motionless until she recognized the woman staring back at her. The woman in the mirror was a carbon copy of her mother. It was difficult to determine the exact moment when Lena began neglecting workouts or stopped pursuing a healthy diet. Her gym membership merely served as a free entry to the best fruit smoothies and panini spot in town, where no one minded if she sat around for hours catching up on magazines articles. Regardless of how it happened, Lena took a long, hard look at years of complacency.

After she'd seen enough, Lena climbed into the steamy water and settled in. She thought about her life, seriously contemplated how much time she had left on this earth, and how she wanted to spend it. Tears flowed down her face when it occurred how much of her marriage had been spent alone, which was brutally painful on occasion and at times even played havoc on her soul. Although imprisoned by an empty bed more often than not, Lena considered herself fortunate to have a good husband who loved her. Even when surrounded by porcelain tile floors, granite counter tops and a three-thousand dollar bathtub filled with satiny bubbles, she felt as though life was sweeping her under and all she could do was cry.

# chapter twelve
# DAYDREAMS SMELL SO GOOD TO ME

Patients flowed through Lena's office without a hitch all week. Margo filled the examination rooms, scheduled patients and baby deliveries like clockwork. Lena's medical practice was firing on all cylinders and so was her staff. The few times Dr. Lena ran late, due to C-Section drama that didn't go according to plan or a pile up on the freeway, patients didn't seem to mind. Their needs were met eventually and everyone left in a much better position, post examination.

Lena made time to chat with her staff at lunch on Friday afternoon. She shared that it bothered her when seeing wealthy clients shopping at the mall, when they owed substantial balances to the practice. "Portia French almost ate the Valentino crocodile purse I saw her buying at Neiman's," Lena said.

"Not the Gucci Soft Stirrup Croc?" Cathy asked excitedly, while smacking on a chunk of gum. "That costs over thirty thousand!"

"Girl, please," Lena answered quickly. "I would have stalked her at the register and demanded the thirteen-hundred bucks she owes me. It was that Gucci evening bag, I like."

Valerie spun around in her chair. "Ooh, the evening bag is hot. How much is that one?"

"As they say, if you have to ask how much…" Lena said suggestively.

"Then you probably can't afford it," Margo added. She glared when Cathy laughed so hard that a wad of gum flew out of her mouth. "Child, you act like you've never heard that expression."

"I haven't but it's the truth," answered Cathy.

"Poor baby, she's so brand new I can still see the price tag," said Valerie. "Pick up that chewing gum and come help me change out the water-tank in the reception area."

After the women left the break room, Margo flipped through a fitness magazine. "You ever notice how differently rich and poor women respond to being told they're pregnant?" Lena fiddled with her cellphone without answering Margo's question. The Office Manager gave her boss a peculiar look when it seemed she wasn't paying attention. "Dr. Harmon?"

"Yes, Margo, I hear you. Poor folks only want to know how much the delivery is going to cost. Rich people always find some kind of joy in it, even if it'll ruin their marriage."

"That's what I'm saying, Dr. Harmon. Betty Fulbright made reservations at the swankiest place in town to tell her husband she was having a baby by the pool boy from El Salvador."

"It was the landscaper, I thought. Doesn't matter, Mr. Fulbright isn't going anywhere. He'll adopt Betty's child and that twenty-year-old immigrant before divorcing her," Lena surmised.

"You think she's putting it on her husband like that?"

"I doubt it. Betty Fulbright's daddy built half of the skyscrapers in Dallas during the eighties."

"Huh, I wouldn't walk away from all that money either. Maybe they'll let the landscaper move in the pool house," Margo joked.

"Whatever Betty Fulbright went out back looking for when

129

she stumbled into Don Juan and repeatedly fell on his penis just might put her husband in the pool house." Lena chuckled as Margo returned to her magazine. "I have to check on something then get my head right for Shonda Petrie's afternoon appointment.

"Oh, that's right. Let me get the room ready while you review her chart."

Lena stepped into her office. The text message she received compelled her to close the door.

ARIES: Hey You. Promised to stay in my lane
so just saying thanks for the other day.

Thrilled to hear from Aries, she stared at the cell phone before answering his text.

LENA: *Glad to help. I'm sure your new
friend loves the perfume.*

Lena didn't care if the woman Aries told her about was happy with her designer fragrance. However, it was the sneakiest way to say something nice while checking the temperature on his budding relationship. She waited patiently for his next text, expecting an elaborate update of his new status and perhaps a few details about the mystery woman. Lena laughed at his message, which was short and to the point.

ARIES: I'll let u know when I do.

When the office clock read 1:30, Lena knocked on the door of examination room number two. She opened it cautiously when no one answered. "Good afternoon, Shonda." she announced, with a pleasant disposition.

Mrs. Petrie laid on the exam table, staring straight up at the ceiling. She stunk up the room like an ashtray. "Oomph, if you say so," she said sorely.

As Lena closed the door behind herself, the patient shifted her weight to ease the tension on her spine. "You're getting up there in weeks Shonda, won't be long now."

"That's twice you called me Shonda. Am I dying or something?"

Lena ignored her question while pulling on latex gloves then helped Mrs. Petrie roll onto her right side. "Alright, turn back the other way. I'll have to see if I can get a reading from this side."

"Ooh, shit! That hurts too bad, Dr. Harmon."

Lena turned on the ultra sound machine. She spread a liberal squirt of lubricant gel on Mrs. Petrie's midsection. "I see the little man in there. Hi'ya doing, Sir?" The patient winced then resumed her saddened gaze. "Your uterus is retroverted, tipped backwards. Being tilted posteriorly is putting a lot of pressure on your spine."

"I wish I didn't have a uterus."

"Your mobility is not good, I'm afraid. You can tell those big shots at Dash Cola you'll need some time off. I'm putting you on bed rest."

"I already took care of that," Shonda smarted back.

Lena continued to poke and prod at Mrs. Petrie's belly. "How do you mean?"

"They strongly suggested I take a leave of absence or be terminated," she answered, short of breath. "I had a bad day, fired my executive assistant and then cussed out her replacement."

"Is it that rough, with your husband being gone?"

"I'm mean all the time and can't stop myself from speaking that anger to my kids, too." Tears trickled down her face and ran into the corners her mouth. "I don't know how I turned into this. I can't lose weight and can't stop smoking. My neighbors don't speak to me anymore and every five minutes I have to pee."

Lena handed her a small box of tissue. "Sounds like a pretty good country song to me," she mused. "I'm going to admit you for a couple of days. Call someone to watch the kids, so you can get some rest here."

"But I don't have time."

"This stress you're dealing with is bothering the hell out of your baby, so all you do have is time." Lena called for Margo to book a hospital room for Mrs. Petrie. When the patient complained, the doctor placed her hand on Mr. Petrie's shoulder. "This is serious, a life or death situation. For once in our doctor-patient relationship, you are going to do what I say." Lena reached into Shonda's purse then dumped everything out when she couldn't find what she went in for.

"You got no business in there, Doctor!" she hollered. "What the hell are you doing?"

"Don't play with me. You already know." When a half-empty pack of menthol cigarettes tumbled onto the floor, Lena stomped on them. "Now I dare you to get your ass off that bed and pick them up."

Margo parked the wheelchair near the door and waited for Shonda Petrie to get froggy enough to jump. When her resentment dissolved into pity, Margo felt sorry for the pregnant bully. "Let me help you, Ma'am. We'll get you situated in the hospital." The patient was still seething when Lena left the room.

As if Lena's behavior was a clear affirmation, Shonda whined softly. "Dr. Harmon hates me."

"No, ma'am, the doctor likes you a lot or she would have run you out of here a long time ago. I'm the one who doesn't much care for you. Now, relax before you get real upset about choking your baby with those cancer sticks."

Cathy peeked in from the doorway as Margo gathered items from the counter and returned them back to the patient's purse. "Can I help with anything Margo?"

"No, it's better now. This situation has been handled."

Lena heard Shonda Petrie's loud sobs as Margo wheeled her out of the office. It wasn't often that strict measures had to be taken to protect a late term pregnancy but Dr. Harmon OB/GYN willingly stepped in when duty called for giving the child a chance to live.

As the afternoon zipped by, Cathy assumed Margo's responsibilities while she ensured Mrs. Petrie's hospital check-in and subsequent assimilation went smoothly. Valerie called to pre-certify new patients and worked double time to answer the phone that seemed to ring off the hook.

After the last patient of the day settled her bill and exited, Cathy quickly locked the door as if another one might slip in if she didn't. Valerie strolled into the restroom and locked herself in for at least a dozen hits from the vapor e-cigarette; she swore she'd given up. Lena grabbed a bottle of soda and bag of chips from the vending machine at the end of the hall before returning to her office. It was finally time for some junk food and solitude. Since there were only two patients in what Lena called the *go zone*, within 48 hours of their due date, she felt almost certain that her date night with Ledger would go according to plan.

"Hey honey," she said, when Ledger answered the phone.

"I'm wrapping up a tour of the plant in Montego Bay. Maybe we should buy a villa here and soak up some of this Caribbean sun."

Lena munched on a salty-lime potato chip as if it was a made in Heaven. "Promises, promises. I'd settle for an occasional frozen Bahama-Mama and some fried plantains at the jerk chicken joint on the south side."

"Come on now, Lena. I can do better than that. Why don't I have Chef Vivian come by the house tomorrow and whip up whatever you like?"

She laid the chips down after noticing something on her desk. There was a small blue velvet bag sitting on the far end. "That sounds wonderful but what about our dinner arrangements tonight?" she said, while lifting the beautiful sack off of the desk. "A reservation at Sable's is hard to get, especially after I've canceled two times in a row." She loosened the draw strings to open it.

"If I bought *Sables* like I suggested a year ago, we could get a table anytime we wanted," he joked. "Hold on a second, Lena. The chief foreman needs me to speak to some guy stalling on my building permits."

Lena held the bottom of the velvet bag then pulled at the top of an oddly shaped glass container inside. "Sure, I'll wait," she said, long after being placed on hold. She examined the bottle with a slender neck and squared base, which had apparently been designed to resemble a guitar.

"Yes-yes, please get the luggage and locate my pilot," Ledger ordered.

"What bags?" Lena asked, still mesmerized by the bottle.

"No-no. Not you, Lena. I'm trying to stay on schedule and make a date night with my wife for a change. Hey Winston! Go and check the hotel bar if the pilot isn't in his suite."

"Sounds like you got your hands full. I do appreciate your efforts to get home on time." Still unsure what the bottle it was doing in her office, Lena read the name etched on the side of the bottle. "Day Dreams," she said, just above her breath.

"With some luck and a westward tailwind, I'll be wheels down by 8:30," Ledger said. "There will be a car at the airport when I arrive. He could swing by and pick you up first, if you'd like."

Lena twisted off the cinnamon colored top then drew the fragrant into her nostrils. "That is divine."

"Excellent, glad you approve, dear."

"Approve of what?" she asked, amply distracted by the perfume.

"Hello? We're good, right? Franky will send a car for you around eight-ish."

"I'll see you tonight, honey. Have a safe flight." She ended the call then quickly picked inside of the bag. A thin piece of paper fell out onto her desk. It was no bigger than a fortune cookie slip. *Inspired by you Lena. Nicolas agrees with the name*, she read. She sniffed at the clear liquid in the bottle again. A fresh bouquet of aromas swept across her face. The sensual collection of Brazilian rosewood, bergamot, lemon citrus, ginger and a splash of peach smelled like sunshine. "Day Dreams, huh? Aries, you shouldn't have." She sniffed once more and gushed with pride. "Sun-kissed peaches and day dreams." Suddenly a knock at the door startled her. The perfume bottle spilled onto the desk mat.

"Dr. Harmon, you in there?" asked Margo.

"Just a minute," she replied nervously.

Lena sat the container up right then pulled a napkin out of the top drawer to wipe up the liquid. Before she knew it, her entire room smelled like a field of dreams.

"Dr. Harmon, you alright?"

When there was no use in trying to hide the gift or its brilliant scent, Lena gave up. "Come on in, Margo."

She walked in and looked around suspiciously. "You don't have a pool boy stashed in here, do you?"

"Don't be ridiculous. I just knocked over this bottle of perfume and tried to clean it up."

"Sure you weren't trolling those porn sites, when you thought we had all gone home?"

"I don't need porn to get my kicks," Lena replied, with a pensive chuckle.

"Whew, I know I need something to help me forget all that time I spent with Shonda Petrie."

"She got under your skin?"

"No Ma'am. I promised her a fresh pack of Newports cigarettes after she gets released from the hospital."

"Are you nuts?"

"What? It worked. She's checked in and soundly sleeping."

When Margo reached for the perfume bottle lying on the desk, Lena almost grabbed her hand but it was too late. Margo had quickly twisted the cap off and whiffed a hearty snoot full. "Ooh-wee, Dr. Harmon. Now, this right here is TheTruth.com," she howled. "Smells so sweet I don't know whether to dab some on or sip a little bit."

"It is nice, probably concentrated," Lena said, awkwardly.

"Long stemmed roses and velvet sacks of *Day Dreams*," Margo read aloud. "A girl could get used to this."

"Well, it doesn't suck."

"Your husband is busy building empires but he didn't forget about courting his wife."

"That's very nice of you to say. Thanks." Lena secretly wished that either of the gifts had been sent by Ledger. In actuality, Margo couldn't have been more wrong. Ledger had long since forgotten the merits of courtship and the old adage, *'what is done to catch her is also required to keep her.'*

"Speaking of husbands, we managed to get a hold of Mrs. Petrie's husband, Michael. He was not happy to get thirty-three calls from her cell phone but I told him all he had to do was answer the first one." Margo leaned her head back and cackled. "Bully Bad Ass was lying there co-signing and eating it up until those horse tranquillizers took her down."

Lena shot Margo a side-eyed glare. "Bully Bad Ass? See, you were doing just fine until then."

Margo threw both hands up to defend her slight on Shonda Petrie. "You know I don't like that woman but I am trying to see things from her point of view. It can't be easy dealing with life after your man decides he's more interested in something or someone else."

"I hope they can work it out. Three kids and a lot of years invested ought to count for something."

Margo twisted the top back onto the bottle. "Sometimes I wonder if marriage is worth it all."

"Why would you say something hopeless like that, Margo?"

"Well, most of the married women I know are either cheating or wish they had somebody decent to cheat with."

"It can't be that bad out there."

"Afraid so, Dr. H. Membership in the Cheating Wives Club is spreading like wild fire. They even have this website, Dolly Madison or some such name, for ladies who want to step out on their men."

"Ashley Madison. I've heard of it."

"Can you imagine a website for picking up stray men without caring who sees you doing it?"

"No, can't say that I could."

"All out in the open like that, too. I'm no saint but at least have some shame in your game," Margo huffed, disappointedly. "Good thing your relationship is very pulled together though. It gives me something to look up to."

Lena was comforted by her office manager's Cheating Wives Club rant, even though she had spent waking moments imagining what another stolen kiss from Aries might have been like. Now confronted with the pressure of Margo's righteous indignation, she felt more strength in her resolve. Lena was determined to keep her desires for another man hidden, beneath the surface and out of his reach.

## chapter thirteen
# THREE KINDS OF WRONG

The Wine & Spirits Depot offered hundreds of suitable dinner wine options. Lena's mind ricocheted all over the place while browsing rows of imported labels and local vineyards making a name for themselves. She kept thinking about the thoughtful gift from Aries and wondered when he could have had the opportunity to sneak it into her office. He must have acquired help, she thought, and figured it must have been Cathy because Valerie couldn't hold water. She would have blabbed her head off. Lena still hadn't decided whether to keep the perfume or how to tell Aries how much the gift meant to her. She didn't know any women with a signature fragrance and many of her patients had money to burn.

The last conversation Lena had with Margo played back in her head a dozen times. Lena remembered dozens of married women who came to her with an STD from the new boyfriend, a one-night stand or some old flame whose fire flickered far too long. There was a whole other world out there and Lena didn't want to be corrupted by that lifestyle.

Lingering in the back of her mind was Shonda Petrie's condition. When Lena called the hospital before leaving her office, the charge nurse answered on the second ring. She reported that Shonda was resting peacefully then confirmed that Mr. Petrie was in the room and anchored by his wife's side. Lena felt sorry for Shonda's situation and kept her phone at hand, in the event that something changed.

Five minutes after Lena departed from the store, she headed home with a box of assorted liqueurs and tasty adult beverages. When her cell phone chirped loudly, she turned the car stereo down then pushed the telephone icon on her digital console.

"Hello, this is Dr. Harmon."

"I hate to bother you, doctor, but it's your patient, Shonda Petrie. She woke up very irritated, demanding the pack of cigarettes she said someone from your office promised her."

"You've got to be kidding," Lena said, angrily. "Listen, I'm not mad at you but is there something you expect me to do about it? She's in no condition to be smoking or demanding anything except an excellent standard of care."

"I agree Dr. Harmon but she's upsetting other patients. She's had two sedatives already so I can't offer her anymore."

Lena glanced at her dashboard. "It's almost seven o'clock. I'll turn around and head back that way."

"We tried to calm her down before contacting you," the charge nurse said, "but she's a handful." Her sorrowful tone suggested she had no other choice.

"No problem, you're doing your job. I'll be there shortly and make sure you tell Mrs. Petrie that," Lena added, as she whipped a U-turn near her subdivision. "It's very important that a distressed patient knows help is on the way."

"Yes doctor and please hurry or we'll be forced to restrain her."

"Don't you dare further aggravate the situation! I'll be right there."

Lena disconnected the call and shook her head. "Damn it Shonda," she hissed. "Bully Bad Ass strikes again." She poked the telephone icon again. "Call Ledger's cell."

The voice-automated system repeated her command. "Calling Ledger's cell now." The phone rang three times before a recorded message started in.

"I'm not able to take this call. Leave a brief message."

"Honey, it's me. I'm on the way to the hospital to see about a difficult patient. I'll call you when I can. Sorry about dinner. Gotta go, bye."

Loud wailing could be heard from the elevator as soon as Lena stepped off on the eighth floor. The armed security guard outside of Mrs. Petrie's room could have been a Terminator movie stunt-man. Lena couldn't see past his broad shoulders and he didn't seem interested in letting her pass. "You need to move," she said, as calmly as she knew how under the circumstances.

"Uh-uh, no family members allowed. I have strict orders to wait for the doctor."

The charge nurse, a middle-aged white woman in blue scrubs, came striding hard from the workstation. "Let her in there. She is the doctor." The giant oaf hesitated. He blinked at Lena then ducked aside. "I'm sorry, Dr. Harmon. He's new," the nurse explained.

"Doctors do come in black nowadays," Lena growled, through clenched teeth. "Go stand guard over a donut or something. I have work to do."

"Somebody get the doctor before I have all your asses fired!" shouted Mrs. Petrie. "Try me and see what happens." She squirmed sorely, holding her belly and sweating profusely. "Ouuuch! Feels like my head and my stomach are splitting open."

Lena exhaled before entering the room to composure herself. "Shonda, it's me. Dr. Harmon. They called and told me that you were experiencing discomfort so I rushed right over."

Between deep moans, the patient rolled over to see who was talking. "Hmmm! Oomph, it is you Dr. Harmon. Ouch, this hurts like hell. Not like the other babies. He's mad me."

Lena looked over the hospital charts then read the blood pressure monitor. "I can see why he might be. Your blood pressure is through the roof and that stress is not good for him." She finally peered up from the notes then noticed a clean cut slight-build black man, about forty-five years old. He sat by the bed quietly, looking as if this was his first rodeo as Shonda twisted and turned in immense pain. "I hope you're Michael," Dr. Harmon said, matter-of-factly, "because we might be heading to delivery." He grimaced when Shonda squeezed his hands so hard it mashed his fingers together.

After Lena called for an ultra-sound machine, she suggested Mr. Petrie step out of the room to get a cup of coffee. He bolted for the door like an escaped convict. "Get that cart in here," Lena said, when she saw the charge nurse wrestling with it by the door.

"This wheel is stuck," she said.

Immediately, the gargantuan guard lifted the cart off the floor with one hand. "Thanks but you can go now," Lena told him, after he loitered around longer than she liked.

"I didn't know, Dr. Harmon," he apologized. "I'm sorry."

"Yeah, me too. Please step out of the room, now." There was no malice in her voice but it wasn't the time for making up. The nurse turned on the machine as Lena folded the sheets half way down the bed. It was soaked with sweat. "Are you the one who called me?" Lena asked, sharply.

"Yes, Dr. Harmon. I'm Nurse Jessica."

"Good job, Nurse Jessica," she said, while pressing various places on Mrs. Petrie's massive abdomen. "Next time, call sooner."

"Yes, doctor."

"Shonda?" Lena called out, when her patient's damp forehead was cold to the touch. "Shonda, wake up now. I need to ask you something." She nodded for Nurse Jessica to use her digital thermometer. "We need her temp, immediately."

The nurse pulled an instrument from a holder on her hip that looked more like a tool found in an electrical shop. She waved the Non-Contact Infrared Thermometer back and forth over Mrs. Petrie's forehead. Instantly, it beeped then displayed an abnormally high temperature of 102. Nurse Jessica wrote it on the chart. Afterwards, she looked to Dr. Harmon for her next assignment.

Lena used the ultra-sound to view the baby's position. "Okay, it's go time Nurse Jessica. Please call the O.R. and tell 'em we need a room, stat." The nurse hit her long stride again as she left the room. Once alone, Lena placed her hand on the patient's face. "Shonda, we're going to delivery now"

"I'm so tired and hungry. Who bought the peach cobbler?" she asked, after smelling remnants of the perfume Lean cleaned off of her desk.

"It's just spilt perfume but I need to ask you something, Shonda. When was the last time you felt the baby move?"

"Hmmm... I don't know. Right after I got here and fell asleep."

As the nurse returned, she eased passed Michael who had been standing in the doorway. He overheard his wife's responses and had cause to be concerned. "Is she going to be okay, Dr. Harmon?"

"It's likely an infection Mr. Petrie but she'll be fine after a round of antibiotics."

"Shonda's allergic to penicillin."

"Yes, it's written on her chart. We'll take care of her, Sir."

"What about the baby?"

"We'll do all we can," she answered quickly, as two men arrived to transfer the patient to the operating room."

Nurse Jessica couldn't look Mr. Petrie in the face but did her best to comfort his wife while on the way to the O.R.

As soon as she arrived, Lena took control in the large room with a birthing bed in the middle of it and a small rectangular table near the foot on the right side. An operating room nurse and an anesthesiologist stood by.

"Let's start a round of antibiotics then get on with the delivery. The patient is allergic to penicillin but no other known drug reactions." She looked at Shonda's eyes, half closed as if she already knew what came next. "Somebody please find her husband and get him in here," Lena demanded firmly. She was preparing for one of the toughest jobs an obstetrician had to do. There was no way to lessen the sting of telling a patient, a mother, that time had come to induce labor and endure the entire birthing process only to deliver a dead child.

After Mr. Petrie was located and dressed in medical scrubs, he was escorted into the O.R. Lena pulled him near the bed, where his wife laid. "There's no easy way to say this. The baby didn't make it."

Shonda's lips quivered as she groaned and gasped for breath. Michael looked at her through tear-filled eyes that begged the question how this could have happened. The cloud which hung over the operating room was thick, black and ominous.

Time stood still during hours of contractions, blood, sweat and unbridled tears as grim circumstances prevailed. Regrettably, there would be no congratulatory celebrations from the staff to welcome a brand new child into the world. Lena pronounced the baby dead at 11:19 PM. They named him Lewis Calvin.

The physician's parking garage was almost empty when the underground elevator door opened. Hospital security walked Lena out then kept watch until the white Mercedes exited the cement structure. She made a right on Greenville Ave. and headed south for a block then turned into a strip center. Lena pulled into a parking space at 3rd Shift Tavern, a greasy spoon bar-and-grill that stayed open until 2:00 a.m. and catered to medical students and hospital personnel. It was common for doctors and nurses to stop in for a cold beer before calling it a night. After the hellish ordeal Lena experienced, she was looking for something smooth that packed a stiff punch.

Her phone displayed one voice message and two texts. She contemplated calling Ledger but he would have asked her to come home and she was in no mood to be in a quiet place where her thoughts could run havoc over the remainder of her night. Lena needed a quick escape and a really tasty cocktail.

The Tavern was nearly full when she walked in. Rowdy college students sang loudly at the karaoke stand near the front. Waitresses hustled burgers, bar food and beers. The distinctive clatter of balls slamming into one another was in the air so Lena knew it would be a while before either of the pool tables was available. She was lucky when a booth opened near the back of the bar. As soon as she took a seat, a skinny waitress with tattoos hurried over. "I would like something cold and lite," Lena said, "and a shot of Tequila with that. Thanks."

Lena flipped over the laminated menu a few times when everything on it appeared appetizing. She still couldn't decide when her drinks were delivered, so she settled for two dishes. "I'd like a fried shrimp basket and the chicken quesadillas. Bring me a coke, when the food is ready, if you don't mind."

She stared at a shot of golden tequila on the table next to the tall frosted glass filled to the rim with lite draft beer. "To hell with it," she said to herself, while raising the short liquor glass. "Here's to you, Lewis Calvin." With a quick flick of the wrist, Lena tossed the drink in her mouth, swallowed hard and whistled. "Whew, that was hot!" She took a long sip from the cold beer then looked for that waitress to order another tequila shot. Instead she found a familiar face walking towards her.

"Lena, I thought that was you," Aries said, feigning a surprised expression. "Are you expecting anyone or would you mind if I joined you?"

She looked at his black motorcycle-styled boots, worn jeans and thick gray t-shirt then peeped over his shoulder suspiciously. "If I didn't know better, I'd think you were stalking me."

"That would be hard to do seeing as how I was already here when you walked in. Even waved hello from the pool table but you looked right through me."

"Sorry, I didn't recognize you dressed down like that. Besides, I had a rough night." She didn't offer for him to sit, so he continued standing oddly by the booth until the waitress returned. Lena looked through Aries again, this time on purpose. "There's my friend, right on time," she said, speaking of the waitress. "Please check on my food order and bring back two more shots, with salted rims this time."

When the brunette looked at Aries then back at Lena, she was confused. "Will he be joining you?"

"I could leave, if I'm intruding. Although I was here first" Aries added, with a light chuckle in his voice.

Lena glanced up to see what was worth laughing about. Her eyes landed on his charming grin and perfect teeth. Finally, she pushed out a tired sigh then gestured for Aries to sit. "Why do you have to be so cute? Go ahead and sit down."

"I'll take what she's having," he said, ordering another round before taking the seat opposite of Lena. "This rough night you're having, want to talk about it?"

"I don't think so."

"Or we could just... be, if you'd like that instead."

"Be what, exactly?" she asked, in a somewhat dubious tone. Lena wasn't in the mood to be alone but far from seeking membership with other cheating wives.

Aries flashed that grand smile again. "You don't have to be afraid of me."

"You didn't answer my question. Just be, what? You sent me flowers then some beautiful perfume, which I absolutely adore, thank you. But that's beside the point. I'm not accustomed to the attention I'm getting or the way you seem to pop up just when I need to breathe. Tell me Aries, what are we doing?"

"No explanations, not expectations," he answered. "We could simply be in each other's company, sharing the same space."

Lena searched her mind for all the places she'd rather be but couldn't come up with a better one than she had at that moment. "Oh I see. That does sound rather inviting." Even though Lena had been checking her cell phone for his random daily text messages from Aries and wondering what he was doing as she climbed into bed alone most nights, she still hadn't come to grips with sharing her inner-most thoughts with the man she wanted to climb.

Aries had given this potential affair all he had and it felt like the walls were closing in. It was his good fortune that Lena decided to dip into the tavern on her way home. Flea had been camped out near the hospital parking garage when Lena left. He was in utter disbelief when he tailed her to the place Aries used to blow off time waiting for a chance to get deeper inside of Lena's head. He knew she frequented the bar on occasion but meeting her there was a long shot, one he greatly needed. With the long shot now in his pocked, Aries was two-steps ahead and prepared to go all in.

The next hour glided by as they debated over the best Black Exploitation films of the 1970's then named as many titles as came to mind. Lena was floating in tequila and Aries wasn't too far behind. It wasn't until the karaoke machine went on the fritz that the bar quieted down enough to share some personal thoughts that mattered. Lena recounted her evening in its entirety, from her stand-off with the overbearing security guard when she arrived up until the still birth had concluded. However, she omitted signing the papers announcing the baby was deceased. Lena downed another shot then tried to push Shonda's emphatic screams out of her mind and Michael's desperate pleas for God to awaken his child but it was useless. Although Lena fully understood the complications associated with fruitless deliveries, it never made accepting a loss any easier. Lena simply wanted to forget it all.

At two o'clock in the morning, just as the last customers stumbled out of the bar, Aries pushed wildly on the Women's restroom door. With a killer buzz and a hint of apprehension, Lena followed him inside.

It was late.

She was tipsy.

He was determined.

Before that very moment, Lena must have imagined pressing her lips against his at least a hundred times. Now eagerly tasting his mouth and remnants of expensive tequila, Lena found herself wanting to do a lot more than just imagine.

"You're so damned sexy," he said. "I want to give you something."

"We shouldn't be doing this Aries," she answered, while being backed against the wall. "I should not be—oh my God you feel so good against me."

"Here. In here is better." Aries whisked Lena into the last stall on the end and then slammed the door shut.

"Damn, this is crazy," she argued. *But I'm tired of waking up with soaked panties, steaming hot and unsatisfied*, she thought. "I want you, I mean really bad but you are not suggesting I throw my legs open in–in here are you?"

Aries slid his hands underneath Lena's blouse, his nimble fingers massaged her breasts. She moaned as he planted sensual kisses on her neck then eased her breast into this mouth. Lena fell back against the metal door as he slid her pants down around her knees. She kissed his head as he explored her body with his tongue.

When Lena realized his hands were spreading her thighs and the erotic gasps spilling out into the restroom were hers, she stammered nervously. "Wait-wait-wait. This is crazy." Lena's mouth popped wide-open as Aries dipped two fingers into her seeping wet vagina. *This man is amazing*, she thought. *He knows the right buttons to push and— oh my goodness! Oh-My-Goodness!* "Grab my ass," she demanded. "Harder!"

Aries gripped Lena's butt and squeezed. "Damn girl, it's chunky and round."

"Go deeper. Deeper, baby!"

"That's it, right?" he asked, in a way that confirmed he already knew the answer.

"Yes! It ! Is!" *Got me all up in here breathless and open like a hussy in heat,* she thought.

Aries worked his magic touch until Lena's eyes rolled back in her head. The moment Lena's clitoris swelled larger than she thought possible, she panicked. *What am I doing? Good girls don't let men massage them in places their husbands don't even know existed. Good girls don't give it up in public restroom stalls. And, good girls don't get treated to three, four unassisted, orgasms that leave them yearning for more.*

"That's what I've been waiting on, Lena. Don't hold back," he whispered seductively, in her ear. "Let it go!"

She sunk her tongue deep into his mouth when passion overtook every rationale for regret, then it happened. Her chasm exploded! Lena screamed so loud that Aries was forced to hold his hand over mouth to muffle the unbridled chorus of high pitched moans. As her legs trembled uncontrollably, Lena watched Aries lick her juices from his fingers.

"Still think this is crazy?" he murmured, in a soft deep voice.

Lena thought twice before answering. Her voice was low, shaken, and stirred. "No, not crazy. I changed my mind about that ten minutes and two orgasms ago. You've got me feeling invincible, Aries."

"That's a good thing, right?"

"Hell no. It's at least three kinds of wrong but somehow exactly what I needed."

# chapter fourteen
# LAST NIGHT AND LULLABIES

Lena sneaked past their bedroom door carefully, with both shoes tucked underneath her arms. Ledger snored so loudly that she failed to notice the little blue pill he'd placed on the nightstand. He had intentions to make up for the last intimate debacle and treat his wife to a spirited welcome home romp but the long trip wiped him out.

Lena rehearsed the same lie all the way home. Merely another long delivery and a short nap at the hospital, was the story she'd concocted and albeit believable still a lie. One, she was prepared to ride all the way to the grave if necessary but as it turned out, Ledger wasn't up to demanding another shot at pleasing her sexually.

After slinking into the guest bathroom and locking the door, she felt safe. Not from her sins but immediate culpability. Lena flicked on the light switch, recoiled at the brightness then she pushed the dimmer nearly all the way down. Staring back at the guilty reflection in the mirror lessened her shame but she refused to apologize. The charge of electricity she experienced in that dirty restroom stall was still coursing through her veins.

Feeling the fire of a man as fine as Aries, who was capable of manufacturing a multi-orgasmic tsunami that allowed her to cope

with the Petrie's grief of losing child, was not going to be easily forgotten. Although Lena didn't consider what she'd done with Aries
a total skank move, she was forced to contend with betraying her
husband and their marital vows.

Lena knew it was reckless. The way she behaved was inexcus-
able but resulted in the most powerful orgasm in years. She wanted
to ignore the way Aries moved her but couldn't deny it. He had
awakened her spirit and made her smile down to her toes.

*One naughty round of steamy kisses and wicked foreplay in a
dirty women's room didn't really equate to cheating but it has to
stop,* Lena told herself. Ledger's a good man. He's always been
enough for me and that's how it has to be, she decided. Then, she
showered and fell asleep in the guest room down the hall; trying her
best to believe it.

The following afternoon, Ledger was determined to use that
little blue pill, if it killed him. He chased Lena around the house
as she made up one skillful excuse after the next. First, it was a
perfectly timed headache then she complained of feeling bloated
after drinking too much water with an aspirin. "Honey, please
let me run in the bathroom and tinkle," she pleaded, after being
cornered in the utility room. With a great deal of reluctance, Ledger
released the playful bear hug around her waist.

"Alright, I guess. If you really need to go."

"And I do, excuse me."

She quickly made her way into the nearest restroom, locked the
door then paced the floor. Lena couldn't explain to her husband why
she dodged his sexual advances because she wasn't too clear on the
reasons herself. Just a few days ago she would have paid him to
buzz around her like a sex-starved maniac. Now, she wasn't in the
the mood and faking headaches.

"Come on out or I'm coming in," Ledger sung sweetly, just outside the door.

Lena freaked out when she remembered what happened the night before in a restroom with another man. She answered with a slight hitch in her voice then flushed the toilet. "No-no-no! I'll be right there, Honey." She pretended to wash her hands then opened the door wearing a manufactured come-hither leer. "You want me? You got me, big daddy."

Ledger tried to push through the doorway with a full erection and white cargo shorts falling down around his ankle. "You don't have to go anywhere. We can get it on in there." He was grinning like a Cheshire cat but deadly serious.

"Uhhh, I'm not trying to do that," she mewed.

"Come on now, woman. I want to get raunchy and try some of that new sex you wrote about in the magazine. I've never done it in the restroom so that'll be new sex to me."

Lena brushed her hair back with both hands to gather her nerves then she put on a happy face. It was time to surrender. "Okaaay, guess we'd better get it on then." She moved aside to invite him in.

"Hey, you don't have to close the door," Ledger said, as he unbuttoned his short-sleeve shirt, slowly and methodically, like an over-the-hill male stripper. "We're all alone. Leave it open and live a little. Hand me one of those fluffy bath towels and that loofah. This is going to be fun."

After Lena got down and dirty in the second washroom within twenty-four hours, she needed to work out the troublesome feelings attacking her from both sides. Breaking away from her normal Saturday routine of boutique shopping and coffee sipping to pass the time, Lena found herself at a packed fitness facility. She was amazed how many people marched excitedly through the doors to ease pent up frustrations and sweat out the toxin they'd slurped down the night before. College students, singles, mad moms in minivans and business executives darted past her perch in the small café on their quest for better health.

Lena began to notice women her age, nearly all dressed in cute and colorful outfits, strutting their flattering results in and out of aerobic lounges and hot yoga studios. She closed her medical journal and tried to remember the last time she actually went to the gym to exercise anything but her prerogative. When Lena replayed her encounter with Aries, she hopped up from the comfortable padded chair. It didn't register during the throes of passion but it was clearer now, he'd gripped her round behind and called it chunky. She checked herself and frowned at the nonchalant attitude that made her believe being pretty was an exemption from ever having to exercise. Perspiring had been out of the question. However, Lena's new revelation provided ample reason for a woman who desired to be healthier and more productive.

Short of breath and slightly dizzy after climbing the seventeen steps leading to the upper level, Lena quickly realized two things, getting into shape would take more determination than she thought, and every woman who made a lifestyle change deserved to flaunt her hard-earned results.

Later that evening, Aries poured Cherry a second glass of Margaritas on the rocks while lounging on the second-floor balcony of his loft apartment. Raja licked his lips and shoved his glass closer to the pitcher in order to get a refill ahead of Flea. "All the way to the top this time," Raja begged.

"You greedy jerk," Flea said, as he wobbled on the rattan barstool.

Aries watched them go at it like five-year olds on the playground. "Do they always fight like this?"

"Whenever free drinks are flowing," Cherry answered. She sneered as Flea attempted to drink from the pitcher after Raja quickly chugged from his full glass. "Hey, quit it Flea! There's enough for everyone."

"Not if he puts his lips on the pitcher spout!" Aries barked.

The foursome had been called together when Cherry overheard Flea and Aries discussing the interlude that heated up the bar restroom. She interjected when they argued about the next logical step to lure Lena to a preselected venue for outright proof of a sexual affair. Everyone was excited about the tawdry touch and tickling but there were no angles to get video footage, even if Flea had known in advance.

"I told Aries the next time he gets the bright idea to intimately acquaint himself with a target, send me a signal or something first."

"I didn't even know it was about to happen," Aries said. "Maybe I should have seen it coming."

"Ha ha ha. Seen it coming?" Raja laughed. "That's very puny."

"You're very drunk," Cherry hissed. "It's time to lock the hyena cage. Let's make sure we're all on the same page before another opportunity is squandered. Christopher won't ever admit it but he's starting to disconnect from this score."

Flea sat up straight in a feeble attempt to steady himself. "Don't speak that into being," he said. "No one's talking about pulling the cord."

Aries looked worried. "What are you guys are talking about?"

"Cutting you lose, my man!" said Raja, with a blank gaze. "But that won't happen as long as I'm…"

Aries turned to see what happened to Raja. He'd passed out cold on the wicker recliner. "No way, he just went to sleep."

"Yes way. Now I'll get to finish the drink he couldn't," said Flea, with a mad dash for Raja's glass. "Sleep well, sucka!"

Cherry rolled her eyes at Raja, slouched over on his side. "This is so embarrassing. Sorry to litter your place with these light weights, Aries. Please notify Flea the next time Dr. Harmon feels like dusting off the old front porch."

"I would like to capture you putting in work," Flea quipped. "Maybe you could slap that ass for me a time or two."

"I will not be thinking of you when I'm doing my thing with Lena."

"Ewwwah," Cherry gagged. "Did I just throw up in my mouth?"

Flea glared at her. "Why did you have to say it like that? Just because I'm not an Asset doesn't mean I can't bring it in the sack."

"Okay, now I'm uncomfortable," said Aries, with his hands thrown up defensively.

Raja popped up like a jack-in-the-box. "There's a ninety percent chance of vomit in the forecast if I don't find the bathroom quick." Aries hurriedly passed the ice bucket to him as the others looked away. After Raja violently heaved up his guts, he pushed out an enormous belch. "I feel much better now. May I have another drink?"

"That's a hundred percent chance of hell no," Aries objected. Cherry cringed at the thought and Flea wobbled endlessly on the stool. "This was pointless. I'll give Lena some space to think about our recent poke and pinch session then chill a minute. Soon enough, she'll miss me enough to call. As for this meeting of the minds and that intoxicated nerd herd over there, I can't sanction this again. Next time, we're doing it at your place, Cherry."

"That's cool," she agreed. "No free liquor, no problems."

# chapter fifteen
# A THOUSAND DEEP KISSES

Keeping a watchful eye on Lena became more difficult as she departed from her typical schedule. Flea set up surveillance on the usual spots she visited for weeks without detour but lately she was a no show. Tired of spending useless time without getting any closer to catching Lena in the buff, he used the car tracker to see what she had been up to. Three days later, he reported back to Aries what he learned.

"Geez, it's hot out there. Thanks for the water," Flea said, as he wiped moisture from his forehead. "Why didn't you tell me your target was changing her routine?"

Aries sat on the sofa in gray running shorts and a red racer-back tank top. He laced up his shoes and listened while his shooter filled him in on Lena's recent change of pace. "I had no idea. Me and Cherry thought it best to go with a cooling off period. You know the whole *'absence make the heart grow fonder'* approach."

"I wish someone had given me a heads up on that strategy shift. When Lena chose not to show up to the nail spa on Tuesday I didn't think anything about it. On Wednesday, she must have left the house early because she was at the office by 8:00 in the morning."

"I thought she took Wednesday mornings off?"

"Me too but not this time," Flea answered. "Want to know where she went after work and spent darn near two hours?"

"Okay, I'll bite. The mall?"

"Not even close. The gym! She carried her thick and lovely little self over to Fit Quick."

Aries committed her schedule to memory, so he mulled it over in his head before rationalizing her new moves. "So, she got bored and changed it up some. Sounds like Lena swapped out her Tuesday mani-pedi appointment for her gym time sit and sip."

"That's one possibility but get this, instead of chillaxing in the café she put in two solid hours with a personal trainer."

Aries gave Flea a look that reflected what he was thinking.

"This trainer of hers, male or female?"

"See, now you feel me. It's a guy. He's no Idris Elba but he's got some swag to him." Flea lowered his head to keep from laughing.

"You got pics?"

"Of what?" he said, playing dumb to the hilt.

"Of the trainer, you idiot."

"Sure I have some. I got two flicks of him coming out after work. I knew you'd want to get a look at the competition." Flea handed the camera to Aries. "I don't know, he's probably a beast in them sheets."

Aries leaned forward to get a good look at the man on the LCD screen display. There was a picture of a pudgy black man dressed in gray nylon sweats, who was almost as round as he was tall. "I must've forwarded a few frames by mistake, there's a fat little critter on this with a played out shag."

"What's that?"

"A black man's mullet."

"Yeah, that must be the guy who cleans the dressing rooms. Click to the next one."

Aries concentrated while bracing himself for a muscle-built maniac who measured up to his physical prowess. Instead, it was a photo of an older gray-haired gentleman who had to be at least sixty-five. "You must've deleted the pic by mistake Flea. This is an ancient dude, who looks retired and run down."

"That's the one!" Flea howled loudly. "Don't sleep on the AARP."

"Ha ha, very funny. Ass clown."

"I had you going though. Didn't I?"

"Whatever."

"I got you good and you had it coming for making me sit on Lena's 'sweating with the oldies' workout routine."

"You're twisted and I'm overdue for some cardio. So, unless we're both hitting the trail, lock up on your way out." Aries tossed the camera back and chuckled as he walked toward the door. "So we're even now?"

Flea shook his head and looked under the couch pillow for the TV remote control. "I don't think so, my friend," he answered, under his breath then turned on the sixty-inch flat wide-screen and fumbled with the controller. "Hey, you have cable on this thing?" When the door closed, Aries was in the wind.

On the running trail, Aries passed several attractive women. Some of them smiled when he approached and others did as he passed. He'd seen tons of women vying for his attention but he had money on his mind, real money for a change. Christopher was correct. The cost of spending his time with another woman presented a set of unnecessary hazards, so Aries ignored each of them and kept it moving.

After his third mile, Aries began to think about Flea's ploy and the old man who he suggested was after Lena. It made him think about her changes in habit. He thought about her quirky attitude, the way she struck back when challenged and how her kisses turned him on. He was beginning to wonder how long it would take Lena to miss him when the phone strapped to his arm by a runner's band, vibrated. Aries slowed down to see who was calling. It was Lena. "Hey, you, I'm running," he said, attacking a steep hill without breaking stride.

"Then I'll call you back later."

"Not until you tell me why you called."

"But you're working out," she argued.

"And, I want to hear what's on your mind."

"Just been thinking."

"About what, Beautiful?" Aries listened but didn't hear any response. "Lena, you there? Lena? Go on and hang up on me then, with your sexy ass." Aries sprinted down the other side of the hill and motored pass two men slowly merging onto the same trail.

Lena was still on the phone, secretly listening to him breath for several minutes. She almost gave herself away when letting out a giggle for his *sexy ass* comment. She sat in the bathtub with her knees pulled against her chest, enjoying a secret moment in time. And, it felt like heaven.

Later that evening, Aries sipped from an imported-beer bottle on the second floor balcony of his apartment. He looked down at the busy sidewalk below. There were a number of couples enjoying the coolness of the evening, arm and arm and in love. Although he didn't feel capable of falling that hard for anyone, it was nice to see men, his age, who did. Being alone was always hard.

Aries was accustomed to keeping a crowded bed for fear of spending too much time wishing for something he didn't have, a real family. Growing up in the Denver Colorado foster system, Aries became a lot of things, a charmer, scammer and a young man that couldn't stand the thought of being by himself too long. By the age of eighteen he'd developed two distinctive gifts, playing the piano and boosting cars. The latter earned him three stints in the Division of Youth Corrections, kiddy prison, for Grand Theft Auto. On his eighteenth birthday, he received a certificate in the mail from Denver County and a check for $100. Without any viable skills to make a living or anyone to give a damn about him, Anthony Mitchell was pushed out of foster care and onto the streets. Credit card fraud kept his belly full. A half dozen Petty Larceny beefs for minor credit card theft kept him on the police radar. Dreams of having money and prestige kept him hungry.

After people-watching wore off, Aries stripped down to his turquoise boxers and stretched out across his Modcrest black lacquer platform bed and stared up at the ceiling. He'd purposely left the balcony doors opened so he could listen to the traffic and chatter from the street below. Restless and ready to spring the trap on Lena, he was trained to be patient as well as how to woo a married woman, and even suffered through a crash course in humility. Sleep would have come easier if only someone had shared an ounce of insight on overcoming loneliness.

The next morning rolled in with bright rays of sun peeking through the window. Aries squinted at the cell phone when it vibrated on the table next to his bed. "I hope this isn't some *meet me in five minutes and half way across town bullshit* from Christopher," he growled. As soon as his eyes focused on Lena's name atop the text scroll the screen, he was delighted.

LENA: *Almost texted u last night but u might have replied. Can't have that...*
*Hubby was home.*

ARIES: U O me something & I want it bad.

Aries yawned and urinated while awaiting Lena's response. It wasn't long before his phone buzzed. He looked at it peculiarly then read her text.

LENA: *Your wish is my command.*

Aries mulled over responding with something clever that wouldn't have come off as cheesy. He typed it in and pressed send.

ARIES: If that were true, u'd b here already.

Quite pleased with himself, Aries returned to his bedroom and plopped down on the bed. "Five, four, three, two...," he counted down, betting she would call. He answered on the first ring, when it did. "Hello Lena."

"Good morning. You sound asleep."

"Just sleepy," he said, using his sexiest early morning voice. "So, what time does my wish become your command? I hope before noon because I could use some breakfast."

"You're going to hold me to that?" she asked. "My last text, I mean."

"I'm a lucky guy to be talking to you. I'll take what I can get."

"Breakfast could work but I have some papers to sign at the office then I'm free for the day."

Aries pressed his ear to the phone, thinking he'd misheard her. "Way'ment, did you say you had a free day and implied you'd spend it with me?"

"Depends. Did you say way'ment?" Lena laughed so hard, she

snorted. "It feels good to hear your voice. You have no idea how much you've been on my mind lately."

"Anything naughty you'd like to share?"

"Not at the moment," Lena answered, with a sly smile. "But, it is the thought of you I'm growing attached to."

"Good thoughts, though?"

"Yes, of course. Your words have inspired me in a half million ways so far."

"I'm not sure what to say. A loss for words is new to me."

"Then we've said enough, for now, Aries Dupree." Lena allowed a long pause to pass between them then asked the question she'd held onto since he said hello. "Can I treat you to brunch today, if your schedule isn't already booked?"

"Yeah? I would really dig that. Text me the address and I'll be there."

"Does the type of restaurant matter?"

"As long as you show up, not one bit." Aries ended the call then jumped on the phone with Fleas as quickly as possible.

"Flea, wake up. You won't believe what just happened." Aries explained the discussion he and Lena shared. He was tickled at the excitement in Flea's voice and anxious for an opportunity to work on the score.

"Good thing you're listening to me for a change," Flea teased. "I'll shadow you today but won't get too close. Try to have fun, look natural. It plays better that way in the demand package."

"What's that?"

"It'll detail all of the juicy pieces of proof we need to convince that stiff husband of Lena's to pay us off."

"Alight, I'll forward the location. This date couldn't have come at a better time. Last night was rough."

"You didn't invite that Pandora chick over again?"

"I'm horny and bored, not stupid."

"Two out of three ain't bad," Flea joked. "Three out of three could get your cord pulled. See you in a few minutes. Keep up the good work."

The mid-morning breeze danced with the plastic table cover when Aries joined Lena on the patio of a small ham and eggs establishment in the neighborhood. Aries drove passed it twice because it was sandwiched between a washateria and convenience store. As if that wasn't peculiar enough, the numbered address painted on the rundown pale orange building was faded beyond recognition. He was surprised that Lena chose such an obscure place to meet then it made sense. Aries reasoned that Lena selected a part of town where she wouldn't likely be recognized or run into her husband. He took one look at her appearance and quickly understood why Flea called and warned him.

"Hey, you," she said, rising from a wrought iron chair to greet him.

She noted the sharp crease in his dark blue jeans and loved the way wind blew open his light blue short-sleeve shirt. *He could have stepped off the pages of a magazine,* Lena thought. *Could he have gotten finer since the last time I saw him?* When Aries opened his arms wide, hoping Lena would come in close for a warm embrace, she threw herself at him and planted her face against his chest.

Aries braced himself, held her close for a moment then laughed. He tossed the car keys on the table and sized up Lena from head to toe. She'd put on a blonde shoulder length wig, a sun-dress with a busy southwestern pattern and brown cork-soled wedges. He gave her a questioning look. "Wow, this is different." He slowly took a seat, uncertain why she would dress like a ghetto-fabulous chic hood chick.

"You have no idea why I asked you here, do you?"

"Because you're married and being discreet with your extracurricular activities."

"That could be the reason but no. This is one of the oldest buildings in Oak Cliff. It's rumored to be the last place T. Bone Walker did a show before heading to the west coast."

Aries looked around the room scarcely larger than a donut shop. He tried to envision it as a popular juke joint. "How did you come to know about the history of this place?"

"It was a vacant building for thirty years until some land developer wanted to build a strip mall on this entire street and revitalize the community. Fortunately, he discovered its historical significance and couldn't see tearing it down." She omitted the fact that Ledger was the developer and she put up the fight to save the oddly colored landmark.

After their food was served, Lena dug in and enjoyed the best tasting chicken and waffles this side of Chicago. Aries picked at his omelet until she caught him glancing oddly at her wig. "Something wrong?" she asked, with a carefree wiggle in her hips.

"Nah, why do you ask?"

"You keep staring at my hair. Does it bother you?"

Aries put his fork down before offering an answer. "Well, since you asked. I'm the kind of man who doesn't do wigs."

"Good, I'd hate to see you in one," she quipped. "Oomph, and I thought blondes had more fun." She sipped mimosa from a mason jar then cleared her throat. "If that's the only thing, I'll take it off."

Aries looked terrified. "At the table? While we're eating?"

"Of course not," Lena answered, with a raised brow. "But I am very interested to hear all about this overwhelming objection to alternative hairstyles."

Aries poked at the omelet with his knife like a child who was scolded for neglecting to finish his brussels sprouts. "It's more of a fear than objection in the way a lot people are afraid of clowns."

"Arachnophobia."

"That's a fear of spiders. Coulrophobia is the fear of clowns."

Lena nodded that she remembered then subconsciously scratched at her head. Aries bristled timidly as he leaned away from her. "Why are you acting like I'm a clown with a spider in my wig?" When he hesitated, she searched for the waiter. "Maybe this was a bad idea. You're acting strange and I'm feeling self-conscious about my appearance."

"Lena, please don't take it that way. I'll tell you why." Aries mounted the courage before sharing why he behaved so peculiarly. "Nobody knows this so I'd appreciate it if this stays between us." After Lena agreed, he continued. "When I was a boy, no more than ten, my mother was killed by some guy she brought home. She picked up tricks, men who paid for sex, when the rent was past due. This one dude didn't pay her afterwards, so she fought with him."

"That's terrible."

"She made me stay in my room when she had clients but I heard everything they said, did, every time. Well, that last night I thought my mom must've talked the man into paying up because the fighting stopped suddenly and he left. I came out to find her lying face down on the floor in a pool of blood." The ghostly expression on his face suggested he had traveled back in time to relive it all over again. "Her head was bashed in."

"I'm sorry, Aries."

"I tried to shake her, hoping she'd wake but she didn't." He paused to take a deep breath when Lena rubbed softly on his hand.

"When I turned her body over, her wig fell off and rolled onto the floor. Half of her skull was still in."

"No child should have to deal with that."

"I'll never forget how her exposed brain freaked me out. That's why I suffer from Maliaphobia, the fear of wigs. I usually turn away when I see black women wearing one. It's kind of funny but wigs don't affect me at all on white women."

Suddenly Lena wasn't sure what to do about the wig she wore, so she excused herself from the table. When she returned minutes later, there weren't any traces of Blondie No. 7, the popular wig style. Aries nodded his appreciation but didn't say another word until brunch was over. Lena was seriously concerned that he never received proper psychological help for the trauma he experienced as a youth.

"Aries, you okay?" she asked, as they exited the restaurant. "I hope you're not blaming yourself for what happened all those years ago."

During their short walk to the adjoining convenience store, Aries lagged behind. He avoided eye contact initially. "While my mother was screwing for rent money, I hid," he admitted, behind thinly-veiled shame. "When some man was killing my mother, I hid."

"Come here," Lena whispered, as they stood next to a tall rack of overpriced potato chips. "I don't think any less of you for your wig-a-phobia. Way'ment, do bad weaves scare you too? They frighten the hell out of me."

Aries chuckled and nodded as he pulled her close to him. "Yeah, most weaves are terrifying but for a whole other reason."

"Kiss me," she demanded. Aries pecked her sweetly on her lips but it wasn't satisfying enough for Lena. "Uh-uhhh, don't hold back."

Aries stood his ground. "I have a better idea. Let's get out of here." Once they reached the parking lot of the ratty orange building, he couldn't wait to offer his own brand of southern hospitality. "I'll bet you're great in a strong arm challenge," she said, batting her eyes.

"Sounds like it could be fun. What is it?"

"It's a game where two people find themselves alone with nothing but skin on skin and their imaginations between them."

"Really?"

"Oh, I think you'd dig it."

"What are the rules?"

"Who said there were any?" Lena mused, with a false bravado. "The way it works is simple. You dare me to do something that pleases you and I have to follow through or lose."

"So far, so good. What's next?"

"I tell you what I like and you must comply, no matter how freaky or demented. It goes back and forth like that until there's a winner."

"No wigs though," Aries kidded. "That would be an unfair advantage."

"I wouldn't do that but I am known to be crafty up in them sheets," she lied.

"So, now you're cool like that? How do we declare the winner?"

"Once a participant punks out on a challenge, the game is over."

"Come back to my place. I'll give you anything you ask for." Aries was itching to get Lena alone. Christopher had the loft apartment wired for sights and sound. Flea was chomping at the bit to record his Asset's sexcapades in High Definition.

"I might be inclined to see you again, in a more intimate setting but it won't there. I don't want to be taken to the same place where you've slayed all of your other women." Lena opened the door of her SUV when Aries refused to argue the point. "While I do think you gave up too easily, I am glad you didn't push."

"Obviously you're in control of this, us. You left me no choice," he argued.

"And to think, I'd planned on being with you all day long but you seem content to watch me drive away."

"Wait, now I didn't say that." He leaned his head in the car window to show her how wrong she was. Aries gently met her lips with his, kissing her with a degree of naked aggression that proved how much he wanted to continue their date.

"Why don't you hang tight for a minute?" she moaned. I'll call you in a few." Lena's soft expression revealed her vulnerability and decision to enjoy herself with a man who seemingly fell into her lap. Coincidentally, it was liberating to finally admit how intensely her desire burned for Aries. After he'd shared the story about losing his mother, Lena was touched. She realized at that moment how far she was willing to go.

He was surprised at how much he enjoyed Lena's company and how fast she ditched Blondie No. 7 after the gory details he shared. When Flea had sent him a text previous to arriving, a warning about Lena's alternative hair style, he begged Aries to make the wig disappear in order to get better pictures of Lena's face. After Aries' tearjerker, Flea got plenty of damning photos and considered the date a booming success although he had no idea the story that almost brought Lena to tears was true.

## chapter sixteen
# NINJA TRICKS

Aries pulled into the grocery store parking lot and waited for Lena's contact. After forty minutes, he made his way inside to kill time. Before he knew it, there was a small tray of fresh fruit, cheese and fancy crackers in his cart. A picnic would have been nice, he thought, if Lena didn't have a movie in mind. Either way, he'd be in her presence and that meant being closer to her than ever before. He kept an open mind about their rendezvous while he shopped casually and continued to wait.

The text message Aries had been waiting for arrived fifteen minutes later. He read it then shook his head in disbelief.

*"Wine sampling and Miniature Golf?"* he said. "What?" Aries was not in the mood for playing around unless it ended with a big pile of money. He believed that going straight at Lena was his best move and was anxious to show off his sexual acrobatics. "I'll pass on the putt-putt doctor," he said while typing his reply.

> ARIES: No games today.
> Rather sample u instead.

Once he pressed send, the ball was in Lena's court again. He was not surprised when his phone rang immediately.

"Hey."

"That was a very direct answer," Lena said calmly.

"What does it get me?"

"Come to the Ambassador Hotel and find out."

"At the lobby bar?" he asked.

"Room 918. Hurry."

Aries took an instant inventory of his grocery cart items. *No, this won't do*, he thought. *I'll need a can of whipped cream, two bananas, and some duct tape.*

Flea didn't like the news when he got a call from Aries explaining Lena's offer to meet right away. "Nah man, that doesn't work. You'll be spinning your wheels if you do her without getting any pics of it," he argued. "Maybe there's a building next to the hotel with a view of the room she's in."

"It's the 9th floor, dude. Let it go and take some time off. Catch a flick or some miniature golf but don't interrupt me. It's been a minute since I honey dipped so nobody's stopping me from knocking the dents out of that ass."

"No, wait. Let me get Cherry on the line to see what she thinks," Flea said. "Oh, and I'll patch in Raja so he can analyze the odds on going in with nothing to show for it but a quick nut." Flea was unnerved by the silence on the other end of the phone. "Hello? Aries? You there! Hello!"

The Ambassador was a local legend. A number of rock stars, movie sirens and at least three sitting presidents had slept there. The hotel was made of white ivory stone and accented by black iron. Intricate masonry carvings at the four corners of the hundred-and-five year old building provided a charming walk-up appeal. A young valet attendant took the car keys when Aries arrived.

"Will you be long, Sir?" he asked.

"Man, I sure hope so," Aries answered, with a confident smile.

When he stepped off the elevator and followed the narrow south wing hallway until it reached the end, he found room 918. It was the last door on the left. He knocked a few times, wondering what she was doing on the other side of that door. "It's that man, you ordered," he joked, when Lena asked who was knocking.

The door opened slightly. "Come in but *don't* turn on the lights," she said, shielding herself behind the heavy slab of oak. Her behavior was peculiar but refreshing. Having no idea what to expect, turned Aries on. He was used to women swinging the door open with bottles of flavored vodka and a long list of buck-naked fantasies.

Aries walked into the room and sat the vinyl grocery bag on the Mahogany desk. The drapes were drawn completely so it took a few seconds for his eyes adjusted to the dim light, emanating from three small scented candles Lena placed throughout the room. He watched her back up slowly then take a seat on the queen-sized sleigh bed.

"You going to keep standing over there or come and take off my clothes?" Lena said, as if she'd rehearsed it all morning long.

"Just like that, huh? No small talk, no chit chat?" As Aries took a step towards her, Lena stiffened bashfully.

"Okay, you're right," she squealed, then moved farther away on the bed. "I was acting like I'm used to this sort of thing but it isn't true. I still can't believe I'm here with you."

"I could come over there, sit down, and talk about it."

"Not yet. What are the rules?"

"Rules?"

"Did you bring protection?"

"Yes."

"Good. *I* need to be responsible. Wait, not that you don't need to be responsible too but I'm married. Jesus, I'm married. What I doing here?" Lena stared at the floor, mulling over her next question. "Is it alright that I don't do oral? I think that's too much on the first encounter."

"That's not a problem," he answered, almost amused at her lack of experience in such matters. "I'm a gentleman and I won't do anything you're not comfortable with."

"But I want it hard!" she said, quicker than she meant to. "Not rough though. I can't go home bruised down there." Lena muddled nervously through a few more pre-qualifiers then gave Aries a skittish grin. "I'm probably turning you off with all of these silly conditions. I'm sorry."

"No, it's refreshing to be with someone who's reserved and cautious. Usually women show up to the door holding a drink and a list of naughty things to try, while wearing nothing but a smile."

Lena glanced at the nightstand where a bottle of peach flavored vodka and a glass chilled on the rocks. "That's so trashy," she said, embarrassed by her previous thoughts of greeting him the way he'd described.

Aries shifted his weight onto the other foot when he wasn't sure what came next. "I hope there's nothing else because I cannot wait to please you."

"You always know what to say, Aries. I think I'm ready but don't take me too fast."

He walked closer to the foot of the bed then held out his hand. Lena climbed to her knees and crawled towards him. "Come on sexy," he said, in low calming tone. "I won't hurt you." When she reached for his hand, he kissed it softly and slid two of her fingers into his mouth. "Wow, that tastes sweet," he whispered, knowing where her fingers must have been recently. "You couldn't wait for me to get here?"

Lena blushed and turned her eyes away. "I was anxious to see you so I masturbated a little before you came. Okay, twice."

"Bad girl. I like that. Promise to let me watch next time?"

"I could never do that."

Aries pulled Lena against his thick chest. She melted as he treated her with soft, tender kisses that convinced her tongue to dance with his. He pulled away, teasing her before lunging in again with long passion licks along her neck. Lena moaned in short, excited sighs. "I'm so hot right now. I don't usually get this wet."

"I need to wash up. Don't move and don't take off your clothes. That's my job." She nodded her compliance as he walked into the bathroom and turned on the faucet.

Lena heard water run as she waited impatiently. Still a bundle of nerves, she took a long swig of vodka, coughed when the liquor went down too fast then hastily poured another glassful.

"I missed you," she said, when he returned. "Please take your shirt off. I've wanted to see your chest since, well let's just say for a long time now." When he began to unfasten the first button, Lena stopped him. "On second thought, I'd like to do that."

She grabbed Aries by the collar and pressed her lips again his. As she unbuttoned his shirt, excitement grew until the last one came undone. His chest was chiseled like a stone carving. "Oh, my goodness you're one fine man." She kissed his chest, slowly then more ferociously.

"Slow down baby, I'm not going anywhere." He let his shirt fall to the floor then kicked off both shoes and unzipped his pants.

"Your shoulders are incredible. Ooh, look at your arms. They're rock hard."

"Yeah, so is this." He gently guided her hand down his pants. The shocked expression on her face brought a naughty grin to his. "You like that?"

"What *is* that?" she asked, holding the long shaft in her palm.

"You built it, you know. Every inch was erected in your honor."

She pulled his jeans and maroon designer boxers down to take a thorough look at his hardened rod. Lena's eyes widened when she gave it a tug. His thick erection stiffened even more.

"It's like a damned trophy. How do you walk around with this all day?" she asked, in utter amazement.

"Whatever, it's not that big."

"Compared to what?" Lena placed both hands on it.

"Let me know when you're finished inspecting my body so I can get to discovering yours."

"I'm enjoying yours. It's very impressive, like somebody drew it with lots and lots of chocolate-mocha crayons."

Aries nibbled at Lena neck then on the other side. "I know what's going on here. You're stalling." He pulled her sun-dress down past her breasts.

Lena covered herself with both hands. She was self-conscious about their age difference and firmer breasts that Aries was more likely accustomed to fondling.

"Don't laugh. They're not that young anymore or perky like the tits you're used to."

He lowered his mouth to meet them, kissing each one delicately. "They are spectacular... for any age."

Lena's nipples became erect, as if his words and affection were received with great appreciation. She raised her hips off the bed when Aries rustled the dress down past them.

"You don't give yourself enough credit," he added. "Now, not another word about how imperfect you think you are."

Lena nodded again, feeling at ease and treasured. She was thankful when he took the time to lay her dress across the chair so it wouldn't wrinkle. "You are so sweet," she whispered.

Aries smiled as he sized her up once again, keeping a certain number of orgasms in mind for Lena. "Now, lay back and enjoy," he said, knowing she would thoroughly delight in what he had in store.

Lena did just as commanded. She fell into the fluffy pillows and groped his strong shoulders as his tongue circled her nipples then traveled to her quivering stomach. Her body responded to every kiss, touch, playful bite. Lena was enthralled by Aries' patient style and didn't want to rush a single moment of it. As the heat between her thighs continued to rise, his skillful caresses eased away every ounce of apprehension. She was in the moment and loving the way he made her feel like she belonged to him.

As he laid ample kisses on her shoulders, nape of her neck and earlobes, she shuttered helplessly. When Aries traced her hips and inner thighs with his lips, he cast his eyes upward to note Lena's reaction. It excited him more when her back arched and body twisted with anticipation. He propped two pillows beneath Lena's hips, to elevate her behind then nibbled at the valleys between her thighs. Instinctively, she shoved his head into her moist honey pot. Obviously the oral copulation she swore off earlier, did not apply to receiving it.

"Right there, right there," she sighed. "You're so good at that. Oooh, I love it." Lena opened both legs wider as he inserted a finger inside of her. "I can't believe how wet I am. It's embarrassing."

"Uh-uh, not at all. That's what every man hopes for, the wetter the better. And, don't let nobody tell you different." Aries reached for a condom on the nightstand. He rolled it down with one hand while massaging Lena's breast with the other."

"I can't take all of that," she whispered, in a reluctant tone. It didn't matter how much of him she was capable of taking in as long as she got as much as she needed.

When she locked her legs at the moment of penetration, Aries playfully slapped her on the behind. "Uh-uh, relax those hips and thighs baby. Loosen up. I got this."

Lena agreed to trust him and was quickly rewarded with long, steady, pleasurable stokes that ignited her inside. "Careful," she pleaded, "or you'll knock the back out." Lena locked her wrists around Aries' neck and her heels around his waist, graciously accepting his large endowment and pace. His sensual gyrations brought out the woman in her. Passionate screams poured into the darkened room as she craved more intensity. Echoes of ecstasy bounced off the walls room 918 as Lena's unbridled, high-pitched sighs of satisfaction encouraged Aries to go deeper, longer and stronger.

He crossed her legs at the ankles then hoisted them over his left shoulder. After several downward thrusts, Lena began to claw at the bedsheets. She grappled for something to hold onto when the intensity shot up her thighs; causing her vagina to contract around his throbbing wand. Aries licked and sucked feverishly at her calves then guided her toes into his mouth. He felt her body contort and pulsate as her breath quickened. Lena panted deliriously without control or remorse while Aries worked her g-spot like a magician.

"Ohhhh Aries! You're driving me crazy!" she screamed, hitting high notes she never had. "Ohh-ohh-ohhhhhh Yessssssssssssss!" Aries pushed himself deeper inside her, completely filling Lena's orifice while her legs trembled unsteadily.

"I want you to remember everything you're feeling right now."

"I'm shaking. Why am I shaking?" Tears rolls from her eyes when Aries brought forth a second orgasm with his tongue.

VICTOR McGLOTHIN

"That's not fair. You're too good."

"That's only the first act," he said, without blinking. "Told you I'd take it easy. Wait until I show you some of my ninja tricks."

Lena gave him a worried look. "Whew, can I catch my breath first? I'm not used to getting flat-out handled in bed. I need some ice water, lots of it. And, a nap."

Aries watched Lena drifting in and out of sleep for an hour before treating her to another sultry session, commingled with lewd acts of debauchery. Aries was cautious not to take Lena too fast or too far so he slowly guided her body through her seventh mind-blowing orgasm. She tried to keep a count but they fired off too quickly, one intensifying more than the last.

When Lena collapsed onto the bed, Aries smacked her backside as it jiggled. Because of the electricity traipsing up and down her spine, Lena felt no shame. She'd been to the mountain top and experienced every inch of euphoria, on her way down.

Afterwards, Aries played in her hair while feeding her strawberries, pineapple and a selection of premium cheeses. Lena valued the way he remained attentive after their wild interlude but she thoroughly appreciated his innovative use for whip cream during the last round. Lena felt at home nestled on his masculine chest as Aries laid on his back, chomping a banana. She ran her outstretched fingers over his unbelievable six-pack abs.

"Who knew," she said, as if lost in a thought that consumed her.

"What, that you liked having whip cream licked off your ass?"

"You sucked it out of every nook and crevice of my body? But no, that's not all of it. Guess again," she said, tickled that he was playing along.

"Uh, lemme see. Oh, I know. You had no idea how much fun the Kidnapped Débutante routine would be?"

Lena turned her head so she could see his face. "Duct taping towels around my hands and feet, so you could have your way with me, was a routine?"

"You were my best hostage, though," he answered, honestly.

Lena wanted to be his only hostage, although the mere thought of being any more than a conquest was out of the question. She understood what they meant to each other and couldn't risk upsetting their complicated situation. "You're not going to dick and dismiss me are you?" she asked, as concerns persisted.

"Is that your way of asking if we can do this again?"

"Yes. I guess it is. My body has never reacted to anyone like this. You have me yearning, scratching, begging. And you didn't once ask me to *say yo' name*," she joked.

"I already know my name."

"But you did demand that I tell you when I orgasmed."

"*Orgasmed?* Is that a verb?" he said, laughing aloud.

"You know what I mean, silly. I'm not the type to divulge that much information during sex."

"You cannot be serious? You're willing to throw your legs in the air and wave them like you just don't care but notifying your lover when he's setting off a symphony in your pussy, is asking too much?"

"Well, when you put it like that I sound selfish, although I did kind of feel like a circus act when we played hide the banana."

"What can I say? You bring out the beast mode."

"I didn't have a chance to do anything for you. All I did was take-take-take and quake-quake-quake," she said, laughing at how cheesy it sounded. "I was raised to be a good girl and always thought of men slapping my ass as demeaning."

"Then who was that up in here shouting *slap it! Spank it!*" he chided.

"You almost had hotel security beating at the door."

"Forget you Aries. You're a mess."

"I only popped that ass when you were about to come. It heightens the intensity, if you smack it at the right moment."

"Yes, it did!" she revealed. "Who taught you that kind of stuff?"

"You live, you learn," he answered. "Especially if you pay attention."

"So where do they teach that Master's Course in sexual satisfaction because I need to send my husband. Oops, I'm sorry. Is it off limits, to talk about him?"

"Well, it doesn't do a thing for me. I'm here to bring you joy, so it's up to you what we talk about when together. You have a lot on your plate, Lena, I ain't tripping."

Lena turned and scooted closer to Aries. She kissed him gently then rested her head on his shoulder. "You're busy too, building your clientele can't be easy. I know how doctors treat drug reps." Lena realized what she said may have offended Aries until she heard an awkward laugh.

"No worries. I just rep-wrecked you seven times in the past hour."

"Seven? I thought it was five. I did not have that many orgasms," Lena debated.

Aries shrugged. "Okay, we'll call it five."

"Only if you're willing to make up the difference."

"You think you're slick, Dr. Harmon. But I can't help you with that, we're out of condoms."

"How many came in that box?"

"Three."

"Next time get two boxes. I think I can go again."

"Oh, really?" he asked, shocked she would even contemplate more pelvic pounding.

Lena swung her legs off the side of the bed to stand up. She took one step towards the restroom and her knees buckled. "Oh second thought, that was plenty. I can't even walk."

"I love your optimism. Come back and lie down. I'll run your bath water."

Lena eagerly obeyed. She sipped peach-flavored vodka while soaking in the tub. Aries washed her back and listened to her complain about issues common to obstetricians in private practice. He patiently pampered her while devising a strategy to incorporate himself deeper into her life. Regardless of how much he enjoyed their stolen moments or how good he made her feel, it was all meaningless. Aries was simply playing a role, nothing more. Such is the life of a schemer.

## chapter seventeen
# HANGING ON TOO LONG

The telephone rang at 7:31 P.M. Aries stepped out of his shower and grabbed a towel. It was Christopher telling him to come by the W Hotel for a briefing. Aries agreed to meet with the charismatic leader of the traveling crew of takers and handsome heart-breakers. Although he hadn't nabbed a ridiculous sum of money for the Men of M.O.E.T., Aries was content in the work he'd done and the way things were playing out.

Since he was summoned to the penthouse suite for the first time, it was fair to assume that Christopher was finally cutting him some slack. Spending an inordinate amount of time and energy court-ing his target had born fruit, theoretical. There was no denying it. Cashing in before the score city got too hot was imperative. Men, who paid off M.O.E.T. Corp. to keep quiet and go away, meant just that. Leaving town was a necessary part of the negotiation process and understood by all of the parties involved. Sticking around after extorting money from the wealthy wasn't only irresponsible, it was like poking his neck out then waiting to see who would take a swing at him first.

Aries left his black luxury SUV with the valet. On his way into building, he checked his reflection in the large pane glass window. The tan seersucker suit hung perfectly on his long frame. Chocolate brown designer loafers completed his casual yet ritzy ensemble. Aries looked like new money and that's how he felt, crisp and clean.

As he walked towards the elevator, two men in dark suits approached him. Both were over six feet tall, fit and sharply attired with short cropped hairstyles; suggesting they were ex-military goons for hire. Aries didn't recognize either of them but something told him they knew precisely who he was.

"Come with us, Sir," said the smaller of the men, then lead him to the last elevator on the right. "Mr. Denmark has been notified of your arrival."

"I see," Aries grunted. "Chaperones."

"Three coming up," whispered the larger escort, into a microphone hidden in the barrel cuff of jacket. Aries felt more uneasy than protected as the men stayed behind him throughout their ride on the Penthouse elevator.

When the doors opened, Aries saw two enormous men standing guard outside of the penthouse suite. They were dressed identical to the escorts who remained on the elevator headed down to the ground floor. "Please extend your arms to the side, Mr. Dupree," one of the menacing sentries said, as if it were an option. Aries put his hands out but kept an eye on the bulge in the man's waistband while he was being frisked for weaponry.

"I work for Mr. Denmark," Aries said, annoyed by the extensive search.

"It's procedure, Sir. You may enter. Have a good evening," he added, plainly.

Suddenly, the doors swung open. Aries walked in, a lot less

certain of his worth than when he arrived. He continued along the marble walkway leading farther into the brightly lit sitting area with contemporary blue-velvet furniture and elegant crystal chandeliers. Aries heard voices ahead so he kept going. When he wandered through the next set of doors, he saw Christopher sitting alone and talking on the telephone in a language he didn't understand. His best guess was Farsi, of Persian origin, and widely spoken in the Middle East.

Christopher was dressed in silver linen slacks and matching short sleeve shirt. He waved to Aries amicably, gesturing for him to choose something to eat from the buffet on the granite bar, then he returned to his call. Aries looked around the grand living area. An 80-inch flat screen TV played the sports highlights. Most of the westward wall was aligned with tinted glass, undoubtedly to provide guests with picturesque sunsets every evening. Two doors on the adjoining wall were closed but a third was opened. It was a game room entrance for two pool tables, a bank of Xbox controllers and another 80-inch screen serving as a video game monitor.

Aries was fascinated by the ostentatious appeal and could only guess how extravagantly the bedrooms were furnished. He wasn't invited to sit, so he stood until Christopher ended his call.

"There he is," his mentor cheered. "Hey Aries, get yourself something to eat. Big guys gotta eat, right?"

"Sure, I'll take a piece of this chicken."

"There's lobster and calamari there and even some caviar to nibble on."

Aries noticed Christopher's disappointed look. "What? I like what I like. Chicken."

"Ahh, what the hell, I like chicken too. Save me a few hot wings for later."

Christopher poured himself a glass of Big Red soda then joined Aries in the lounging area. "You can't get this everywhere. Big Red goes good with almost everything but they don't sell it in the northwest. And, forget about finding any on the East coast."

"I'll try to remember that," Aries said, while his concerns mounted.

"Eat up. We have some things to talk about."

As Christopher discussed his interest in buying a NASCAR team and an English soccer franchise, Aries ate chicken and listened carefully. Christopher shared dreams of controlling other people's lives with a checkbook and granting them million dollar salaries with the swoop of an ink pen but Aries remained anxious to talk about Lena and the progress being made with his target.

"I drove by the MOET office today and the place was pad locked," Aries said. He knew something had changed and wondered if it affected his potential score.

"Yeah, we no longer needed the facility once you slept with Dr. Harmon. It's only a short matter of time before we're finished in Dallas and long gone. So, how was it?"

Aries shrugged, nonchalantly. "Sex with Lena? It was a basic slang and bang. I did my thing, she liked it."

"Outstanding. Where's the proof?" Christopher asked.

"She invited me to the Ambassador but selected the room and got settled in before I even knew where she was."

Christopher winced as if Aries' explanation literally caused him great pain. "Flea couldn't record this alleged *slang and bang* but I'm supposed to take your word for it?"

"You think I'm lying on my dick?"

"You could be, I'm just saying. Last night I fisted the Duchess of Cambridge up the ass while her husband the Duke watched. No, wait. I gave Alice in Wonderland the best head of her life on a dirty mattress in Time Square. Get my point?"

VICTOR McGLOTHIN

"Yeah, you want something we can sell." Aries replayed Fleas' ridiculous plea to avoid sleeping with Lena until he could record it. "It's not like I had a choice?"

"You could have waited Aries, until we were in position."

"I had a shot so I took it," he said, in his own defense.

"A shot. Sometimes a single shot is all an Asset gets. One freaking shot!" Christopher raised his hands to calm himself. "Contrary to rumor, I don't like being adversarial but we're in the proof of pussy business, you understand. We show incontrovertible evidence that the woman in question has grabbed her ankles, given it up, and taken a high hard one. No proof of pussy, no deal!"

"I'll get it again."

"There are no guarantees in this game, man. That's what Flea was trying to tell you. What if, now she's so full of remorse that she never takes another call from you? Or let's say you had an off night and your performance sucked. If that's the case, she's *really* sorry she gave it up."

Aries couldn't stop thinking he'd done the right thing by getting Lena to give in and trust him. Getting Christopher to agree was impossible so he put on an apologetic face. "I didn't see that as a potential problem at the time but you're right."

Christopher accepted Aries apology even though he had some doubts about Aries. "You're a difficult guy to manage. You know that?"

"No. Never been told I was difficult before."

"Really?" Christopher smiled then sipped on his red soda. "You've never worked at any place more than 90 days in your life. Yeah, I looked into that before bringing you aboard."

"How did you get that intel on me?"

"Don't worry about it. I know what I see and that's a maverick in a tailored seer sucker suit. Nice duds, by the way." He leaned

186

back against the comfortable sofa and spread his arms along the top of the cushions. "You can tell a lot about a man in the way he responds to a simple gesture of hospitality."

"I'm a pretty good judge of character too," said Aries.

"Not character, more like instincts and trust." He glanced at the buffet in the kitchen area. "By the time it took you to get here, from the moment I called, I doubt you had time to eat anything. You came hungry and got a royal escort on the way up. That had to be unnerving even for a tough guy like you, who was probably sizing up my security in the event you had to fight. Next, you got to be impressed by all of this lavishness. I sure pay enough for it. Then, I offered you a nice layout to choose from. Good food. First you refused my hospitality altogether then you selected the cheapest thing on the platter."

Aries wouldn't let on that Christopher was correct on every point he'd made thus far. "What are you suggesting?" he asked, in an accusing tone.

"That you don't like owing anyone anything, which suggests you're a maverick who does what he wants regardless of the rules. You don't respect authority and neither do I but in my house, the Men of M.O.E.T., I am the authority. I've done right by you. Now, respect is due."

The only thing Aries could do was agree to stick to the script Christopher set before him. He was given two weeks to close the deal or call it quits. There was a premium placed on common sense in the extortion racket. Be good, be smart, and be gone. Accidentally bumping into an angry millionaire who recently forked over a ton of cash would have been catastrophic and seen as rubbing the mark's nose in it. It wasn't smart to create a deadly case of buyer's remorse. Christopher explained that was the reason for top-flight security at the hotel and why he couldn't be seen in Dallas by the rich, angry husbands. He further explained that the two M.O.E.T. Assets, who connected with their targets weeks before Aries had, were either vacationing or setting up the next score in another city. Two weeks was all the time Christopher felt comfortable risking being spotted. Aries had to compromise his target or come up with the money Christopher fronted him. All of the planning and plotting had come to this. With his scheme ticking down to its last fourteen days, Aries shoved a chicken strip in his mouth and marched out of the penthouse suite like a man on a mission. Christopher raised his glass of Big Red and bid Aries good luck.

After his favorite Asset was securely on the elevator, Christopher summoned his overnight guest from the closed master bedroom. Cherry slinked out in a long, gray, flowing negligée and matching velvet high heels.

"He's going to come through," she said. "Trust in that."

"He'd better."

Aries stopped in for a stiff drink at a Tex-Mex cantina down the street from his apartment. He replayed the conversation with Christopher and the number of days he was given to bring a promising project to fruition. He thought it was plenty of time to romance Lena's heart, twist her mind, and provide all the slang-and-bang her eager vagina could handle. Keeping her off balance and satisfied, that was his plan. Easy as 1-2-3. Aries needed another tasty concoction followed by a good night sleep before rolling out phase one of his program.

# chapter eighteen
# SMART IS THE NEW SEXY

Lena zipped by the long line waiting to be seated at Magnolia's. She dismissed the pushy hostess who tried to question her as Aries gained her attention from the back of the trendy salad and salsa restaurant. "I'm with *him*," Lena said, with a great deal of pleasure. "Isn't he pretty? I know he is, you don't have to say it," she added, while making a bee line to her lunch date.

"Wow, you're glowing today," said Aries, as he stood to greet her.

"Hey, so glad you asked me to this new place," Lena replied, as she approached his table near the window. "And thanks for coming early to get a great table."

"You've been very busy. Please have a seat." He looked at her scrubs, hanging loosely on her shoulders and the drawstring bunching around her waist. "And look at your clothes, falling off."

"I've lost seven pounds and I needed to. Got to get back to the old me." Lena enjoyed an eyeful, as she appraised his brown fitted suit and polished shoes. "I like the way you put things together, always so stylish."

"Thanks," he said, gazing deeply into her eyes. "I thought about you last night."

"Sounds interesting."

"Then I woke up." He flashed a sexy smirk, adding a huge dose of *bashful* to reel her in further.

"Are you blushing? Ooh, it was that kind of dream?"

"Guess so. My boxers ended up on the floor somehow."

Lena inched closer to the table and softened her voice. "Boy, don't make me jump over this table, in front of all these people," she teased. "You trying to send me back to work with my panties soaking wet?"

"You could leave them with me."

She flirted back with her eyes as they undressed him ever so slowly. "See, that's why I can't fool with you in public. You're too damned sexy, that's your problem."

A waitress stopped by to take their orders. Lena found an entrée that sounded delicious then noticed two women at the next table checking out Aries. When their food server dashed off to grab an ice tea, Lena's disposition changed. "Do you see those women clocking you over there?" she asked.

"Tangier and Makella? No. I haven't noticed, lately."

Lena laughed uncomfortably. "Tanqueray and Magnesia? Are they some of your old friends?"

"We just met. They sat down a minute ago. I was alone so they chatted me up." Aries accepted his drink from the waitress, pretending to be oblivious to his immediate surroundings and Lena's increasing tension.

"Did they ask for your phone number? I know they did."

"You need to stop," he said, shaking his head.

"Maybe you should tell me what y'all got all chummy about." She looked at the women again, both very attractive and at least ten years younger than her.

"If you must know, they asked who I was, if I were dining alone and if I happened to be single."

The hairs on the back of Lena's neck stood up. "Well, are you single?" she said, sorry for the question as soon as it left her lips. "Scratch that. I have no right to expect exclusivity from you." Lena shot a nasty little sneer in the ladies direction when they made eyes at Aries then giggled like star-struck teenagers.

"You're not jealous, are you?"

"You're just eating this up," she whispered, through clench teeth. "Go ahead and admit that you love having strange women screwing you with their eyes."

"Ha ha ha. Hold on now. First of all, I told them I was seeing someone and then you appeared so there." Lena gave him a grateful smile then quickly thought about the implications.

"Wait. Now those chicks think I'm your girlfriend?" She turned her face toward the window, to shield it from their full view. "What if they were my patients? Or work for my husband?"

"Calm down. I didn't say you were mine but it does bring up an issue I've been worrying about. What will you say when we do run into a patient or someone else you know?"

She envisioned him, sweat dripping and skin glistening, without a stitch of clothes again.

"Built like that, nobody's going believe you're my accountant."

"Then I'll be your fitness trainer or when dressed like this, I'm a personal shopper for your husband."

Lena nodded her agreement. "Hey, that might work. Fitness trainer I can see but a personal shopper? I don't know."

"That's what Tangier over there does." He skillfully brought the conversation back around to Lena's potential competition at the next table.

"And how would you know that? She just told you all her business?"

"Why are you rolling your neck? Don't go there," he mused.

"She gave you her number too?"

"Yeah, it was on her business card." He almost spit out his food when Lena slapped the table in opposition. "You are really showing out, right now. And, it's kinda cute."

"That's it, I'm not letting you go out in public alone ever again. I can't take the aggravation. Check please!"

"But I'm still eating."

"And? I've lost my appetite. You're not staying here at this hookup joint with thirsty personal shoppers trying to get at you."

"Lena, I'm a grown man. I can handle myself and I'm quite capable of saying no to beautiful women."

"Which one of those crows do you think is beautiful, Aries?" She flashed a *mind your own business* glare at them, when it became obvious they had overheard parts of the discussion.

"If they didn't think we were lovers before our first spat, they do now."

"Which one is Tangerine?" she asked, calmly. "She probably works at a cheap mall store."

Aries' answer came reluctantly and under extreme duress.

"*Tangier* is the one with the white top."

"Oh, she is pretty and I like that blouse but her friend looks like Shrek, with Donkey's ass."

"Don't be mean," he said, staving off a hearty laugh. "She's probably very nice." He thought about paying Makella a worthy compliment but knew better than pouring gasoline over that fire. Instead he placed the Styrofoam to-go containers inside of white plastic bags with the restaurant's name on them.

"Here you go."

"Thank you for a fascinating lunch," she said, her words drowning in sarcasm. "Let's do it again some time, at the chicken shack, where women with gold teeth know how to stay in their lane."

Lena was late getting back to work after trailing Aries to a nearby running trail to be alone, park and spark. They were both worked up after several minutes of hot and heavy foreplay. Lena left Aries with a severe case of blue balls. Lena changed her panties in the restroom stall and laughed at her behavior during lunch. She considered making an apology, one Aries wouldn't soon forget.

He read a litany of funny texts Lena sent during the afternoon. She asked if he still liked her after seeing her horns come out. Aries replied with a smiling-face sticker but offered no written answer. Lena wondered how he honestly felt, if he were being dismissive or if he were merely too busy to respond. She could barely wait to hear his voice after her office closed.

"I'm sorry to blow up your phone with IMs all day," she said, testing the waters. "I hope they didn't distract you too much."

"I was calling on doctors from the south side. Office hopping as usual," he lied. Aries had been watching cable news from his sofa for hours. Flea was bored to death and nodding off on the love seat. "Not one of my docs wanted to discuss products though. The news story about that white girl who's pregnant by the Mayor's twin sons has everybody mesmerized." Lena wished she could have blabbed what she knew firsthand about the newsworthy patient; who happened to be in her office, less than an hour ago for a checkup.

"Yes, I've heard about that," she answered, instead. "What are you getting into later?"

"I can be available. Anything specific in mind?"

"You seem preoccupied. I'll let you go."

"Come by and see me on your way home. I'm fighting traffic but I can meet you at my place."

"You know I would love to see you, anywhere except there," she answered sweetly. "Don't be mad. It's a woman thing."

"A Lena control thing?"

"You have so much power over me Aries. Other than giving myself to you, when and where I do it are the only things I can control. Please try to understand."

"I do, sort of."

"That's good enough for me and it presents the perfect opportunity to invite you out to finish what we started at the park today."

Aries sat up on the sofa. "Sure, I'd like to finish what we started after lunch," he said, to wake Flea and clue him in on the conversation. "You paid for the last hotel room. I'll get this one." Flea's eyes widened. He yawned and motioned for Aries to keep pushing that scenario along, so he could get in the room early and set up hidden cameras.

"Didn't we just talk about this?" she asked.

"I heard you loud and clear."

"Perhaps but were you listening to me?" Lena said, with a twinge of disappointment in her voice.

"Now you're hurt. I won't ever ask you to meet me again or beg you to let me fund our rendezvous or pay for lunch or for coffee."

"You think you're funny, don't you?"

"No. I didn't like the tone you used to accuse me of not listening. I want to be a joy to you."

"You've been all that and more. Can you meet me at our place after I've gone to the gym? I'll see if they have the same room available."

"Yes, it's always great seeing you."

Aries shook his head at Flea, signifying his failure to back Lena down from her stance on selecting the venue for their next wild romp. "Hit me with the room number and I'll be right there. Want me to pick up anything?"

"Your desire to be with me is more than enough. I'll bring the condoms. Extra-large, right? Got it. I'll see you later."

Aries arrived at the Ambassador with flowers in hand and good intentions. Lena answered the door, in the same darkened room but she left her clothing neatly folded on the oak desk. "Come in handsome," she said, hiding behind the door.

Once inside, Aries closed the door and kissed Lena sweetly then presented her with a bouquet of colorful daisies. "These are for you," he said, impressed by her fresh Brazilian waxing. "Nice landing strip. When did you get it?"

"Before I went to the gym. I hope you like it."

"It's hella sexy. Of course, I like it." He leaned forward with a tender kiss on her forehead then tattooed more of them on her cheeks and neck. "I've missed you. More than you know," he added, with his hand caressing the rise in her behind. "You're getting toned."

"I'm... I'm... trying to keep up with you," she said, breathlessly. "The way you're built is unfair."

"I'm not going anywhere." Aries swept Lena off her feet in one effortless motion and carried her to the bed. "I want you and can't seem to think of anyone else." Lena's eyes were trained on his face until he began to peel away his clothing. Her attention shifted lower when he pulled his boxer shorts down to reveal his long brown shaft.

"Ooh damn," she marveled, as if it was her first glimpse of it.

"There it is."

"You are such a freak," he jested. "What happened to that prim and proper lady doctor who ran me out of her office?"

She crawled to her knees then quickly took him into her mouth, easing it in and out. "You, happened," Lena answered seductively, while bobbing her head and stroking his penis with both hands. "Now, this is what she wants." She backpedaled on her prudish stance on non-oral activity from her side of the mattress. Aries stood next to the bed, barefoot on the floor as Lena demonstrated her passion for him and a surprising sensual talent for fellatio. She played with his tool, gripping and moistening it. His toes clawed at the plush carpeting as his lover licked and sucked then stroked and slurped.

"Wow. You've been holding back. Baby, I can feel it in your throat."

"Uhhh-hmmm," she cooed. "Had me sloppy wet all afternoon thinking about this." She pulled his hand between her legs to examine her claims of excessive juices. Instantly, his fingers glided easily into her slippery pleasure pit.

"Talk about unfair," he groaned. Aries loved the way Lena's back arched as he manipulated her enlarged clitoris with his fingertips. "You're sexy as hell, Lena. I want some of that." When he could not endure another moment of her talented tongue, Aries climbed on to the bed to give her what he came for.

Suddenly, Lena pushed him onto his back then straddled his lap. "Not yet," she moaned, kissing his nipples while dry-writhing on his swollen rod. "I don't know how you do this to me. I'm so hot." She raised herself a few inches above his lap and guided his sword of satisfaction inside of her.

Aries pulled his hips back and yanked his penis out immediately. "What are you doing?"

"Huh? What?" she asked, somewhat confused by his actions.

"Protection? I thought you brought rubbers."

Lena leapt off of Aries when it finally occurred to her that she had inserted him without a condom.

"I'm sorry. What was I thinking?" She thought about her patented speech given to hundreds of promiscuous teens, irresponsible adults and married women who were impregnated during a wild romp without a protective barrier. She'd doled out the self-righteous, accusatory tongue lashing millions of times and never once understood how it was conceivable for passion to overwhelm a person's good judgment. Yet, there she was only moments ago, riding bareback and getting her kicks just like the patients she reprimanded.

"It's alright," he said, to calm her down. "But as a rule, I don't go raw dog. I'm not ready to be a father."

"That's very mature of you. Whew, I was too horny for my own good."

She sat on the bed with a bewildered expression. Aries rubbed Lena's back then worked his way to her shoulders, massaging them gently. "Thanks, that feels nice." His tender hands relaxed her. She closed her eyes and surrendered to his gifted fingers. Within minutes, Lena's powerful thirst for him returned. Her yearning was made apparent by shortened breaths and heavy pants. "Why don't you get the condoms from the top drawer," she said, reflecting on her previously blunder.

The primal craving Aries exhibited during their first two encounters was noticeably absent from the slow, sinful grind-fest that he delivered flawlessly during this episode. Nonetheless, Lena enjoyed a number of window-rattling orgasms the way she had before and was exceedingly grateful for each and every one. "Whew! You are incredible," she sighed, wiping perspiration from her forehead with the bedsheets.

"If you aren't the best lay on the planet, I don't need to know who is."

Aries flashed a soft smile as if it were all in a good day's work.

"Joy bringer," he whispered, in her ear.

"Yes you are and so good to me." Her fingers danced on his chest playfully then suddenly stopped. "But why were you different this time?"

"How is that?"

"Your speed and pace were deliberate, almost methodical," she answered honestly. "I'm not complaining because it's obvious that you know how to put it down in any gear."

"I've had a lot on my mind. You know as well as I do that building a business is full of ups and downs."

Lena playfully nipped at his chin. "So is really amazing sex."

"There you go, when I'm trying to be serious."

"Okay *Serious*, what's behind that slow and steady screw you whipped on me today?"

"Making my next move, my best move. It'll all work out. Always has, so far."

Her interests grew until she gave legitimate thought to his plight. "What would you like to do next?"

"You really want to know?" Aries thought twice about his question after floating it.

"Yes, I care about what's on your mind."

"I want to create wealth and become a millionaire," he answered, truthfully.

Without blinking, Lena fired off another pointed question. "What would you do if you had a million dollars, two million or three million?"

"Figure out a way to flip it, make my stacks multiply."

"You're a man, alright. Money is never enough with y'all." Lena shimmied towards the head of the bed then repositioned her body to get closer to Aries.

"Come over here baby," he beckoned her. Lena gladly accepted his invitation to lay her head on his chest. "Yeah, that's better. I like having you there."

"You're making it so easy to fall for you. Who's going to catch me if I do?"

"A crush is supposed to hurt a little, right?"

Lena placed her hand on his then loosely intertwined their fingers. "See, there's more to being successful at life than making piles of money."

"Not for me. Growing up in foster care keeps you hungry. Fear of being that broke again keeps you hustling."

"I get that. A real man needs to chase his dreams to keep them alive but you sound like most ambitious business men. They're so driven they tend to miss what's right in front of them." She noted an oil painting hanging on the wall above the desk. It was a sailboat, docked in a shallow harbor with the sails stored away. "Take that boat for instance. It probably carries the owner to ports all over, thousands of miles every year but look at it in the picture. That worthy vessel is docked, and the sails are put away. It's resting like the owner is. Even sailboats are meant to relax at times. That's what beaches are for."

Aries took Lena's words to heart. She made her positions on life and leisure crystal clear. "That's brilliant how you came up with that analogy, right off the top of your head?"

"Easy to see makes it easy to say," she replied, knowingly.

Lena had mentioned slowing down to Ledger on many occasions. He blew her off each time and bragged about how much

199

money he'd made or the vacation houses purchased because of his refusal to take breaks.

"I dig your business savvy, Lena. You're a talented doctor and serious medical professional. I can see why your practice is booming."

"Thank you. I work hard too, *when* I'm setting sail."

"I appreciate the time you make for me. I don't take it lightly."

Lena rubbed her hand on top of his then looked Aries in the eyes.

"There's no description for the way you make me feel. I'm thankful but I have been wondering something. When tons of women like those two at lunch are constantly throwing themselves at you, why me?"

"Why not you? You're beautiful and your type of smart is the new sexy," he said, sincerely. "Most of all, you feel me on a level that goes deeper than physical attraction. You get me and that's everything."

"I'm falling and do not want to stop," she pouted. "You'd better catch me. You promised!"

# chapter nineteen

# I GOT SUNSHINE

Morning came fast. Lena crawled out of her bed and stumbled into the bathroom. As the steam rose toward the vaulted ceiling, she walked into the spacious shower with her eyes half-closed. She pulled on the plastic floral shower cap then plopped down on the granite seat to feel the hot water washing over her body. A steady stream of running water soothed her. The roaring sound made Lena relax and think about the discussion she had with Aries. She wished she could have remained in the security of his muscular arms and talked about sail boats and beaches all night long. After experiencing sexual bliss and thoroughly relishing every second of time spent with him, there wasn't a single trace of repentance left in her body. Accepting membership in the Cheating Wives Club was a lot easier than she would have guessed and Lena couldn't see giving it up.

When she toweled off, Ledger entered the white-tiled room wearing brown slacks, a white button-down dress shirt and dark paisley necktie. He walked towards the large mirrors then grunted hard.

"Lena, that must have been one hell of a shower? All of the mirrors are streamed up."

She wrapped the towel around her chest, subconsciously concealing her breasts from his line of sight.

"Good morning to you too," she sighed. "Next time I'll try washing up in the sink." She pulled off the shower cap then took a seat on the velvet covered vanity chair to lotion her legs.

"I didn't come in here to upset your day," he said, wiping at the mirror in a circular motion. "I'm running late and can't seem to get this knot right." Without hesitation, she stood and wrestled with his necktie until it was picture-perfect. He looked past her, stared at himself in the clear patch on the mirror then smiled. "You've always been good at that. Thank you." When she returned to the chair, Ledger noticed something that seemed off kilter. "You're spending a lot of time at that fitness place but I must say it's looking good on you."

"Thank you," she offered, flatly, as if he'd told her the sky was blue.

"Maybe next time you go, I could get in a workout. I've been too busy to stop by the country club but you can probably tell, huh?"

"I guess. Maybe a little."

He glanced at her while putting on the pair of diamond-studded cuff-links she bought for his last birthday. "Hey, you okay? Been real quiet." Lena continued to apply Lubriderm on her legs and arms without as much as an acknowledgment of his question.

"Here's an idea. Why don't I pour cooking oil all over my clothes and fire up a cigarette?"

"Don't be ridiculous. You don't smoke."

"Well, I'm not sure I like that answer. What's gotten into you?"

Lena experienced a flashback of Aries and his magical manhood. *You really couldn't handle the truth if I told you what's been getting deep into me*, she thought.

"Oh, nothing. I've decided to call in sick, boss's prerogative. Can you break away from your business today to help me pick out some new things to wear?"

"You mean cancel important meetings, to go shopping with you? While I'm sure that would make for an interesting day, I don't have that kind of time to waste." He flicked at his hair then turned to leave. "I hope you can manage on your own."

After she quickly dismissed Ledger's snub, she rubbed oil on the heels of her feet then abandoned the towel where she sat. Steam had completely evaporated off of the mirrors, providing a clear reflection of her body. Lena pulled and poked her midsection like she did every morning but there was a flatter tummy and slimmer hips than she had seen in years. She resembled her mother less and looked more like the women at the gym. Ten pounds had seemingly vanished but Lena knew it was calorie counting, exercise at the fitness center and sexercise with Aries that helped her shed the unwanted fat.

"Hey girl, where have you been? And, why did you stay gone so long?" she mused to herself. "As long as you stick around this time, I won't hold it against you." She pinched her lower buttocks where it met with her thighs then pranced back and forth while looking back at it. Lena's delightful smile turned into a rewarding laugh.

"Keep it moving Tangerine and Millennia. Aries has all of this to keep him occupied."

Taking her own advice about getting rest and lowering sails, Lena called Margo at the office to reschedule her patients; something she hadn't done in a long while. Margo congratulated her on being selfish for once and told her to enjoy some much deserved *me time*. Lena was excited about the weight loss and flattering results until nothing in her closet seemed to fit. Immediately, she remembered one of Aries' admirers was a personal shopper which was exactly what she needed; someone to help her celebrate a lifestyle change with a whole new style.

Within the hour, Lena stormed through Nordstrom's with two personal shoppers in tow. She was in and out of dressing rooms for hours and grew increasingly more comfortable with shorter dresses and form-fitting outfits selected for her. When she couldn't decide which of the garments suited her best, Lena bought everything hanging on the rack outside of her private dressing room.

"That's right, I want it all," she said, to the surprise of both women who did a magnificent job assisting her. "Send those twelve dresses and all of the blouses and pants to my house. I owe it to myself." She couldn't stop looking at her lean legs in the last outfit she tried on, a denim short set that accentuated her shapely thighs; so she declined to remove it. "Put this on my bill too," she said, striking a fierce Cat Woman stance. "No way I'm taking it off."

She picked out a slamming pair of Gucci wedge sandals then exited the store four inches taller and her head in the clouds. Several women complimented her or smiled pleasantly as she strutted past. Even though she liked the way people noticed the bounce in her step, Lena's new look was unfinished. One call to an old friend who managed a chop shop downtown set things in motion. She arrived at Urban Styles salon with a half-eaten chicken panini and a new hairdo in mind. Lena flipped through magazines casually and munched while on her low-fat lunch until she came across the contemporary cut she wanted.

"This is the one," she said, pointing at the tapered-trim look, made popular by Nicole Murphy. "I want to rock it just like her. Get to chopping before I lose my nerve."

Lena took a deep breath and closed her eyes. She catnapped through an exhilarating wash then kept her eyes closed during an intensive sculpting process. When the stylist finished her master-piece, Lena sat up and carefully opened them. She couldn't believe her eyes. More than half of her length had been lopped off and the result was astounding. Her hair was gorgeous. "I look ten years younger," she said, louder than she meant to. An older client in the next chair agreed.

"It's very pretty on you. Mind if I get the same style on my next appointment? It's about time I looked ten years younger too."

Lena stared at her new and improved coif then passed the stylist a hefty tip on her way out. She wasn't ready to go home but had nowhere in particular to be. She sat in the Mercedes, infatuated with her pulled together appearance. There was someone special she wanted to share her excitement with and hoped he would be available for a spontaneous hookup.

When Aries' voice message picked up, she cast a sexy leer as if he could see her.

"I know you're working but I'd like to show you something." She applied lipstick then snapped a selfie with her cell phone. Acting like a young girl, who couldn't get over herself, Lena laughed out loud then sent the picture in a text attachment.

LENA: *Something new for you...*

Within seconds, Aries replied that he was in a meeting and would call her as soon as it concluded. Lena was disappointed until her phone rang. "I thought you were in a meeting."

"I had to step out when your hot selfie came through my phone," he said, with a lift in his voice. "Damn Ma', I'm feeling what you did."

"Hmmm, you haven't talked street to me before. Say something else like a bad boy from the hood."

"Lemme get back to this client discussion but you know you can get it."

"Okay. Bye, Boo."

"That's funny. Talk you later."

Lena looked at herself in the vanity mirror for the umpteenth time then admired her attractive selfie before backing out of the parking lot. Aries and Flea watched her drive away from a silver Nissan Altima parked across the street.

"I told you Dr. Harmon was up to something when she ditched work this morning," said Flea, with his long telephoto lens pointed at Lena's rear bumper.

"Damn, this picture she sent is nice but nothing like the real thing. Did you see those legs, that hair? Flea, I would make a run at her even if she wasn't my target."

"Yeah, I saw. Too bad you're in a catch and release situation."

"How's that?"

"It's like fishing in a stocked pond. You catch for the sake of seeing what you can hook and reel in but it's against the rules to keep anything."

"Shiddd!" Aries remarked, still marveling at Lena's new look.

"There's nothing in the rules saying I can't play with the feisty fishy a little before throwing her back."

Flea laughed then looked at the last pictured he'd taken of Lena standing outside of her SUV. Her legs were toned, behind firmer and lifted from hundreds of daily squats, arms shaping up nicely.

"Yeah, I'd smash that for free," he howled. "Too bad you can't."

"Like *you'd* ever get the chance," Aries scoffed, putting an end to what he felt was blatant disrespect of Lena.

"Drop me back at the apartment. It's time to go fishing."

It was almost three o'clock when Aries returned Lena's phone call. He had less than two weeks to manufacture quality evidence on her or else. He refused to waste any time on the or else part of the situation.

"This is Lena," she sang amicably, into the phone. She paid for the scoop of Pink Paradise then headed out of the door of Yummy Yogurt. It was the first time she treated herself since turning over a new leaf.

"Hey, what's up with the new everything?"

"You approve?"

"Heck yeah, I approve. Had I known you were thinking of going all glam, I would have paid for it. If you'd let me watch," he added in a low sensual tone.

"You are so nasty. Okay, next time, you can watch."

"That's my girl. Can I get on your schedule for the rest of the day?"

"That's a possibility," she said, flirting shamelessly.

"Oh really? What's the stipulation?"

"It just depends on how badly you want to see me. I have time to pick up a few things then get on home."

Aries listened attentively, waiting on the other shoe to fall.

"Where do I fit in?"

"If you don't mind shopping with me, we could do that together."

"I would ask what we're shopping for but that doesn't seem to matter."

"It shouldn't," she answered sweetly.

Aries stared through the lenses of high powered binoculars as Lena strolled past the dry cleaners on McKinney. Aries licked his lips when she slurped on the pink fruity yogurt.

"You're right, as usual," he admitted, from an inconspicuous parking lot further down the block. "And like all the times before, tell me where to go Lena and I'll be there."

"Preston Crest Town Center. It's a small collection of stores near Royal Lane."

"I know the place. See you in fifteen minutes." Aries lowered the binoculars and placed them in the console between the front seats. *That's awfully close to Lena's home,* he thought. *She either isn't concerned about running into neighbors or doesn't care what they might say if she does.*

When Aries arrived at the strip center, he spotted Lena immediately. She was talking to a clean cut black man in front of an expensive women's clothing store. Aries studied her interaction with the guy who appeared to be early forties as he deliberated swooping into the middle of their conversation and making off with Lena on his arm. Thinking better of it, Aries waited until Lena finished her discussion before he exited the covered parking lot.

Once Lena walked into the boutique alone, the stranger walked down the sidewalk but not before he checked out Lena's pants first. Aries couldn't blame him for that. She was captivating and feeling herself. He admired her confident stride while following her around the store like a suspicious mall cop.

"Excuse me Ma'am but we've received calls of a very alluring black female fitting your description," Aries said, with his hands inside his pockets.

Lena's face lit up when she turned to find him standing there, with the thirsty expression she adored. "But I'm not breaking any laws that I know of," she answered, to play along.

"Well, it ought to be a crime to be that fine. I should run you in for those shorts alone. And I can see that fitted blouse is hiding two concealed weapons."

"Ooh, this is fun," Lena said, excitedly. "Role playing is very erotic."

"Quiet Ma'am, you're trying to confuse me. Just keep both hands visible while I think a minute."

She swung her hips in his direction then placed her hands on them. "What, like this?"

"Oh now you've done it. Store policy says I have to frisk you."

"Then let me assume the position." Lena placed her hands against the wall then spread her legs. "Like this?"

"Yeah, that's nice. Hold it, just like that." Aries took a step towards Lena to continue their game when he heard someone call her name.

"Dr. Harmon? Is everything alright?" asked an older white woman.

Lena straightened up and snapped her head around to see who had walked onto their playground. She found a sassy petite lady with closely cropped silver hair, wearing a fuchsia colored tank top and white denim jeans.

"Ohhh hey. It's one of my favorite patients, Dane Tolliver" Lena said, for Aries' benefit. "How are you, Dane?"

Mrs. Tolliver was still sizing up the situation when she responded. "I should be asking you the same thing."

"Oh him," Lena said, grasping for a way to explain why her tail was tooted up for Aries.

"I'm the loss prevention officer," he said, with a straight face. "It's my job to keep an eye on the unusual suspects."

"And you're following this woman she's here to steal something?"

"Well, Ma'am…"

"We've come too far in this country for you to profile African American shoppers. You ought to be ashamed."

"Believe me, I am."

"No, he isn't Dane," Lena said finally. "This is my fitness trainer. I ran into him outside the store and we were having a little fun."

Dane looked at him, smiled then checked out Lena's shorts and high-heel wedges. "Yeah honey, I get that. The loss prevention officer meets the frisky lady doctor gag, huh?"

Lena was embarrassed at the implication. "Mrs. Tolliver! It's not like that."

"The hell it isn't but I ain't one to judge. Excuse me trainer, I need to get some more panties in a size four. My dates keep swiping them." Aries moved aside to give her access to the rack behind him. "I'll leave you two alone to figure out what game you're really playing but it sure does look like a whole lot of fun." Aries flashed an awkward smile when it was apparent the older woman was thoroughly onto them.

"Yes, Ma'am," he answered, instead of spewing another thinly-veiled lie. It would have merely added insult to injury.

"We are only friends," Lena submitted, in her own defense.

"Lena, save it. That man's got a hankering in his pants for you the size of Florida. Friends or lovers, doesn't matter as long as you're enjoying life. When the ride ends, and it always does, remember to get off before you lose your dignity. I wish someone had told me that, years ago. Well, I'll see you at my appointment next week. Enjoy the ride, Dr. Harmon."

Aries nodded goodbye to Dane Tolliver. Lena lowered her head in shame then glared at her boyfriend's budge in his pants.

"Why didn't you put that thing away?"

"Like sticking your cute ass in the air isn't the reason I'm saluting like this."

"We just got outed by one of my closest patients. How embarrassing."

"I could be wrong but I don't think she gives a damn what you do or who with, as long as you're getting your kicks."

"Then let me see if there's any more of those panties that Dane's dates can't keep their hands off. Maybe they have a trap door."

"If not, I know where we can get some that do," Aries said, as Lena picked through several styles of women's underwear. "By the way, who was that guy I saw you talking to when I got here?"

"Outside the store? He's a surgeon I've operated with on occasion and I'm so glad you didn't come up and introduce yourself. He's a Nosey-Nancy, who lives across the street from me and blabs everything he knows about all the other neighbors."

Although Lena dodged that bullet she still got run over by the Dane Tolliver express.

## chapter twenty
# BEWITCHED, BOTHERED AND BEWILDERED

A very dashing summer-wool suit hung on a male mannequin in the window of an exclusive men's clothing store. Aries stopped to admire it. Lena smiled as his eyes danced with interest. The jacket was designed with three buttons and a tapered cut to accommodate a man with broad shoulders and a slim waist. The pants were made with pleats and a small hidden opening near the front right belt loop for a pocket watch. When Aries nudged Lena gently to continue on down the broad sidewalk, she didn't move an inch.

"That style of suit was designed with you in mind," she said. "Sloping lapels and that pocket watch compartment reminds me of another era. My father owned many high cut trousers like that."

"He had taste. They don't make 'em like that anymore."

"It looks like they're bringing that old thing back and an industrious man such as yourself should own one."

"Maybe in a month or so."

"You have taught me that waiting on something, which should be yours anyway is nonsense. Let's go in and get you fitted. My treat."

Aries was taken aback. While flattered, he was not used to women offering things he hadn't strategically conned them out of first.

"I can't let you do that," he argued. "I'm a big boy who pays his own way."

"The operative word being let," she hissed playfully. "You're not letting me do anything. I'm a big girl who wants to treat her man to something nice."

"It's probably more than you want to spend," he guessed.

"That's why they make the African American Express," she answered, with a playful poke.

"The African what?"

"The Black Card, baby. I thought you knew." Aries laughed as she pulled him by the hand like a reluctant child.

"Okay, I'll let... I mean, I'll go along with you on this but don't make it a habit."

"It's funny, how you think that would be up to you."

Lena took great pleasure in sipping on a glass of Chardonnay while an Italian tailor fussed over Aries, took his measurements and outfitted him with two custom-made shirts and three neckties to complete the package. It was the first, in a long time, Lena could remember delighting in a special gift for someone she cared about. Aries, on the other hand didn't know how to feel. Of course, women treated him to expensive gifts in the past but this was different. Lena wanted to thank him for the rebirth he provided in her life. She presented her Black Card, with Aries' arms wrapped around her waist and didn't blink once when the purchase totaled over $2,000. Every time he argued the cost was too much, she kissed him on the lips until there was nothing else to discuss.

"Thank you Lena," he said, as they reached her vehicle.

"You're very welcome but it's really nothing compared to what you've given me."

"I'm floored by your generosity. Thanks."

She kissed him again. "I like to take care of my man."

"You called me that earlier. I thought it was a slip of the tongue."

Lena blushed but was unapologetic. "You are my man, in my mind at least. A girl can dream, right?"

"What am I going to do with you," he asked, staring longingly into her eyes.

"You could take me to a nice dinner with white tablecloths and candle light."

"When? Just name it. I'll take you anywhere."

"After they deliver the new suit to your apartment," she answered, with a naughty leer. "Maybe we could even spend the night together. Leaving you is always so hard for me."

Aries let out a subtle sigh as if a hurtful thought replayed in the recesses of his mind. "It's never easy watching you go. Like now for instance. I want to snatch you up and unleash that thing you like."

"What's holding it back?" she whispered, kissing his lips softly.

"Really, here in the parking lot?"

"My windows are tinted. The sun is going down. Know what I'm saying?"

Aries was excited. He thought Lena was too much of a prude to get it on like a couple of horny college kids. "You're prepared to get served up in the back of your whip?"

"You hear me saying no?"

"I think that qualifies as a yes. Open the door. Let's get in on the other side so no one sees us."

Lena pressed her key fob to unlock the door. She followed Aries and climbed in the back seat with him then pulled a level to lower the back seat. It slammed down under his weight. Caught by the swift fall onto his back, Aries chuckled.

"You've done this before?" he asked, while unzipping her shorts. She kicked them over the seat then fished into her purse. "Sure you want to know the answer to that?"

"Nah, I'll just pretend this is your first rodeo."

Lena hadn't pulled that stunt in the SUV before but the thought had crossed her mind. Unfortunately, Ledger complained about his knee and blew off the invitation to christen her new truck. Lena liked the idea of Aries believing she had a wild side previous to meeting him, so what could it hurt. However, she didn't enjoy that nearly as much as she did when he spun her around to gain better access to her moist vagina from behind.

Aries buried his tongue deeply inside her to administer a measure of delight that equaled her generosity. "You have to keep watch," he panted. "I can't see nothing but beautiful ass from here."

"Okay-okay. I'll try but it's hard to keep my eyes from rolling back in my heaaad!"

Aries kept thanking Lena until she fell off of him, spent and satisfied. "Dang, it got hot in here. Whew Lena, crack the window."

"Not yet. I want some of this," she said, feverishly unfastening his pants.

"Whoa, I'm too tall for this."

"I know but I'm still simmering. My girl needs some deep tissue entertainment." She waved a condom wrapper in his face, tore it open with her teeth then tossed the latex to Aries. "Strap up big boy. Momma wants to swing on that pole."

"You are scaring me right now," he joked. He hurriedly rolled the condom on and sat up on his elbow when it was clear that Lena had abandoned her role as lookout. "You're gonna get us busted."

"Shut up and take it," she hissed, like an alley cat in heat.

"I've created a monster."

She pulled him down on top of her then locked her legs around his waist. The SUV rocked side to side like a wagon with a broken wheel. Aries kept watch while thrusting himself between her legs. Lena bit him on the chest and sucked on his neck passionately.

"You're driving me crazy. Don't stop!"

Aries froze suddenly and locked his hips. "I think someone's coming."

"Don't you dare stop," she pleaded. "Unless it's the cops I don't care."

He peeped out of the foggy window again as the shadowy figure in the parking lot walked even closer. Aries was relieved when recognized the man. It was Flea, acting like a casual passerby, who just happened to be taking pictures of a certain parked Mercedes.

"No, it's someone looking for their car I think." He waved Flea off with a sneaky backhand to get away. Flea sneered at him but kept on moving so as not to draw attention.

Once the immediate threat was gone, Aries jumped back into the saddle. Lena spat lewd commands until her man literally came through. She dug her nails into his back when she felt his passion explode inside of her.

Aries was breathless, dripping sweat and falling for a woman he knew would never be his. "Wow! That was insane."

"Uh-uh, it was incredible."

Aries pulled out then reached down to remove the condom without spilling his juices on her leather seats. He was shocked when all that remained of the condom was a rubber rim around the base of his penis. "Shit, do you have a towel?" he asked, while searching for something to help with the messy fluids.

"You're drenched. Here, take this extra set of scrubs I keep in the back. You can wipe your face with it."

"I'm afraid it's not my face I'm concerned about." Aries pulled off the remnants of the condom, showed it to Lena then shoved it into his pocket.

"Where's the rest of it, Aries?" She followed his eyes to her drenched vagina. "Oh, no. No way!"

"I could try to fish the condom out, if—"

"Why didn't you tell me it tore?"

"If I had known, I would have stopped!" he said, with a raised voice.

"Don't you yell-at-me!" During her first moment of clarity all day, Lena sniffled at the tears running down her face. "Please hand me those scrub bottoms. I need to clean up and go home." When Aries assisted, she flung his hands away. "I got it. Maybe you should go before someone else comes and finds us like this."

"Lena, I don't have a disease, if that's what you think."

"I don't know what to think, right now. Please, just go."

Aries pulled his pants up, wiped beads of sweat from his face then scooted out of the back seat. He turned back to say the only thing that felt right.

"I'm sorry."

"Yeah, me too. Now, close my door."

Aries hopped in his Porsche and slammed the door angrily but remained in the parking lot until Lena was dressed and gone. He ignored the non-stop ringing phone. After Flea tapped on his window, Aries unlocked the door to let him in.

"Christopher is pissed at you!"

"He isn't the only one."

"You can't keep allowing your little head to *dictate* what the big one does."

Aries stared into space. He couldn't believe how a kinky

interlude played out so wrong. To make matters worse, his photographer almost blew his cover.

"That's not funny Flea."

"For once, I wasn't trying to be. Well, maybe a little."

"Please tell me you got something on that camera we can use."

"Wish I could but the tint was too thick. Only got silhouettes mostly and one outstanding shot of an ass cheek pressed against the side window. Too bad it was yours!" Flea put his camera away then studied his Asset's bewildered expression. "Let's go see the boss before he has to come looking for you."

Thinking back on the armed thugs Christopher had at his disposal, Aries balked at the unfavorable scenario that ended with them hot on his heels.

"No need for that. I got the message the first time."

Flea went to his own car then sped away as fast as he could. A few years ago, he witnessed Christopher split an Asset's head open with a wine bottle, for chronic tardiness. When the boss said come, it meant immediately if not sooner.

Aries heard stories of irrational brutality but one thing was more pressing than Christopher's threats. He sent Lena a quick voice message after the text he formulated failed to adequately convey his sentiment.

"Hey, it's me. I am sorry for the mishap. I saw the look on your face and I know you're worried. Please don't be. I couldn't stand it if that's the last expression I see on your beautiful face. I'll be here when you're ready to talk."

After hanging up the phone, Aries collected his thoughts and prayed he didn't ruin his chances of getting even closer to Lena.

As he backed out of the parking space, a black Chevy Tahoe pulled behind him, blocking the path.

Before Aries realized what was happening, one of the men from Christopher's security detail jumped out and opened the driver's door on his Porsche.

"Come with us, Sir," the man grunted. "Mr. Denmark requests your attendance, pronto." Aries gave up his keys and got into the back seat with armed guards on both sides of him. The Tahoe tires screeched from the parking structure with the Porsche being driven closely behind it.

The ride downtown was a short one, ten minutes from start to finish. Aries couldn't help but wonder how many more times Christopher would tolerate his mistakes. He breathed a sigh of relief as the Chevy SUV pulled into the underground parking garage at the W Hotel instead of an open field in the middle of nowhere. Aries was relieved that he wasn't going to die.

He was taken through the same ritual as before, including being patted down and chaperoned all the way up to the penthouse suite. Flea opened the hotel room door when they handed off Aries to another set of guards outside of the elevator.

"I didn't tell him how it ended with Lena," Flea whispered. "He can't know that she left in a huff."

"How did you know?"

"Shush! Christopher is raving mad in there, so watch your head."

They walked through the enormous living room and into the common area. Christopher studied a chess board in the center of the room. Walter wore a satisfied grin while sipping on a cocktail near the large pane window. Cherry sat on the arm of Christopher's chair, perched like a calculating feline. Raja nibbled timidly on a plate of food near the buffet table. His empty expression revealed how little he wanted to be there.

VICTOR McGLOTHIN

"Aries Dupree, we need to talk," said Christopher, as he advanced his white knight towards a would-be opponent's Queen. "Get yourself something to eat. From what I hear, you've gotta be exhausted." Christopher was still playing mind games and Aries wasn't ready to concede yet. "We have freshly steamed lobster and sea bass over there. Oh, and can't forget the caviar. I think you could really benefit from some caviar. The way it explodes in your mouth is damn near erotic. It's the snack of kings or something like that. Right, Walter."

"That's right," Walter answered confidently.

Raja rolled his eyes and shook his head but he dared not contradict Christopher when he was making a point. So, he shoved another lobster tail into his mouth and kept quiet.

"What will it be, Aries?" asked Christopher, as he stood to face his incorrigible Asset. "What do you have a taste for?"

Aries looked at the buffet table then at the guards by the door. He also noted the bulge in Walter Shuman's jacket.

"Lobster looks great to me but I think I'll start with the caviar first. Thanks for the great suggestion, Christopher."

Cherry offered a silent prayer of thanks. She feared blood being spilled if Aries selected chicken again as a sign of disrespect, like before.

"Good boy," said Christopher. "Eat up." Aries put a couple of lobster tails on a plate then sat it on the bar next to Raja's, who immediately wished he had chosen anywhere else to stand. The boss made small talk with Walter, kissed Cherry on the cheek to calm her worries then he summoned Aries to the sofa for a necessary grown-man conversation.

"Nice hickey you got there. You give your girlfriend a promise ring?" Walter snickered then took a sip from his vodka tonic.

"No, no rings," Aries replied quietly.

"You did bend Lena over in the back seat of her Benz though, like a horny little bastard who doesn't think, he just does!"

"I know you think my decision was a bad one but she's still on the hook. She wanted, I gave. That's the game until it's time to score."

"You don't get it so I'll break it down for you." Christopher lifted a bottle of Big Red from the coffee table to take a drink. Aries flinched. He felt like an instant chump when Walter laughed at him. "Relax. I'm not going to hurt you or it would have happened already," said Christopher. "However, I will share two potentially painful pieces of information. One, is how close you came to royally screwing the pooch today."

"I don't follow."

"Imagine, when you agreed to hump Dr. Harmon in a public parking lot, that someone saw you and called the cops. Now imagine getting arrested on some petty lewd sexual conduct charge and have your target's face plastered all over the news for free!"

Christopher was so distraught by the mere thought of spending all that time and money to set Lena up; only to have it melt down with one careless mistake. When he explained it to Aries in those terms, even Raja was embarrassed for the way their Asset jeopardized the operation. "Now, for the second thing. We're stepping up the timetable to shut down this score."

"You said I had two weeks," Aries argued, his voice cracking under the circumstance.

"You said you'd comply with my instructions but instead you just had to eat the damned chicken."

Raja looked at the chicken strip on is plate then slyly flicked it off. Flea looked at the half-eaten chicken wing in his hand then quickly put it down.

"See, someone has to think things through and others have to be responsible for the execution. Walter there, he loves executions."

Walter nodded his affirmation. "There's nothing like a clean execution, I always say."

"Kill me and nobody gets paid," Aries growled, as he grew tired of being threatened.

Cherry stood up and walked calmly over to Aries. "Nobody's talking about killing anyone. They just talk tough," she said, to ease Aries fears. "Let's remain focused. There's a lot of money left on the table. Christopher has taken down two marks in Dallas already so he can't freely run around town. As you might understand, he's getting edgy. Walter is just being Walter. Bottom line is, we need to get this score settled Aries and disappear fast. I know you're trying, we all know you're doing a great job but it has to end on the right note."

"I told you he wasn't up to it Christopher," said Walter. "He doesn't do what he's told. He takes unnecessary chances and they don't pay off."

"I have my target doing things in the bed she didn't even know possible before I taught her," said Aries. "Lena Harmon is addicted and I'm close to stringing her all the way out."

Walter took a long swig from his glass then turned it up all the way up. "Talk is cheap, loser."

Christopher gave Walter an ice cold look to chill him out then tried to salvage what was left of Aries' opportunity. "Alright look, we still have a couple of days then it's over. No amount of money is worth getting pinched for." Christopher stood then walked behind Cherry. He ran his left hand down her back then smacked her behind.

"Ouch! That stings!"

"See, she's angry now and wants to get even. It's a natural response. Now, the last lesson I'll teach you is this, don't get in too deep. The trap can backfire if the deck isn't properly stacked. Lena has to be remorseful of the affair when it's reveled to her husband. Your target must hate you afterwards and show remorse for her dirty deeds, or the husband might sabotage the deal to embarrass her publicly."

"I'll work it out. Lena can't say no to me."

"I'm sick of this bullshit," Walter huffed. "Someone pour me another drink. Christopher is hemmed up and can't go out while this cocky son-of-a-bitch keeps screwing up the works."

"That's the first thing I heard from Walter all night that made any damned sense," Aries said, with a total disregard for his safety.

Walter was feeling the effects of a third stiff cocktail when he opened his mouth. "Yeah, that's right. Hey, wait a minute, you prick!"

"I am cocky and it's gotten me this far. Things tend to go sideways when I step back."

"Get over yourself," Walter hissed. "Pride goes before a fall, you know."

"Pride goeth before destruction Walter," Cherry corrected him. "It's a haughty spirit that goes before a fall."

"What? That can't be right," said Christopher.

Raja looked at his phone screen and nodded his agreement. "According to Google and Proverbs 16:18, Cherry is one-hundred percent correct." He smiled at Aries and nodded vigorously until Christopher shut him down with a stifling scowl.

"I guess everyone can be wrong. Am I wrong about you Aries Dupree?" the boss asked calmly. "Can you turn this around in three days or come up with an even ninety grand?"

"I'm only into Men of M.O.E.T. for sixty thousand," Aries huffed angrily.

"That was a few weeks ago. I'm in this luxury penthouse with expensive security watching my back and that cost money. We should have been in Las Vegas by now, setting up the next three scores."

"And you're putting that on me?"

"Me and my team are all locked away like prisoners because of you so listen up. I like you and I'm a reasonable man but this is it."

"I'll square the deal in two days if that's the way it has to be. Flea can stay with me so he can get proof of the pussy. Isn't that what you called it Christopher?"

Christopher slapped his hands together loudly. "Now that's the phrase that pays!" He performed a smooth Samba dance step then held out his right hand to Aries. "Let's shake on it. You come through or the life insurance policy pays off for you. Personally, I'd rather see the proof myself." Raja couldn't stand to watch as Aries extended his hand.

"If you shake it's final," Cherry warned, as if he were making a deal with the devil. "You don't have to do this."

Aries grabbed Christopher's hand firmly then shook it. "Yes, I do Cherry. I do." He took the car keys from Christopher, shot a stiff middle finger at Walter then gathered his nerve to head for the door.

"Try to keep up Flea. We're on the clock."

## chapter twenty one
# GOING THROUGH CHANGES

It was Wednesday morning. Lena had been wide awake for hours. She marched back and forth from the luxurious bathroom to the master bedroom, wearing silk peppermint-print panties and red, leather three-inch heels. After she'd grown tired of kicking herself for biting into the condom package and causing it to rip, she climbed out of bed and listened to the voice message Aries left her. His words were kind and reassuring, which was precisely what she needed to sooth her love hangover from the night before. Somehow, he always seemed to know just what to say. She replayed it several times before deleting but the last sentence made her feel cared for and appreciated. *I'll be here when you're ready to talk.* He knew her very well and anticipated her needs, even when she acted out of character. She loved him for it.

Lena turned up the iPad docking station in the bathroom and moved to the music while she put on earrings. She searched through a cabinet drawer for the bangle hoop bracelets she almost never wore anymore because she'd felt too old for them. Now, she was liberated, practically nude and strutting around like an exhibitionist in striped panties and sexy heels.

Eric Benét crooned smoothly about a relationship that got out of hand. Lena didn't know many of the words but danced to the beat, singing loudly and off key to the chorus like nobody was watching. "Oh, that's my jam!" she yelled, when an old LL Cool J hit came on. She wound her hips like a Jamaican dance-hall queen then raised her hands in the air. When Ledger walked into the bathroom, he stopped on a dime. "I love this new Hip Hop station. Want to dance, Ledger?"

"I want to go to work but I had to wait until the delivery guy unloaded all the things you bought at the mall yesterday."

"Good. Did you put them in the bedroom?"

"And throw my back out? Hell no, I didn't."

"Go Brooklyn! Go Brooklyn! Just doing it wild," she sung, while dancing closer to Ledger. "Don't sweat it. I'll have the pool guy to bring them up."

"The hell you will," he objected.

"Why not? You think Fernando might come up here and try to seduce me?"

"You mean Ferdinand, who's almost my age and his back is worse off than mine?"

"Whatever. I'm in a good mood and not interested in having anyone ruin it."

Ledger gave his wife a peculiar look then surveyed her body thoroughly for once. "Hey, what happened to your clothes?"'

"They're on the valet in my closet. Can you run and get the bra I left on the bed?"

"Run and get," he mumbled. "What the hell?" Despite his protest, Ledger wandered into her spacious walk-in closet then backed out when he forgot why he went in there. He noticed the red satin bra on the bed and remembered it was the reason he was dispatched. As soon as he reentered the bathroom, Lena shimmed over to him and demanded he put it on her. Ledger played along and even copped a frisky feel as she stepped away.

"Hey, you did something different. Did you change your hair?" he asked, while looking her over, peculiarly. Lena didn't answer right away. Instead she continued to sing along with the radio. "Yes, your hair is shorter. That's it, right?"

She tossed him a patronizing expression in the mirror.

"Yes, that's it Honey. My hair is about eight inches shorter. Glad you finally noticed."

"You've been practically living at that fitness place. You bought out half the store and cut your hair." After an interesting thought came to mind, he stared at Lena's animated dance moves. "And now you're dancing damn near naked in the bathroom with some high heels on." He squinted in a suspicious manner then nodded as if he were on to something. "I think I know what's going on. Oh Lawd, you're *waiting to exhale.*" he whined. "Just don't set my T-bird on fire. I love that car."

"True, I might be going through something but your car is safe," she answered, with the radio turned off. "I would leave you before torching your precious whip."

"My what?" Ledger wasn't quite sure how to take that so he followed Lena into the bedroom.

She sat down on the chaise longue then slipped on pantyhose. "I can remember a time, long ago, when you'd buzz around me like this and watch me get dressed."

"Yeah, it's been a while. Guess I'm guilty of being lax on a number of things I used to do. Cute panties and red pumps can make a man re-prioritize though."

"Do I hear a hint of regret in your voice? So, no more of that dogmatic *'I even got white women who would love to wear your shoes'* bullshit?" Lena laughed while playfully mocking him from the words he'd spat in a previous discussion that went terribly wrong.

"That's not exactly what I said and you know it Lena."

"That's what I heard. It's certainly what you intended to convey. But I'm glad you no longer feel that way." She stepped into a pair tapered black linen slacks and a thin white Casper jacket, with black trim on the lapels. "I'm running late."

"Where are you going, happy hour?"

"Ha ha ha ha. I'm going to work."

"All that time you spent in the mirror, I couldn't tell."

"Have a good day," she said, with a friendly peck on his cheek. "Oh, do be a dear and help the women's charity with the clothes I'm donating. They're in the closet."

Ledger remembered her vast collection of designer blouses and dresses, many with the tags still on them. He walked to the front staircase as Lena carefully descended on them. "How will I know which clothes they can have?"

"None of it fits me anymore. They can take everything!" she announced proudly. Lena needed something more her speed, like a new man to suit her new needs. She was having new sex and lots of it. No longer complacent with the meager time Ledger committed to their marriage, she was done but had yet to realize how over it she truly was.

"Let me take you to lunch today!" he shouted, urgently. "I can put off my meeting until this afternoon."

Lena grabbed a bagel and her car keys on the way out of the door. "Sorry, I'm booked. Maybe next time."

"Go on and leave me high and dry then!" he hollered, well after Lena left.

Ledger peered down at the protruding knot in his trousers with great disappointment. "I'm getting too old to waste a perfectly good erection. What the hell?"

When Lena arrived at the practice, she slipped in the back door. The staff was busy setting up examination rooms and checking medical charts for the proper forms so no one noticed her. She arranged the pictures on her veranda, dabbled on a hint of the signature Day Dreams fragrance that Aries designed then rubbed her wrist together.

"Hmmm, that is divine," Margo said, as she walked closer to the desk carrying a handful of charts.

Lena turned to greet her good friend and second in command. "Good Morning. Yes I know, right. It makes me feel sexy too."

"And look at you Dr. H! Your new style is fierce."

"Thank you. I've been going to the gym to do more than sit on all of this fierceness for a change."

"It shows. Trimming down is what's up. I'm talking about that jazzy cut though," said Margo, looking at Lena with a bright smile. "I know Mr. Harmon was doing back flips."

"Girl, he hardly noticed. But he's a man so I let him slide, this time."

"Most black men are all about the hair. The longer the better, even if it's polka-dot."

As a private thought about a secret lover crossed Lena's mind, she blushed and smiled ever so faintly. "My man isn't that shallow. Long hair or not, he knows what he's got."

Margo chuckled heartily. "He'd better because this kind of fabulous will have a lot of heads turning."

Lena accepted the compliment and snapped back into focus.

"Who's the first patient up today?"

There was no immediate response so Lena held out her hand review the top chart that Margo held onto. She read the name on the tab and nodded with a subdued expression. "Shonda Petrie."

"I feel so bad about her loss. I wasn't ready to deal with the sadness that comes with still births so I asked Cathy to put her in room one."

"It's never easy for anyone involved. Go on and get the other patient's comfortable. I'll see about Shonda right away."

Margo left the office with her head hanging down. She felt awful about calling Shonda "Bully Bad Ass" before her pregnancy faltered and even worse that she was too ashamed to face the woman afterwards. Lena understood the difficulty in being fond of patients, who made it hard to do so but the loss of a child warranted the best bedside manner possible. If Margo wasn't capable of providing it, asking Cathy to step in was the right thing to do.

After a light wrap on the exam-room door, Lena opened it and walked in slowly. Shonda sat on the examination table in a loosely fitted gown, leaning against her husband for support.

"Hello Shonda. Michael. It's good to see y'all this morning." Lena flipped through several pages in the folder to buy time when neither of the Petrie's returned her salutation. Michael looked as if he was about to fall over too and his wife had clearly dropped at least twenty pounds. Lena laid the chart on the counter top then turned back to address her patient. "How are you feeling? Any reactions to the medicine I prescribed?"

"No Doctor, none at all," Shonda replied stoically. "Can we get on with the exam, please? We've got a meeting in an hour and another appointment after that."

"Okay, then," Lena replied, softly. She knew there was something behind Shonda's unusual demeanor, besides the obvious.

"Mr. Petrie, you can have a seat over there." Michael gave his wife a hug then sat on the chair on the other side of the exam table. He pulled a cell phone from his pocket then busied himself with a game that didn't require having to think or feel.

"You look different," Shonda remarked, when noticing Lena's elegant upgrades. "The hair is very becoming. It makes you look younger, prettier."

"Thanks, you're not looking too bad yourself. Here, turn this way." Lena continued the examination, ensuring that no placenta remnants remained. Patients in Shonda's condition were susceptible to serious infections or disseminated intra-vascular coagulation; which could cause hemorrhaging and in severe cases even death.

"I'm going to do a lot of things differently this time," Shonda said, calmly.

"In what regard?"

"Everything. I'm turning over new leaves in every aspect of my life. Michael is helping me with the kids and to make sure I take it easy at home. My company thinks I'm crazy, so they're giving me time to grieve and come back on a flex schedule."

"Sounds like a lifestyle change. Good for you." Lena pushed on Shonda's stomach gently, while noting her responses to pressure points. "Tell me about this flex schedule?"

"It means I can work half days or an abbreviated work week."

"Are you seeing anyone? A grief counselor?"

"Yep, right after the marriage counselor." Shonda turned her head slightly to gage Michael's comfort and mental stability. "We're going to work on us. I lost my baby and can't see losing my husband too."

"It does help to talk about emotions and moving past losing a

231

part of you. Families have to stick together, especially in the midst of a storm." After Lena concluded the exam, she hugged Shonda for a long time. "Is there anything else I can do for you, today?"

Shonda wiped her nose with a tissue then nodded her head. "Yeah, send me some of that peach-cobbler smelling perfume you're wearing. I remembered you had it on the night I delivered the baby. It reminds me of Lewis Calvin and I like that."

"This fragrance is still in development but I promise to send you a bottle when it goes on the market. Goodbye, Shonda. Michael, hang in there."

He offered a half smile then stood up from the chair. "I don't get a hug? I lost a son too," he said, plainly. "I like the smell of peach cobbler."

Lena laughed almost as loud as Shonda did. "Of course. Bring it in." The three of them hugged it out until Cathy knocked at the door to prompts Lena's departure.

"Thanks, I really needed that y'all," Lena admitted.

"We're good then?" Shonda asked. "You're not transferring my care to another doctor?"

"Wouldn't think of it for the world. I'll be here when you need me and rooting for your marriage from the sidelines. Take care."

Lena left the room feeling better than she expected. It was therapeutic and necessary. She knew how much it would have meant to Margo, had she been there to witness that touching moment, whether she felt worthy enough or not.

During the lunch break, Lena called Aries to apologize. She wanted to explain for being short when they parted ways and hoped to sort things out. He didn't return her call until her office staff returned. Lena knew there would be a number of interruptions so she put a sign on the door that read 'The Doctor is Out' to ward off any disruptions.

"Hello, this is Lena."

"Sorry I couldn't talk earlier. What's going on?" Aries asked, with an ounce of uncertainty in his voice.

Lena leaned back comfortably in the leather chair and slowly delved into the reason she'd reached out to him. "Thanks for calling me back. I didn't know if you would after the way I behaved." Out of sheer necessity, she minced no words to be transparent and openly share how vulnerable she felt. "I hope you don't think I'm a head case but I was scared. Accidents happen and I understand that. Still, it shocked me when I looked down and didn't see the condom where it was supposed to be."

"Lena, you don't have to say another word. I get it."

"We were being responsible and things got carried away. I shouldn't have freaked out and snapped on you. It was uncalled for. Can you forgive me?"

"Unless there's something else you're holding back, I'm already over it and still very much into us."

Lena rocked nervously, back in forth. "That's nice to hear. It's funny how you value something a lot more when it seems that it could be taken away," she said, deep in thought about tossing and turning the night before. "I fell asleep last night angry, although you've done nothing but gone out of your way to please me. I said I wasn't going to tell you this until sure there was still going to be an us."

"Okay, now you're making me nervous," Aries said, wondering what she found so hard to get off her chest.

"Don't worry, unless me loving you is a frightening thought."

"Really? You're feeling me like that?"

"I had a bad dream that I almost lost you. It sounds so stupid every time I have to remind myself that you... are... not... mine."

"I am yours, Lena. I have been since we laid together that first time." Aries didn't have to lie. He honestly believed they were meant to be together but only for the time being, regardless of how soon it was destined to end. "You're mine too, you know. When I'm with you," he added, solemnly.

"Aries, why did we have to meet under these circumstances?" Lena had no idea what she was saying as her world inched closer to spinning out of control. "It feels so natural to be with you. I want more of it every day."

Aries sipped from a cold bottle of water as Flea sat across from him, hanging on every word. "We could do something about that. Let's meet for drinks tonight then see where it goes from here."

"We both know where it would end up," she said, biting her lip.

"The same place it always does."

"And, where's that?"

"Between my legs."

"See, you're wrong for putting that visual on my mind. Now I'm sitting over here on bone with no way to relieve all of this tension." Aries shot a playful middle finger at Flea, for frowning at the thought of him sitting there with a massive erection.

"I have a full schedule this afternoon so you'll have to handle that yourself, literally."

"Look at how you do me. I was hoping you could handle that instead, later tonight."

"Sorry, I can't. I'm doing dinner with the hubby when he gets back from Ontario. We have a lot of things to talk about." As Aries held his comments in check, his silence bothered Lena. "Are you there?"

"Yeah. Still here and still wishing I can see you." Aries shook his head dismissively at Flea, who was adamant that he push harder towards orchestrating another backseat quickie. After Flea's gestures grew more insistent, Aries gave in. "Is it possible for you to meet me somewhere dark and out of the way, for about fifteen minutes?"

"And then run home unsatisfied to my husband? I might be a bitch at times, Aries, but I'm not a dog. That's too much wrong to ask of me, even if I hate saying no to you." Now, it was Lena's turn to sit quietly and let Aries stew in the pot he stirred.

After he flicked another dismissive bird to Flea for suggesting it, Aries acquiesced. He felt horrible for putting Lena in that position. "You're right. My bad."

"Glad we agree. I need to go and see about my staff. They're awfully loud out there."

"I hope you don't hold my desire, to be with you, against me."

"We're good, me and you. I'm still very much into us too," she said, using the words he had earlier. "Talk to you tomorrow."

Lena ended the call feeling justified in her decision to tell Aries she loved him, just as much as her refusal to meet him for a quick thrill then scurrying home to her husband's arms. She had to draw the line somewhere.

Aries stared at the wall, looking at his bleak chances at getting Lena to perform for Flea's digital camera. He was also fixed on the 36 hours he had left, to make a miracle happen or lose everything.

# chapter twenty two
# FADE INTO YOU

Aries marched circles around his apartment. Flea watched him pensively while throwing every idea he could think of against the wall, hoping something would stick. Aries wouldn't agree to drug Lena in order to manufacture a fictional sex tape. He also rejected the lame-brain trick of picking up a stray female from a bar and seducing her as Flea filmed them from certain angles, making it appear the woman was Lena. Although Aries had to admit it could have worked, if the video was delivered along with the mountain of photos and footage they already had on her. Nonetheless, Aries passed on setting up his target that way. Besides, she could have claimed it wasn't her and their entire scheme would have fallen apart on flimsy evidence in an otherwise perfectly good collection of lies.

After hours passed, Aries couldn't deny that the walls were closing in. He had to get out of the house and breathe. Thoughts of making a break for it crossed his mind a few times. With only sixteen dollars to his name and keys to the rented Porsche SUV, leased in Christopher's name, he wouldn't get far. Flea didn't argue when Aries decided to go out for an evening run to clear his head. He had to come up with a viable plan.

Ten minutes away, Lena sipped on a second glass of Chardonnay while reorganizing her walk-in closet with all of the new clothes from the recent shopping spree. It was seven-thirty when the call she'd waited on, finally came. To avoid being pessimistic, she put on a brave face and answered the phone.

"Hey Ledger, how are you?"

"It was a good day, dear. The venture capitalist I've been meeting with all day has signed on as the vice chairman. It'll strengthen our position before making a public offering next month."

"That's good. You worked this deal really hard and now it's coming through," she said, knowing that's what he wanted to hear. She could not have cared less about how much more money Ledger stood to make unless it meant he would slow down and spend more time with her. "So, you're boarding the plane in Ontario then?" she asked, with fingers crossed.

"Nope, but I'm looking right at it. This area has been pelted with heavy rain all afternoon," he explained. "It did let up for a while then we were hit with another downpour. I'm cooling my heels at the platinum lounge with my old friend Jack." Ledger ordered another Jack Daniels, on the rocks, as the bar continued to swell with irritated passengers, who had nothing better to do than ride out the storm. "They're canceling flights left and right but I'll be on the first thing out of here."

"Okay. Do the best you can to make it back tonight," she said, like the million times before. "I'll keep the porch light on for you."

"Thanks Lena. I know you had your heart set on dinner and stretching your legs. It'll probably be too late when I get in but there's always tomorrow."

"I know. Text me whether you get on a plane or not. I like to set the security alarm when I'm here alone."

"Will do. Talk to you later."

Lena didn't have to wonder if her husband would get a flight out. By the way he sounded, it was only a matter of time before Tennessee whiskey put him down for the count. Ledger was a lightweight when it came to hard liquor. After a full day of intense negotiations and calculating financial risks with teams of corporate lawyers, his stood little chance of being able to find his way onto the plane, much less catch the right one home.

Torn between feeling sorry for herself and calling Aries, Lena drew a hot bath. She poured herself another glass of wine as satiny bubbles multiplied in the tub. The discussion she'd planned on having with Ledger, regarding their relationship and spending entirely too much time alone, had to be postponed. Lena was tired of putting off a long overdue conversation, tired of sleeping alone, and sick of pretending it was enough to sustain her marriage. She wanted joy, the magnitude of bliss she felt when with Aries. Until her demands were hashed out with Ledger, Lena thought it best to touch bases with her other man. When her phone call went unanswered, she left a simple message that gave him precisely what he wished for, a thin slither of hope.

Aries returned from his long jog even more committed to taking a lion's share of his Ledger Harmon's money then make it out of Dallas alive. Unfortunately, he couldn't find a back door into that treasure trove. Lena held the key and kept perfect guard over it unknowingly. Time was running out on Christopher's well-crafted scheme, Lena's secret love affair, and Aries' life.

Moments after he stepped out of the shower, Flea awakened to inform him that his elusive target called while he was out. Aries didn't think much of her message initially but nearly dropped the phone when he listened carefully to her sweet voice the second time.

"You're probably out running the streets and I don't blame you. Ledger's plane was grounded in Canada, so dinner is off. Wish you were here. Well, not here since I'm at home but you get the picture. Hee-hee-hee," she giggled playfully. "Guess I had too much wine. Miss you baby. Good night."

Aries listened to the message again while growing more excited. He nodded assuredly when realizing he had not only been given a key to Ledger's treasure trove, the door was left wide open.

"Flea, wake your ass up!" he shouted, towards the other room. "Suddenly, I feel like a late night swim."

A golden, harvest moon hung beautifully amidst the shining stars over Dallas and gentle winds pushed a herd of thick clouds across the night sky. Aries peered up to admire it before diving into the backyard swimming pool with excellent form. It was exhilarating to breathe for a change. Aries felt like a goofy kid nailing a flawless canon ball in the deep end.

"Whoo-hoo!" he yelled. "And for my next trick," he said, as the lights inside of the house came on. "Hey, Flea, go ahead and make the call."

Flea dialed Lena's cell number and pressed send from Aries' phone, handed it to his Asset then vanished in the tall shrubs along the eight-foot wooden fence. The moment Aries heard Lena's voice on the other end, he flashed a bright smile. He knew she wouldn't have answered if she weren't still alone.

"Aries, I'll call you back. Some neighbor kids are playing around in my pool again," she said heatedly.

"Not this time. It's me. Sorry, I couldn't resist," he apologized, without an iota of sincerity. "Come on in, the water's fine."

Lena flipped on the backyard flood lights, which illuminated the pool and spa area. She opened the door cautiously then wandered out of the house wearing a flannel housecoat, leather slippers and a paisley head scarf. Aries chuckled at the sight of her wielding a wooden rolling pin for protection.

"What the hell? That really is you!" she spat, with shock pulsing through her voice. Lena was beside herself. "Aries, what are you doing back here? You have to go!"

"Good to see you too, baby," he teased.

"This is not the time to be playing with me. What if my husband was here?"

"But he isn't," he replied sharply. "Look, I know this is foul to drop in on you like this."

"You think!"

"I couldn't sleep, Lena. Not a wink."

Lena looked around to see if neighbors happened to be peeping out of their windows but with such a great distance between the large houses, it wasn't very likely. "I was sleeping just fine until I heard some damned splashing out here."

Aries swam to the edge of the pool then placed his elbows on the cement deck near Lena's pointy house shoes. "This is a great pool you got here. Come on in for a midnight skinny dip. It could be fun."

"Are you crazy!" she answered, louder than intended. Lena grimaced nervously when she heard a dog bark in the distance. "This is ridiculous. You have to get out of there now!"

He shrugged harmlessly as his lips curled into a sinful grin. "Well, if you insist."

Lena huffed angrily until he climbed out of her swimming pool with water dripping off his chiseled body, like diamonds sparkling in the moonlight. Her mouth fell open once she noticed his epic erection. "Oh my goodness," she mouthed quietly. "Why is it sticking up like that? Man, you have to put that thing away before one of my nosy neighbors see it." Aries bent over and picked up the bath towel off the ground then hung it on his penis. "Oh my damn!" Lena cursed, excitedly. "You know that's not what I meant, with your fine ass."

Aries gestured at the pile of clothes he'd placed on a patio chair. "Can I get my things and come in to dry off before I go?"

"I guess that would be okay," Lena agreed. "And, hurry up!" She kept her eyes trained in his every move as he collected his clothing. "Just sexy for no reason, scaring me with all that splashing around. Come on in the house and put on some clothes, so you can leave." Lena slapped his muscular behind then she followed him into the kitchen and locked the door.

Aries knew his risky move paid off as soon as he saw Flea ducking behind the sofa in the den.

"Whoa! Sorry Lena, I'm tracking water on the floor."

"Be still and I'll dry you off, big ol' baby," she joked.

Aries handed her the towel then did as he was told. He didn't move an inch when she wiped moisture from his back, broad shoulders or stiffened penis, although he tried to relax when she caressed his frame with her probing hands.

Flea used the night vision setting on his camera to snap a litany of photos with Lena kneeling down in front of Aries. From the camera angle, it appeared she was satisfying him with her mouth. Flea was ecstatic. With the collection of images he had amassed over the past month, there was plenty of evidence to initiate the payoff package. The only order of business left was texting Cherry to inform her of a successful outcome then signal Aries to get out before something went awry.

After Flea sent the text, he scooted stealthily to the end of the sofa, jutting his head out to flag Aries, only to be surprised that no one was standing where he last saw them.

"Oh shit," he whispered, unsure of what to do next. He began to gnaw on two nubby fingernails while sitting on the floor to update Cherry. Flea swallowed hard when Christopher sent a sharp response instead.

> CHRISTOPHER: He won't leave until he knows
> you're free and clear. Give Aries
> the signal, get him out and bring
> him home! I'll be waiting.

Flea read the message and shook his head sorrowfully. "Uh-oh, somebody's in big trouble." With his marching orders in hand, he placed the small camera in its case then slung the strap over his narrow shoulder. There was no way to know where Lena had taken Aries so Flea crept around on the first floor, slinking from room to room, terrified that he might accidentally run into them.

When his search on the first level proved unsuccessful, Flea ventured up the front staircase. Upon reaching the second floor landing, he heard cries of passion spilling out of the third room on the right. He tiptoed down the hallway then stooped to his knees near the lover's doorway. He was anxious to see what sounded like an animal being driven wild by her mate, just a few feet away. Flea chewed on another fingernail while he listened to Aries deliver unrivaled ecstasy to Lena, on the guest-room bed.

"Tell me you love it!" he demanded. "I can feel another explosion coming."

"Oooh-ooh. Yes, I love it, Aries!" she squealed. "You got me open, baby."

"Just let it go. Don't hold back."

"Give-give-give!"

After Flea gave it some thought, he figured the best time to risk a quick look-see was at the moment Lena moaned the loudest because she would likely be overwhelmed by an orgasm then. With baited breath, he inched to the mouth of the door, pulled his camera out of the case and carefully slid along the floor so he could view the live action, on the small screen, and pull it back if necessary.

The image Flea saw gave him major wood. He pressed the record button hurriedly as Lena's head hung off the bed with her legs spread wide. "Go man go!" Flea cheered, silently. "Make that money." Flea captured about fifteen seconds of Aries' signature slang and bang on the camera then put it away.

Several more minutes passed, with dirty talking, tongue dancing, butt smacking and orgasms aplenty. Flea had grown annoyed of the high-pitched shrieks from Lena. He was ready for the ear-piercing screams of seduction to end but he wasn't prepared for what he heard next.

"Promise me you'll never leave," Lena moaned. "Ooh, promise. Mmmm… promise me."

"I won't leave you," Aries grunted. "I promise."

"Ohhh, shit. I'm coming again! I love you, Arieees!"

"I love you too, Lena."

Flea's eyes widened when he heard Aries' confession. Assets were allowed to say almost anything to get in the panties but voicing 'I love you' during intercourse was strictly forbidden. Aries had been warned that those three little words carried far greater potency when uttered during the throes of passion. Flea vowed to omit what he heard if and when Aries ever finished his thrill-a-minute marathon. Assets weren't allowed to break either of the sacred rules or all hell would break loose as a result.

Rule #1: Don't get caught.

Rule #2: Don't get caught falling in love with a target.

A certain level of decorum was expected by all of the Assets. Expectations had to be met and rightfully so. Without rules, seeds of discords were inevitable and certain to wreak havoc wherever they sprung up. Flea believed in the rules and expected Aries to hold fast to them as well.

As soon as Lena fell asleep, Flea crawled into the room and tapped Aries on the foot. Startled, Aries gained his bearings then pulled himself off of the bed. Flea snapped one last nude photo of Lena with his cell phone, before Aries covered her with a soiled bed sheet. Flea flinched when Aries scowled as if he considered snatching the phone away.

During the short ride to Aries' split level-apartment, Flea was unusually quiet. He couldn't wrap his head around his Asset's nonsensical behavior with Lena. Aries couldn't have known that he didn't have to seduce her after Flea took compromising photos down stairs. On the other hand, Aries must have known how dangerous it was to share his feelings, especially if they were honest. Flea gazed silently out of the SUV window. He was jumpy, disappointed and reasonably scared. A dedicated photographer, on fourteen successful scores, Flea was convinced he had seen it all but he couldn't have been more wrong.

Christopher was livid when they finally arrived at the loft apartment. He stomped angry circles around Aries until he decided how to handle the delicate situation that swimming pool stunt put his crew in. Cherry sat on the love seat next to Walter. It was difficult to distinguish which of them was more uncomfortable. Raja stayed a far distance on the second-story patio, concerned that he would lose his million-dollar bet if Christopher lost his temper and Aries matched his emotion with flexed muscle. Flea dug his teeth into another nubby fingernail and listened to his boss's grand tirade.

"What is with you, Aries!" he shouted. "You went to the mark's house? His home!"

"Please bring it down, Christopher," Cherry pleaded. "The neighbors might call the cops."

He unbuttoned his brown linen jacket and eased it off his shoulders. Christopher handed it to Walter and took a moment to compose himself. "Whew! I shouldn't get worked up but some things defy logic and I don't do things I don't understand."

Aries counted four armed men sitting in black town cars downstairs and two more in the black Tahoe parked across the street. He had to keep a lid on his feelings to get what he deserved, respect and a rewarding pay off. "I was running out of time Christopher and running out of options."

"You'd better hope Ledger Harmon doesn't try to have you killed and that slut wife of his too," he added, to stick it to Aries. "Money is power. It buys you things that matter, like not having to pony up for some guy banging his woman, *in his own home!*" Christopher raised his hands to stifle Cherry's second reprimand.

"Ledger Harmon built that house, not you," he spat sharply. "There is a code among schemers. A man's home is off limits unless he has it coming. You had no business going there."

"So it had to happen in the man's home," Aries said, as humbly as he knew how. "And I would go to hell and back again to get what we needed."

"There was a lot at stake Christopher," said Flea, in Aries' defense. "He had to do something."

Christopher shot his old friend a look that cut to the bone. "You shut your damned mouth, Flea! You're in this shit, waist-deep, just like him. There is always a gentlemanly way to go about doing things but you guys didn't think to find it." He shook his head angrily then shrugged as if dismayed with Flea's alliance to Aries and lack of trust in his leadership. "You've been with me too long to take his side on this. Maybe I should blow town and forget about this score. I got a bad feeling about this whole thing," Christopher huffed. "It took too long and now stands a big chance of coming off the rails."

"We got the evidence, Christopher," Aries insisted. "Proof of the Pussy! Wasn't that the goal?" His comment was meant to question Christopher's motives for being so belligerent, regardless of the methods taken to bag the confirmation.

"What good is baking the cake if you can't eat it?" He ran both hands through his thick hair and chuckled. Aries glanced around the room for glass bottles within Christopher's reach as he continued. "I like cake. I *really* like cake. Let's not leave this one half-baked." He angrily ran both hands through his hair again. "This is what you and Flea are going to do, immediately, and without fail."

Always two steps ahead, Christopher explained a number of details that needed to be executed before the night ended. Everyone paid close attention and took their assignments seriously. Raja performed a statistical analysis on the back of a dirty napkin then concluded that Christopher's line of reasoning was overwhelmingly correct. The cake was indeed half-baked and required an infusion of heat or risk of falling apart under its own weight. Everyone in the room bought in on the Christopher's plan and vowed to see it through. Each of them wanted a taste.

# chapter twenty three
# PAPER HEARTS

At sunrise, Lena was awakened by a ringing telephone. She rolled off the guest-room bed and wrapped herself in the flannel housecoat she almost tripped over on the floor. When she answered the house phone, an unfamiliar voice ran down a host of pertinent information regarding a problem at her office. Lena gathered her senses while connecting the dots but the man on the phone was talking too fast and it was simply too early in the morning to keep up.

"Hold on Sir," she said, eventually. "Now back up and go slowly. You said someone broke into my office?"

"Yes Ma'am. I'm with hospital security, Dr. Harmon. A cleaning woman found your back door cracked open. Nothing seems to be taken as far as we can tell but someone clearly went digging through things in your office."

"Was anything broken?"

"Only the lock and a bottle perfume."

"Shaped like a glass guitar?"

"Looks like it could have been, yes. We suggest you get down here and take an inventory in case we missed something."

Lena hung her head and glared at the digital alarm clock on Ledger's night stand. "It's seven-twenty now. I'll be there within the hour. "

The hospital maintenance supervisor was repairing the door lock when Lena reached her office. She felt violated, knowing someone had bashed in the door and intruded her personal space. Two security officers walked her through the burglary protocol associated with break-ins or thefts in private practices. They watched her take an account of petty cash, prescription pads and other items commonly taken from a doctor's office.

"Nope, my business checkbook is right where I left it and all the office cash is in its bag," she said. "I don't keep narcotics on hands and can't see anyone breaking in to steal contraceptive samples."

Lena signed off on the new door lock then watched the team of hospital employees file out of the office space she leased on the sixth floor. Other physicians experienced thefts from disgruntled staff members or light-fingered housekeepers from time to time but nothing like this. Lena was hopeful that whoever crashed in during the night either found what they were looking for or reached the conclusion that Lena's practice didn't possess any of it.

After sweeping up glass from a broken picture frame, Lena pulled the photo of Ledger out of it. She sent a text asking him to call when his flight landed at DFW Airport. Next, she called Aries to check in while reminiscing on their uninhabited sexploits on the guest-room bed, although determined it would never happen again; under any circumstances.

Lena eased back against the desk chair while the phone rang. She hung up when hearing a generic message instead of the silky smooth voice that made her tingle. Two more attempts proved her concerns that something was wrong with Aries' number as it continually defaulted to an automated greeting. *Perhaps he lost it,* she thought, *or maybe he deleted his personalized message by mistake.* Lena yawned as she blew it off for the time being. She presumed that Aries would see the missed calls then contact her instantly. Her next order of business was getting something to eat and changing her guest-room linen before Ledger made it to the house. Covering her tracks was a necessary evil but she had no clue what lengths it took to hide every dirty, little, lie.

Rain came down in buckets all afternoon, further delaying Ledger's plane. He was excited to be home finally and apologized for welching on another dinner date. Lena wasn't salty the way she'd been all those times before. Instead, she appeared pleasant and unfazed. She was even rock solid when telling him about the office break-in and seemed unusually interested in hearing about his business trip in detail. Her attentive behavior went unnoticed by Ledger but he noticed something else was off right away.

Soon after hanging up suits and neckties in his closet, he walked out wearing a perplexed expression. "Did the cleaning ladies come to the house while I was gone?"

Lena shook her head slowly, wondering if Ledger had stumbled across a pair of her panties among his belongings somehow. "No one has been here, why?" she asked cautiously.

Ledger was meticulous about his things and didn't like a single item out of place. "Huh, that's odd," he said, with a puzzled look on his face. "You're sure that no delivery or cable guy had been here for service since I left for Ontario?"

Lena was terrified that someone saw Aries leaving or God forbid taking a naked midnight dip in their swimming pool. "No, no one that I know of. Uh, what is this about Ledger?"

"Then I need to get the police on the phone because my vault was open. I'm missing a Rolex, that antique pocket watch you bought me in London and some diamond cuff-links."

"Are you positive, honey? Is there a chance you took those things to Canada and left them at the hotel?"

He held out his right arm to show Lena the watch on his wrist. "I'm still wearing the one I took on the trip. That Rolex is a Presidential collector's edition. It's worth thirty-seven grand so I only wear it when closing a deal. My initials are laser-stamped on the inside clasp. You wouldn't even notice it was there unless I showed you." Ledger looked exasperated as he dialed 911 to report the apparent theft in his home. He spoke to the dispatcher in an easy tone that threw Lena for a loop. She knew he was considering another explanation for the jewelry disappearance.

Ledger didn't utter another word about it until a police squad car parked in front of their home. He greeted them at the door then examined each of the door locks. As Lena observed her husband discussing particulars with the police, she also checked her jewelry box and closet safe to see if her prized possessions were all accounted for. Nothing looked out of place but her anxiety climbed when she began to suspect the robberies were somehow connected.

Before the police officers left, they asked if anyone new to their surrounding had access to their home and the doctor's office. When Aries came to Lena's mind, she had to excuse herself. Suddenly, she felt sick in the pit of her stomach.

Lena flew into the downstairs bathroom. As panic flooded her senses, she dropped to her knees and threw up into the toilet. She didn't want to fathom Aries screwing her brains out then stealing from her husband and rummaging through her office, all in the same night. Lena spent the remainder of the day replaying conversations with Aries but there was nothing out of line. *He's a successful sales rep, drives a beautiful vehicle and dresses in fine clothing. He's polished, fit and gorgeous,* she thought. *Aries couldn't be more perfect if someone invented him.* There had to be another explanation she reasoned. So many questions plagued Lena throughout the weekend. Ledger was unnerved as he continuously checked the door locks, looking for clues that simply weren't there. Lena couldn't discuss her suspicions with Ledger and Aries was off the grid. He hadn't answered or returned her calls and all of the texts she sent remained in *undelivered* status so she knew he hadn't read any of them. Lena felt alone and desperate. She was living in a giant home and in a private hell. She tormented herself for foolishly getting involved with a man she hardly knew.

Monday morning couldn't have come fast enough. Lena sped straight to the office and unlocked the back door at eight o'clock sharp. She opened her desk drawer then rambled through it, tossing out several items that got in the way of locating what she hunted for. After dumping half of the contents onto her desk pad, she found it. The first thing Aries had given her, a business card, had been used as a book marker for the medical journal she promised herself to finish reading. She pulled it out and looked at it. Aries Dupree, the sales representative for Veritas Pharmaceuticals was avoiding her but she needed answers. Maybe the company could shed some light on his unexplained departure from her life.

Lena was embarrassed to call her lover's job because it was beneath her as a physician. Unfortunately, her integrity and judgment as a wife were both already in question, so chasing a man down was not that far of a leap. Lena's hand trembled as she dialed the home office number located on the front of the business card. Somewhat shaken, she paused when a woman answered.

"It's a great day at Veritas Pharmaceuticals."

"Uh, hello. This is Dr. Lena Harmon, I'm an Obstetrician from Dallas Texas."

"And, how may I help you Doctor?" Cherry asked, in her best customer-service associate voice. She knew the call would come because it always did once the Asset collected the proof and disappeared. The business card was one guarantee, the one link every target turned to when the relationship they cherished began to come apart at the seams. "Doctor, are you still there?"

"Yes, I'm looking for one of your sales reps. I owe him a meeting but have been extremely busy. Is there a way you can reach him for me?"

"That shouldn't be a problem. I'll put in a request to have you contacted today. What's the rep's name?"

"Aries Dupree," Lena said with excellent enunciation.

"Hold on please, I'll look him up."

Lena felt pathetic, like a jilted lover grasping at straws. What she learned next sent chills though her entire body.

"Thanks for holding Dr. Harmon but we'll have to get someone else to meet with you. That representative is no longer with the company."

"What! What do you mean? When did he leave?" she said, angrily.

"I'm sorry but I can't divulge that information. However, I can have another very capable associate contact you or I could patch you through to my supervisor."

"No, that won't be necessary," Lena answered, softly. That was the last link to Aries and now that it was broken she wanted to burst into tears.

Lena closed her door and locked it when she heard Margo singing a hit love song, loud and off key. She wasn't in the mood to confront her work day just yet and the intense smell of Day Dreams perfume, from the broken bottle, made her feel nauseous. Lena dipped into the restroom and vomited again. Her nerves were tattered but her schedule was full. Despite how terrible she felt, it was imperative that she picked herself up and pushed through the day. Her patients deserved it and she needed something to occupy her mind as every empty moment was spend worrying about Aries and wondering how he could up and vanish without saying good bye.

Experiencing a myriad emotion, she was unseasonably quiet. Despite attempts to disguise her pain, the office staff sensed that Lena wasn't all there. The doctor still managed to see everyone on the patient list and then responded to an instant message from her business checking account at the end of the day. The bank flagged it when a check was submitted in the amount of $5,000. Lena assumed it was a mistake. She pulled up a copy of the check on-line, that was made payable to cash. The photo copy was grainy but it visibly displayed a copy of her signature. The endorsement on the back was a scrawled mess and could have been anyone's name, so Lena didn't waste time trying to decipher it. The ID used was a foreign driver's license and a dead end.

"Check number 4122," she said, while flipping through her business check binder. She gasped when a blank space appeared between two checks, where a third one should have been. Because it was taken from a sheet, near the back, it would have gone unnoticed for months otherwise. Lena didn't know what to think about her bad luck or who to blame for it. Still, there were so many questions and not a single answer. It was like a bad dream that continually worsened. The most excruciating part was not being able to tell anyone. Ledger was suspicious and Aries was missing in action.

Lena called the bank to put a freeze on the business account until further notice then searched through her personal checkbook. There wasn't anything out of ordinary, nothing missing or unexplainable withdrawals. Still, she was beside herself with uncertainty and humiliation. Before she called the police and came clean on her affair that may have ended with a cleverly planned theft, Lena made sure everyone was out of the office then she dialed the number used to contact Aries from the very beginning.

As the telephone rang, Lena took a deep breath. She was preparing to choose her words carefully, if he did happen to answer her call. When the same automated message begun to play, she slammed the phone down on her desk. "Damn it Aries!" she screamed.

"What did I do now?" he answered, from her office doorway.

Lena was startled. She leapt from her chair then studied his relaxed demeanor and casual attire. Dressed in jeans, a blue V-neck pullover and loafers, he didn't seem concerned in the least. However, Lena was as shocked by his appearance as his sudden vanishing act.

"Aries, how did you get in?" she asked, in a purposely subdued tone.

"I used the key pad. Cathy told me what it was weeks ago, so I could sneak in the flowers and perfume. Smells like you poured out the entire bottle in here."

"You and Cathy?" she asked. Her expression was pensive and accusatory.

"There's nothing between us. I told her I wanted to get your business and she couldn't wait to help me out."

Aries wore a smug grin that Lena didn't recognized. She had dozens of questions and had no idea where to begin. She was hesitant to confront him because there was an outside chance that he didn't take Ledger's expensive gifts from her home or steal the missing check from her office, but she kept her distance from Aries' overly confident swagger.

"You changed your phone number and didn't tell me how to reach you so I called Veritas Pharmaceuticals. Why aren't you employed there anymore?"

"It wasn't working out."

"What does that mean? You were knocking on doors and building their business right?"

"Yeah, something like that. It was a good relationship until they became convinced that I committed bank fraud and forgery on one of their biggest clients. Go figure."

Lena immediately thought about the forged check she'd been grieving over for the past hour. "Oh my God. Did you steal the check from my business account?"

Aries chuckled then smirked at her as if it wasn't a big deal. "Look, I came to talk about us."

"Us! How can you say that after stealing from me?" Lena was so disturbed that her hands trembled. "I trusted you. I gave myself to you. Hell, I changed myself for you!"

"And I am thankful. I enjoyed it so much that I'd like to step up our relationship Lena. Leave your husband so we can start a life together. Let's get married."

She couldn't believe her ears. Lena laughed to keep herself from crying. "Sure Aries. Let's do that then rob a bank together."

"What?"

"Yeah, let's get married tomorrow and spend our honeymoon on a bank robbing spree all over Texas."

Aries gave Lena a patronizing stare then chuckled again. "You think this is a game?"

"Isn't this a game we're playing? You say something ridiculous like 'leave your husband and run away with me.' Then, I get to say something more ridiculous to top yours?"

"I do care about you and want to be taken seriously so please hear me out. I could be a big benefit in your life as well as in your practice."

"So, you're a doctor now? No wait, you'll be my receptionist?"

"I'm going to be your silent partner. You know, behind the scenes. And, before you decide, it'll only cost you the low-low price of fifty thousand dollars."

"Man, have you lost your mind?" she said, finding it difficult to look at him. "Please get out of my office before I call the police."

"And tell the cops what, Dr. Harmon? That I made you have sex with me. No wait, you can show them this while you're at it." Aries casually tossed seven photos on her desk, one after the next. Lena's knees weakened when she recognized her naked body in the pictures, sweaty and sinfully intertwined with his. She collapsed in the chair and analyzed them individually with a disgusted look in her eyes. When it became overwhelming, she tried to hand them back to Aries.

"No thanks, I have another copy," he announced. The thought of other people seeing her like that, bent over and exposed, made her feel nauseas. She pushed past him and darted into an interoffice restroom. He heard her vomiting into the commode. "I can see that you're busy Dr. Harmon," Aries shouted from outside the closed restroom door. "I'd hate to send my copy of the pictures to your husband and the hospital medical board."

"Why are you doing this to me?" she cried. "I just want you to go. It was a big mistake ever giving into you. Please get out of my life."

Aries felt conflicted about taking her through this painful phase of the scheme but it had to happen. Christopher sent him to break into the office and steal the check then disconnect himself from their relationship; including the removal of his personalized voice message. Targets were known to lose it over listening to an Asset's voice repeatedly and subsequently committing suicide or worse, running to the police with evidence to be used in court. It was Aries' own decision to slip back into Lena's home and take Ledger's jewelry. Aries wanted a trophy, something special that Lena purchased, so he took it. Christopher would not have allowed it, therefore he had no idea it had taken place.

"I can still feel you out there," she whimpered, sorely. "And I don't ever want to see you again."

"Get a money order from your bank, in the amount of fifty gees and you won't have to," he said, with great resolve.

When Lena heard him walk in the other direction and the outer door close, she unlocked the restroom then ventured out warily. After obtaining more answers than she could process, Lena was distraught. Her entire affair with Aries was a lie that she helped to create, one lie and one laugh at a time. Several steamy pictures laid on her desk, chronicling the darkest hours of her life. What she had been reduced to was painfully revealing. $50,000 was a small price to write it off and pretend it never occurred.

Lena sat in her luxury SUV in the physician's parking lot with the windows rolled up. The motor hummed quietly as tears poured from her eyes. She couldn't go home but there was nowhere else to be, not with puffiness and obvious disgrace painted on her face. She tried to clean herself up but it was no use, so she put on a pair of dark sunglasses and closed the vanity mirror on her overhead visor. A soft knock at the window made her to jump. Fearing Aries had returned again, Lena fumbled with the pepper spray canister on her key-chain until she realized it was a woman trying to get her attention.

"Lena, it's me. Dane Tolliver," said the lady, who was gesturing for the doctor to lower her window. "Hey Doc. I'm always taking a wrong turn and ending up in this parking lot. You feeling okay, Hun?"

Lena avoided eye contact while hiding behind her thick sun shades. "I'm fine, really. I just had a very bad day."

"Oh, I see. Man trouble?" she asked, mostly guessing. "Take off those glasses."

"I have to get home, it's really nothing I can't handle," Lena offered, more annoyed now than upset.

"Lena, you might be my doctor but you're also my friend. Let's have a look at your face?" Reluctantly, Lena removed the thick plastic frames. Dane gawked at Lena's eyes and sneered disapprovingly. "Oomph, I figured as much. Well, at least he didn't beat on you."

"Hell no! Nobody is going to hit me," Lena announced, staunchly.

"Yeah, that usually comes later." Dane didn't waste any time making her position as plain as she could. "Look, you don't have to tell me you're hurting. That's clear. You might not need the police on this one but every woman needs a peace of mind. She pulled a snub nose .38 pistol out of her purse.

"Hey, watch it, Dane! I don't believe guns solve problems."

"Well Doctor, it'll believe in you every time this trigger gets pulled."

"I'm just upset, it's not like that," Lena argued.

"You damned near jumped through the windshield when I walked up. That's fear if I've ever seen it. You're too smart and too pretty to be squirrelly behind some fella. Take this peace of mind and keep it in your purse."

Lena opened her designer handbag for Dane to ease the gun inside it. "I don't know how to use it Dane."

"It's not rocket science but it will blast a som'bitch out of this world. If a man puts his hands on you, plead self-defense after the fact and let a judge sort it out. Just point and squeeze the trigger."

Lena returned the dark glasses to her face and nodded her gratitude. "You're something else Dane, thank you."

"If you don't need that pistol, good. But if you do, well that's even better. There's a special place in hell for woman-beaters and sending 'em home on a bullet train is the least a good Christian can do." She squeezed Lena's hand and said goodbye.

Dane Tolliver saw more than her share of angry men who acted out their disappointments and lack of discipline in violent outbursts that shattered everything around them. As a result, there always seemed to be a woman crying a river of tears in an empty parking lot and another one telling her it would be alright.

# chapter twenty four
# ALL OVER BUT
# THE CRYING

Lena drove straight home and crept in the back door. She told Ledger she needed time alone, that her eyes were irritated by an allergic reaction to a new brand of mascara she'd purchased. Ledger didn't argue or seem overly concerned when she closed herself up in one of the upstairs bathrooms for hours. There was no way to get over what had transpired during the past three days because she didn't fully understand any of it. The man she fell head over heels for was demanding money after robbing her business account and burglarizing her home. She wondered if he was addicted to drugs or had gotten in too deep with a gambling debt. In the midst of a whirlwind that shackled her to a situation she couldn't control, Lena still cared about Aries and the struggles she presumed he dealt with.

The only place she felt comfortable was on the guest-room floor. She grabbed a pillow and blanket off the bed then tossed and turned all night. Each time she closed her eyes, Aries' handsome face appeared. She badgered herself for finding solace in a stranger's arms regardless of how wonderful he made her feel.

"You knew better than this," she muttered, to herself repeatedly. "You are better than this."

Lena wished there was someone to tell about the suffering she was going through alone. She yearned to unburden herself but there was nowhere to turn. After staring into darkness became unbearable, she took two of Ledger's sleeping pills. Eventually her emotional exhaustion gave into the sedatives and allowed her to find sleep. It was the longest and emptiest night of her life.

Morning rolled in slow. When Lena pulled herself together, she stumbled into the master bathroom to shower. There was a hand written note from Ledger leaning against her silver plated tooth-brush stand.

*I don't know what happened to us. I don't know how much of it is my fault. I'm sorry Lena and I love you.*
*Signed,*
*Ledger*

After reading it, she could not allow him to be destroyed by seeing those photos Aries flung on her desk. Lena wasn't sure if the money Aries demanded was the answer to freeing herself from his clutches but she had to do something.

She found herself at the bank, withdrawing money from her savings account. Ledger paid all of the bills so there was over a quarter-million dollars sitting in a low interest bearing account collecting dust. The bank manager asked if Lena were doing alright and why she was withdrawing such a large amount. Although Lena didn't disagree with the woman's questions, she'd earned the money and therefore the right to do with it as she pleased. Her eventual response was that she had to pay a debt that came due but wouldn't elaborate further. Lena didn't like being advised that a money order, for such a high amount, was not the safest way to transfer funds.

Without being made payable to a certain individual, it could have been cashed by anyone presenting it within a whole year. Against her better judgment, the bank manager completed the transaction then handed Lena what amounted to a $50,000 bill.

Lena thanked her then sat in the Mercedes, waiting on instructions and a place to deliver the bank draft. Tired and hungry, she called Margo to inquire if Aries had stopped by. She didn't explain why she needed to cancel all of the patients for the day or why she had been out of touch. Lena simply ended the call then found a small breakfast eatery to avoid seeing anyone who might recognize her.

After two hours of killing time and three cups of coffee, she was on edge. Lena wanted to talk to Aries, give him the money and began to pick up the tattered pieces of her life that he'd torn apart and stepped on. She couldn't wait to get back to being Lena, the woman with her head on straight; the one who would have seen Aries' diabolical plan coming a mile away.

Once boredom got the best of Lena, she felt compelled to make a move. The expensive men's store in which she bought Aries' suit was virtually empty when she walked in. The tailor remembered her and gladly located the alterations ticket with a physical address written on it. Lena was surprised the suit hadn't been delivered so she offered to take it there herself.

Eight minutes after signing the alterations receipt, she was sitting in front of the same apartment building she promised herself she'd never set a foot inside. There was no sign of the black Porsche Aries drove. Despite her bundle of nerves, she read the door number then walked down a short open breezeway until she came to the third apartment on the right. Holding tightly to the purse on her shoulder and the gift-wrapped box close to her chest, she knocked on the door twice. Lena pressed her ear to the door, listening for sounds on the inside. She couldn't hear a thing so she knocked again, with the same outcome. No sounds and no one answered.

At another crossroad, Lena headed back to her vehicle. She deliberated over staking out his apartment until Aries arrived although she couldn't be sure he lived there anymore. With her peace of mind nearby, she walked onto the first-floor patio and peered inside the window. The camel colored leather furniture suggested good taste although there were no visible signs of a woman's touch, whatsoever. It was, for all intents a purposes, a bachelor's pad that Lena imagined came equipped with a revolving door to accommodate his hoard of women. Suddenly, she didn't feel like the only fool on his chain anymore. The thought of other women being duped like she had been almost brought a smile to her lips, then the mood quickly slammed hard against reality when she recognized Ledger's watch and what appeared to be his diamond cuff-links sitting on top of the kitchenette bar.

Lena's unyielding desire to get inside would not be denied as the pursuit for clarity and closure took a hold of the gift box in Lena's hand and hurled it through the patio window. She used her purse to knock glass chards out of the way then quickly wandered inside the spacious room on the first floor. A closer look of the Rolex watch clasp confirmed her suspicions. Her husband's name was laser-stamped where he told her it would be. Next, she searched the downstairs home-gym then in the utility room.

As Lena marched up the stairs, all she could think was finding the pocket watch and getting out of there with all of her spouses' personal belongings. She rumbled through the dresser drawers, dumping things out onto the floor just as Aries had done to her desk. When Lena heard voices outside so she ran to the bedroom window and looked down. A man with a dog was snooping around but kept his poodle back away from the shattered glass on the ground. She knew it was only a matter of time before someone called the police. She had to get out of there.

While Lena made her way to the staircase, something beckoned to her from behind a closed door. She tried to leave but couldn't until knowing what was on the other side of it. Lena disregarded the police sirens in the distance as she approached with caution then slowly twisted the knob. What she discovered brought all of her worse fears to bear.

The walls were covered with pictures taken of her for months. She immediately felt a knot growing in the pit of her stomach as hundreds of photos seemed to mock her. They depicted easy flowing laughter and casual conversations she had with Aries at the charity ball, the coffee bar where he first kissed her and several shots of her entering and exiting the Ambassador Hotel. Lena wanted to die when she saw enlarged photos of damning evidence, dishonoring her husband in their home when making unrepentant love to a slick hustler on her guest-room bed. Lena knew then fifty-thousand dollars would never be enough to push Aries out of her life because he'd always come back for more blackmail. She was determined to call the police and beg Ledger's forgiveness. There was no other way out and she felt deserving of whatever punishment that accompanied such a tragic mistake. However, she was not going to heap on an arrest charge for breaking and entering to the troubles destined to land at her husband's feet.

Police sirens screamed in front of the building as uniformed officers yelled for nosey bystanders to step back away from the patio. Lena hurried down the carpeted stairs as the cops came in the same patio door she entered through. She left the large gift box where it laid then ducked out of the front door while the two officers raced upstairs. Lena jogged down the short breezeway then circled around to the rear of the building. Beads of sweat mounted on her forehead as she stopped to catch her breath.

Composing herself to look as natural as possible, Lena sauntered down the sidewalk then casually crossed the street to her parked SUV. Another police squad car roared to the scene as she pulled away from the curb in the opposite direction, she was beside herself, tortured and torn.

Christopher seethed in the back of a Tahoe as he watched the crowd swell in front of Aries' apartment; which he had the presence of mind to lease, using a false identity, and pay five months in advance. Unfortunately, the loft was hot now. Police were involved, making it too risky to reclaim the clothes purchased and other personal items. Aries' cover was also blown. Once a police investigator was assigned and had a look at the disturbing photo collection of Lena, there was sure to be legal inquiries that couldn't be explained. Christopher slammed his fist against the leather seat then told the driver to get him out of there.

Before the vehicle returned to the hotel, Christopher made a quick call to Cherry, apprising her of the situation they faced.

"Cherry, find Aries. I don't care what it takes. Find him and tell Walter he was right. Asset number twenty-nine's contract has been terminated. Effective immediately."

"But Christopher, he got us the proof we asked for," she said, to appeal to the boss's sense of fairness.

"What he's going to get us, is pinched." Christopher signaled to the driver to bypass the valet stand and park on the street instead. "This score had problems from the start. We should have scrapped it and took our lumps. Aries hasn't checked in for hours and I believe

Flea might be covering for him. It's time to tie up loose ends. Pull the Asset's cord, tonight." Christopher had one more call to make but it didn't leave him much time to redirect the unguided missile he suspected was heading directly towards Lena's heart.

Aries slammed two more shots of tequila then chased them with a tall mug of stout lager. He'd been observing the crowd outside of the apartment from his perch on the cantina patio down the street. His vantage point was limited by the number of people gawking at the hole in his apartment, so there was no way to see Lena's departure. He assumed it was just his bad luck to be victimized by a random break-in that brought the police to his door. Nonetheless, Aries knew it fractured his relationship with Christopher. Getting the million dollar payoff that M.O.E.T. Corp. owed him, for the proof of Lena's adultery, seemed like a long shot at best now. His next move had to amount to something big, he thought, while hot wiring an old pickup truck behind a convenience store.

The evening sun was dissolving into the horizon when Aries slammed on the brakes at Lena's house. Christopher and his men were waiting for him. "Aries, let's talk about this," he said, stepping out of the vehicle and into the middle of the street.

"There's nothing to discuss or you wouldn't have brought those thugs with you." He took a step towards the front door then heard someone cock a semi-automatic weapon. "Really, you're going to do it right here?" Aries barked.

"It doesn't have to be this way, you know. Let's go and regroup over a few beers," said Christopher, in a placating tone.

"I've already had my share of brew," he cackled slovenly. "Funny thing is Christopher, I thought of you and ordered the chicken. Ha ha ha ha. See you around."

"Bet your ass you will," Christopher said, angrily.

He climbed back into the Tahoe then texted Walter the address where he could find Aries. With a hit ordered on Aries' life, it was all over but the crying.

Aries watched the truck peel off down the street and exit the subdivision. He enjoyed having the last laugh as he banged on the door like a mad man.

"I'm here to take you on that fancy date, Lena!" he yelled. "I don't have the snazzy suit you bought me but we can work something out." Suddenly, the door opened. Aries walked inside boldly, as if invited.

He was met by Lena's husband, who was dressed in beige cotton slacks and a matching golf shirt. "I'm Ledger Harmon and don't appreciate you acting a fool on my front porch. This ain't the hood so you can carry your ass on back to whatever rock you crawled from underneath."

Watching Lena walk down the stairs, wearing the same housecoat and slippers from the other night made Aries smile; although her right hand was wrapped in a bandage.

"Hello Lena," said Aries, totally dismissing the man of the house. "How did you hurt yourself?"

"I saw it Aries," she answered. "I was in your apartment today and saw everything you had on me, in the upstairs bedroom."

"Well, good. Good. Now you can tell your father here, that your new daddy is home." When Aries heard the door close behind him, he kept Ledger in his periphery, in case he tried something.

"Tell this man he doesn't belong here, Lena," said Ledger, needing to hear her say it.

"Maybe I should tell you what me and your wife have been up to," Aries spat back at him. "Oh yeah, she did some things you probably didn't know she could!"

"I already told him everything. So you can go now," she answered, as firmly as she knew how. Lena was wounded and weakened by the spectacle she made of her marriage and having to face both men she loved simultaneously.

"Hey Gramps, did she tell you I taught her how to suck and swallow? Huh? Yeah, she was rusty at first but once you stroke that ass right, she'll do damn near anything you want."

"ARIES PLEASE!" Lena cried. "Why are you doing this?"

Ledger bucked up to Aries, once it appeared he wasn't going anywhere unless he was good and ready.

"Somebody should knock your big ass down a peg," he growled.

"Is it going to be you old man? Ha ha ha! Please take a poke at me. Go ahead and take your best shot."

In a bold attempt to protect what was left of his wife's honor, Ledger raced towards Aries and threw a wild punch that missed. Before he knew what hit him, the older man was lying flat on his back with a busted jaw.

"Stop it! Stop!" Lena yelled, as Ledger crushed her boyfriend's knee with a bronze bust of Martin Luther King Jr.

"You old fool! I'll break your neck!" Aries snarled. He grimaced through the pain while thrashing Ledger with thunderous blows to his face. Blood poured from his nose.

"Aries, you'll kill him!" Lena screamed.

Aries wouldn't let up. His eyes glassed over while continually pummeling Ledger with vicious strikes to his face. Aries cackled like a raving lunatic until glancing up to find a very calm and calculating woman, pointing a shaky Snub Nose .38 pistol at his head.

"Hit him one more time and that'll be the very last thing you do."

"Ha ha ha ha! You ain't gonna do shit but come with me and leave this old buzzard to rot."

"Uh-uh. See, you're an intruder who trespassed into my home

with a knife and attacked my husband. Now, I'll have to save his life."

After struggling to his feet, Aries limped across the floor just below Lena's position on the stairs. He was intrigued but unflinching. With a sarcastic grin, he applauded her plan.

"That's not bad but your story has holes in it. You and I have a past so it won't be that easy to wash your hands of me, even after I'm dead."

"That's the problem with a user who doesn't want to work for his food but would rather take from those who do."

"Watch your mouth!" shouted Aries. He didn't like the sound of Lena's disparaging remark.

"You don't get to tell me what to do anymore," she hissed, with tears rolling down her cheeks. "I loved you. I trusted you. Cherished..."

She fell silent with a troubled expression, as if wondering what might have been. She regained focus when she heard Ledger groaning in pain on the floor.

"After the mess you made of my life, I'll take great pleasure separating you from your miserable soul. Yeah, that's it. I'll blow you away where you stand and plant the knife near your body. I may even cry a river over losing you or what I thought you meant to me, then take a long, hot shower to wash it all off."

"Bravo, Dr. Harmon but I don't think so," Aries objected, certain he still held all the cards. "See, I know you better than you know yourself. A woman like you wants a strong, virile stud to smack that ass and make you scream! A horny bitch like you needs—"

Bang!

Bang!

Bang!

Bang!

Bang!

Bang!

Lena kept firing until the gun was empty. Unable to listen to another word, she'd pointed and squeezed like Dane Tolliver instructed. Without batting an eye, she punched Aries' ticket on a one way bullet train to hell. The smell of gunpowder filled the foyer of her four-million dollar home but Lena couldn't get the sweet scent of the Day Dreams perfume out of her mind. Aries was dead, Lena's life would never be the same and she was still in love.

After successfully planting a knife by Aries' side, Lena calmly stared at his body and told her story. Just as rehearsed, she ran it down to the police sergeant, who questioned her, as the crime scene investigators placed markers where bullets fell onto the ground.

"I knew him as a pharmaceutical sales rep who called on my office a few times. When he sent gifts to my office, I told him I was happily married and not at all interested in his advances. He stalked and harassed me for weeks. After my husband threatened to report Mr. Dupree, he showed up here today with that knife and attacked Ledger." As tears streamed from her eyes, Lena refused to go on.

The sergeant assured Lena that the intruder got what he deserved then immediately closed the book on an obvious case of self-defense. Lena thanked them for helping her through the terrible ordeal as paramedics revived Ledger, on a gurney. After sustaining a concussion, several lacerations to his face and three broken teeth, he was lucky to be alive. However, the marriage, which he never made time for, was shattered beyond repair.

After the medics whisked him away to the hospital to treat his injuries, Lena took a long bath to wash off the residue of a disastrous affair. She cried a river over losing the man who made her feel alive then she searched for a crease in her life to climb back into, after Aries Dupree rocked it off the axis.

Christopher and the Men of M.O.E.T. crew went into hiding until they were sure none of the tragedy surrounding Aries' death blew back on to them. Cherry had mixed emotions about claiming his remains but there was a sizable life insurance check awarded once they presented the death certificate for Anthony Mitchell.

Two weeks later, Ledger received a call from a man demanding five-million dollars or he would leak copies of lewd photos and sex videos that would have implicated Lena for murder in a sordid love triangle. A scandal of that magnitude would have buried Ledger's chances of launching his multi-billion dollar IPO. His personal attorney sent a wire transfer to an untraceable offshore account in the Grand Caymans. An hour later, Ledger filed for divorce.

Lena, content to face whatever life cursed her with next, agreed to end the failed marriage without contesting a breakup in court. She forfeited more than twenty-million in a potential settlement but walked away with her thriving medical practice and a powerful resolve that nothing could break her after what she'd experienced.

Months later, she purchased a small house in a quiet neighborhood and painted the baby's nursery yellow. Although pregnant and alone, she found joy in the excitement of motherhood and all that it entailed. After returning to work, Lena received a box of beautiful, yellow, long-stemmed roses. She closed her office door and read the card.

*Aries wasn't supposed to fall in love with you but he did. His real name was Anthony.*

Cherry thought Lena deserved to know who the man was that changed everything in her life.

Half way across the country, in a Las Vegas hotel, Christopher paid off the bets he'd lost since Aries did in fact provide the evidence to wrap up the score within the time-frame they agreed upon. He handed Flea and Raja duffle bags with a million dollars in cash. Raja took one look at the large stacks of bills and almost fainted on the spot. Flea bit his fingernails while staring endlessly at his enormous sack of loot. He sincerely missed the friend Aries became but he wasn't foolish enough to give the money back.

Cherry returned to Dallas to place flowers on an unmarked grave. Before leaving in a black limousine, she said her last goodbyes. "You could have been one of the greats, a legendary schemer. We all have to make the best of the cards we're dealt but when it's all said and done, life is nothing more than playing the odds. So long Aries."

# BOOK CLUB DISCUSSION QUESTIONS FOR
# SCHEMERS

1. Do you think Aries truly fell in love with Lena? If so, what was the turning point that made his feelings for her change?

2. Ledger was a very wealthy man. Do you think being a good provider was enough in their mature marriage? Why or why not?

3. Do you think their marriage would have eventually dissolved without the appearance of Aries?

4. Why do you think Dane identified so much with Lena and was willing to go so far on a limb for her?

5. Given the sudden change in Lena's pattern, behaviors and appearance, do you think Ledger suspected an extra-marital affair? Why or why not?

6. If you were Lena's best friend, knowing all the details of the situation, what advice would you have given her after she began to fall for Aries?

7. As a best friend, would you have helped to cover up the murder? Why or why not?

8. Do you think Lena would have taken Aries up on his offer to run away together had the blackmail scheme not been revealed? Why or why not?

9. Why do you think Aries went to Lena's home, demanding that she run away with him?

10. Do you think Ledger should have divorced Lena?

11. Do you think Christopher would have actually followed through on his threats to have Aries killed?

## about the author

Victor McGlothin completed a Master's Degree in Human Relations & Business before penning 14 bestselling novels and three film projects. He lives near Dallas.

CPSIA information can be obtained
at www.ICGtesting.com
Printed in the USA
LVHW082320280321
682786LV00019B/847